Guide to the Holdings of the
STILL PICTURE BRANCH
of the
NATIONAL ARCHIVES

Compiled by
Barbara Lewis Burger

NATIONAL ARCHIVES AND RECORDS ADMINISTRATION
Washington, DC

PUBLISHED FOR THE
NATIONAL ARCHIVES AND RECORDS ADMINISTRATION
BY THE NATIONAL ARCHIVES TRUST FUND BOARD
1990

Library of Congress Cataloging-in-Publication Data

United States. National Archives and Records Administration. Still
  Picture Branch.
    Guide to the Holdings of the Still Picture Branch of the National
  Archives and Records Administration / compiled by Barbara Lewis
  Burger.
      ISBN 0-911333-83-5
      1. United States.   National Archives and Records Administration.
  Still Picture Branch—Catalogs.   2. Archives, Audio-visual—United
  States—Catalogs.   3. United States—History—Pictorial works—
  Catalogs.   I. Burger, Barbara Lewis.   II. Title.
  CD3027.S75   1990
  015.753'037—dc20   90-5834

ABOUT THE AUTHOR

Barbara Lewis Burger is an archivist in the Still Picture Branch, Special Archives Division, National Archives and Records Administration. She has served as the Assistant Chief for Reference in the Still Picture Branch, and as the Assistant to the Director of the Special Archives Division. Mrs. Burger has a master's degree from The Catholic University of America and an undergraduate degree from Howard University. She has worked with still pictures for over twelve years.

Designed by Serene Feldman Werblood

The paper used in this publication meets the minimum requirements of the American National Standard for Permanence of Paper for Printed Library Materials Z39.48-1984.

Cover: 83-G-44021. *Mexican Irrigator. He came from Mexico 12 years ago, works the year round on this large-scale farm. These fields are being prepared for flax; have never had a crop before. Eloy District, Pinal County, Arizona.* November 1940. Dorothea Lange. (RG 83, Records of the Bureau of Agricultural Economics)

TABLE OF CONTENTS

Part I—FEDERAL RECORDS

Part II—DONATED MATERIALS

PREFACE

This *Guide to the Holdings of the Still Picture Branch* describes a significant visual component of the National Archives of the United States. It includes summary information about almost six million photographic prints, negatives, transparencies, posters, and other visual images that are now in the custody of the Still Picture Branch.

Guides such as this one have been prepared at the National Archives since 1940 when the first *Guide to the Material in the National Archives* was published. Over time, new editions of this general guide have been published and supplementary guides have been issued that focus on specific subjects or specific types of records. This guide joins the *Guide to Cartographic Records in the National Archives*, published in 1971, in the latter category. Guides, which are intended to provide an introductory overview of large bodies of records, are supplemented by a variety of other specialized finding aids. For photographs, these include select lists of images of such subjects as the American West, Indians, the Revolutionary War, the Civil War, World War II, Navy Ships, and American Cities. To these lists, the National Archives has recently added *War & Conflict*, a picture book composed of reproductions of more than 1,500 archival images of American wartime experiences from the American Revolution through the Vietnam war.

The images described in this guide portray the work of the federal government with an immediacy that is often lacking in other sources. They range in date from photographs taken by Mathew Brady and associates during the Civil War to slides taken for the Environmental Protection Agency during the 1970s that illustrate issues relating to air and water pollution. The list of talented photographers and graphic artists represented by the varied records in the Still Picture Branch includes such familiar names as Howard Chandler Christy, Lewis Hine, William Henry Jackson, and Dorothea Lange. Whether attributable or not, however, the millions of images comprising the branch's holdings expressively illustrate every aspect of the American experience.

The holdings of the Still Picture Branch have long been recognized by many photo researchers as a uniquely valuable information resource. It is our hope that through the publication of this guide we can bring this resource to the attention of all who seek vivid images of our nation's past.

Don W. Wilson
Archivist of the United States

ACKNOWLEDGMENTS

I wish to express my sincere appreciation to the many National Archives staff members who provided invaluable assistance. Without their help and participation, the *Guide to the Holdings of the Still Picture Branch* could not have been completed. Virtually the entire staff of the Still Picture Branch assisted me at some point over the years, but special thanks go to Edward J. McCarter, Paul White, James H. Trimble, and Patricia Richter whose advice, encouragement, and unqualified support helped me over many rough spots. I am also extremely grateful to Jonathan Heller, editor of *War & Conflict*, who provided first-hand knowledge of the publication process.

Current and past chiefs of the Still Picture Branch, Elizabeth L. Hill, Jack Saunders, Richard F. Myers, and Joe Doan Thomas, supported me throughout this process and assured me during the bleak periods that the guide would be completed. I extend my appreciation to William H. Cunliffe, Director, Special Archives Division, for allowing me the time to complete the guide, and my gratitude to James W. Moore, who as Assistant Archivist for the Office of the National Archives, initiated the project by directing the Still Picture Branch to compile a guide.

Progress on completing this guide would have been slow indeed if not for the initial technical advice and support given by Marie Allen and the other personnel of the Archival Research and Evaluation Staff. Once the technical aspects of producing the guide were decided, it was Sheila V. Mayo and later Holly Reed who labored long and hard on entering the data. Their dedication to seeing this project completed made all the difference.

Virginia C. Purdy, Robert M. Kvasnicka, and Sharon Gibbs Thibodeau of the Archival Publications Staff, and Constance Drakeley reviewed and edited the manuscript. Many thanks also to Susan Carroll who did an excellent job of indexing this guide.

Bobbye West and her coworkers in the National Archives photo laboratory did an superb job of providing quality reproductions. The actual publishing of the guide was the responsibility of Henry J. Gwiazda and the Development and Production Branch staff. Serene Feldman Werblood did a wonderful job designing the cover and layout, while Richard B. Smith steered the guide through the various publication stages.

Finally, special thanks to my husband, Robert, who supported me in this endeavor, and who was my sounding board through it all.

BARBARA LEWIS BURGER

INTRODUCTION

The National Archives and Records Administration (NARA) administers the permanently valuable noncurrent records of the federal government. These archival holdings include documents, maps, drawings, printed matter, photographs, motion picture films, video recordings, sound recordings, and electronic records. The records date from the time of the Continental Congress, 1774–89, and include most of the basic records of the federal government produced by the Congress, the courts, the executive departments, and independent agencies.

The purpose of this guide is to describe pictorial materials among the holdings of the National Archives of the United States and to assist researchers in locating these documents. All of the records described in this guide are in the custody of the Still Picture Branch of the Special Archives Division. Not covered by this guide are photographs and illustrative materials that are integral parts of reports, studies, and other textual records housed in other branches in the National Archives; photographs in the Regional Archives, Federal Records Centers, and Presidential libraries; or aerial mapping photographs among the holdings of the Cartographic and Architectural Branch, Special Archives Division.

The National Archives began acquiring still pictures from federal agencies shortly after its establishment in 1934. Today, the Still Picture Branch maintains approximately 6 million photographs and graphics from over 170 departments, agencies, and bureaus. The branch also maintains a small collection of donated materials.

As with other units in the National Archives, the records in the Still Picture Branch are organized for administrative and physical control by record group. A record group most frequently consists of the records of a single agency (and its predecessors) at the bureau level of government, such as the records of the Children's Bureau (RG 102). The records of the head of an executive department and units with department-wide responsibility may be assigned to a general record group, such as the General Records of the Department of Housing and Urban Development (RG 207). Less frequently, records of a number of agencies may be brought together on the basis of similar function, such as the Records of Agencies for Voluntary Action Programs (RG 362).

Each record group is assigned a number. When the National Archives record group system was developed in 1944, record groups 1 through 190 were established and numbered consecutively in the order in which the first records in each group were accessioned. Subsequent record groups generally have been numbered in the order in which they were established.

Within each record group, the basic archival unit of control is the series, which is a body of records arranged in some serial order or logically grouped together for some other reason. NARA attempts to keep the records within series in the order in which they were maintained by the creating agency, but agency filing systems were designed for administrative purposes and do not always benefit researchers. In order to assist researchers, NARA has prepared subject guides and preliminary inventories for many record groups. These publications provide information regarding agency histories, series titles, series dates, the quantity of records, the types of records, and brief descriptions of the subject content of series.

In this guide the same information is provided, but the emphasis is pictorial records, with attention given to both the type of record (medium) and the content of the series. The diverse nature of the contents of most of the series prohibits the compilation of exhaustive series descriptions, but an effort has been made to identify subjects, events, and personages. Occasionally photographs of unusual interest are mentioned specifically.

It is hoped that this guide will lead the reader to explore more detailed descriptions and relevant finding aids available in the Still Picture Branch.

This guide also should be used in conjunction with the *Guide to the National Archives of the United States* (Washington: Government Printing Office, 1974). The National Archives *Guide* provides descriptions of all the holdings that were in the Archives custody on June 30, 1970, as well as a detailed explanation of the record group concept, and general regulations for the use of NARA records. Most importantly, detailed administrative histories of agencies, and the titles of available finding aids for each record group are included. A new edition of the *Guide* is in progress.

Several NARA publications contain information on still pictures and graphic arts. These publications include Select Audiovisual Records leaflets: *Pictures of Indians in the United States*, *Photographs of the American West. 1861–1912*, *Pictures of the Civil War*, *Pictures of the Revolutionary War*, *Pictures of United States Navy Ships. 1775–1941*, *Pictures from the Harmon Foundation: Artworks and Art Activities*, *Contemporary African Art from the Harmon Foundation*, and *Pictures of the American City*. Also relevant are *Broadsides and Posters from the National Archives* (NARA, 1986), *The National Archives of the United States* (Abrams, 1984), *The American Image: Photographs from the National Archives, 1860–1960* (Pantheon Books, 1979), and *War & Conflict: Selected Images from the National Archives, 1765–1970* (NARA, 1990). A list of other NARA publications is available from the National Archives upon request.

Most of the records described here are readily available to researchers. Some records, however, may be temporarily unavailable or may have restrictions on access. It is suggested, therefore, that researchers query the Still Picture Branch about the availability of records in advance of their visits. Researchers should inquire also about guidelines and the rules and regulations governing research in the Still Picture Branch.

Photographic reproductions of Still Picture Branch records are available for a fee. We do not, however, charge user fees. The majority of records in the branch are in the public domain, but because agencies often acquire photographs from private sources, some items may be under copyright or carry publication restrictions. The owners of the rights to these images may impose certain fees for their use. The information available to NARA about these restrictions, however, is often incomplete. For further information on ordering and using photographs furnished by the National Archives, contact the Still Picture Branch.

ORGANIZATION OF THE GUIDE AND SCOPE OF THE ENTRIES

General Organization

This guide is organized in two parts. Part I—Federal Records describes the accessioned records of the federal government in the custody of the Still Picture Branch as of October 1989, according to the record group to which the records have been allocated. The record groups are in order numerically. The Still Picture Branch does not hold records from some agencies for which record groups have been established; thus, there are gaps in the numerical sequence followed in this guide.

Part II—Donated Materials contains descriptions of photographic and graphic materials donated to the branch and the National Archives. The documents in this section were formerly identified as RG 200, The National Archives Gift Collection. Information on the donations is by collection. The collections are arranged roughly in chronological order according to the content dates of the materials described.

Scope of the Entries

The following key illustrates the important elements of the format of entry descriptions in both Part I and Part II of this guide.

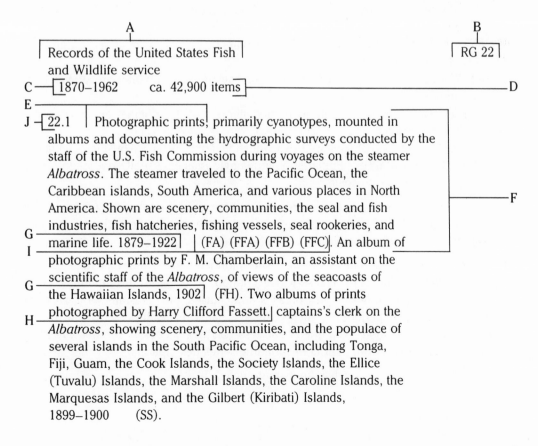

A

Records of the United States Fish and Wildlife service

B

RG 22

C — 1870–1962   ca. 42,900 items — D

E

J – 22.1   Photographic prints, primarily cyanotypes, mounted in albums and documenting the hydrographic surveys conducted by the staff of the U.S. Fish Commission during voyages on the steamer *Albatross*. The steamer traveled to the Pacific Ocean, the Caribbean islands, South America, and various places in North America. Shown are scenery, communities, the seal and fish industries, fish hatcheries, fishing vessels, seal rookeries, and marine life. 1879–1922   (FA) (FFA) (FFB) (FFC). An album of photographic prints by F. M. Chamberlain, an assistant on the scientific staff of the *Albatross*, of views of the seacoasts of the Hawaiian Islands, 1902   (FH). Two albums of prints photographed by Harry Clifford Fassett, captains's clerk on the *Albatross*, showing scenery, communities, and the populace of several islands in the South Pacific Ocean, including Tonga, Fiji, Guam, the Cook Islands, the Society Islands, the Ellice (Tuvalu) Islands, the Marshall Islands, the Caroline Islands, the Marquesas Islands, and the Gilbert (Kiribati) Islands, 1899–1900   (SS).

F

G
I

G

H

(A) In Part I, this is the record group title. In Part II, it is the section heading. Collection titles for donated materials are indicated elsewhere (F).

(B) RG is the abbreviation for record group, followed by the record group number. This does not apply to donated materials.

(C) These are the informational content dates of the still pictures in this record group or collection. This date represents the time period for the subjects pictured and is not necessarily the date the records were created, accumulated, or organized. Those organizational dates, when known, are indicated in the body of the description if they differ from the informational content date. This departure from usual NARA practice was made because NARA believes that the readers of this guide are primarily interested in knowing the time frames of the subjects pictured, particularly since many of the agency files contain retrospective information.

(D) The number of items (discrete images) in a record group or of all of the donated materials under the custody of the Still Picture Branch. The count for individual series is not given.

(E) The type of record or medium if easily identifiable.

TERMS:

PHOTOGRAPHS—A general term that refers to both prints and negatives.

PHOTOGRAPHIC PRINTS—A more specific term. Printing types when known are indicated, such as cyanotypes.

CARD PHOTOGRAPHS—Refers to photographic prints on commercially produced cardboard mounts of standard sizes.

STEREOGRAPHS—Refers to photographic prints only.

PANORAMAS—Refers to photographic prints only.

PHOTOGRAPHIC NEGATIVES—A more specific term that refers to film base items, usually. Where entire series consist of glass negatives, it is noted.

SLIDES—Refers to positive transparencies in cardboard mounts—2″ × 2″ in size.

LANTERN SLIDES—Refers to positive transparencies made or mounted on glass— usually 3¼″ × 4″ in size.

ART, WORKS OF ART—General terms. When specific art techniques are known, they are indicated.

POSTER—Generally refers only to printed items, not the original art from which posters are printed.

PORTRAIT—Refers to photographs of an individual only, usually a bust-length image.

AERIAL PHOTOGRAPHS—Primarily oblique-angle images, usually not taken under mapping purposes to scale.

(F) Series descriptions. Descriptions are usually arranged chronologically. Series with similar content information are often described together. Collection titles for donated materials are indicated here.

(G) Informational content dates for series. The informational content dates are usually found at the conclusion of each series description. When series descriptions consist of several sentences, or complex phrases and clauses, the dates are set apart from the description by periods. In such cases the dates relate, however, to all of the preceeding information. With briefer and less complex accounts, commas are used to distinguish dates from their corresponding series descriptions.

(H) Names of photographers, when known, are noted.

(I) Series designators. Often several series are described together, and so several series designators may follow a description. When referring to series, please cite the record group number or collection title for donated materials and the series designation.

(J) This is the entry number for the descriptions in this guide. When referring to individual descriptions you may also cite this guide and the entry number.

ILLUSTRATIONS

The photographs illustrating this *Guide to the Holdings of the Still Picture Branch* were selected from approximately six million images in the holdings of the branch. The images will give the researcher some indication of the breadth and variety of pictures maintained by the Still Picture Branch of the National Archives.

Captions

The photograph identification number (example: 111-B-36) precedes the caption. Italics denote original captions. Paraphrased captions, or those created when no original information was available, are in roman type. Dates and photographer credits are from the original item, whenever possible. We relied upon the original item for accuracy of this information. In most instances when dates are not included in the original caption, we provide an approximate date.

Several original captions are edited for length. In three instances information in brackets is added to aid the reader in understanding the image. When known, locations are mentioned. Occasional misspellings or colloquialisms are retained. In addition to captions, dates, and the names of photographers, the title of the record group from which the image was selected is indicated.

How to Order Reproductions

To the best of our knowledge, all of the illustrations in this guide are in the public domain and there are no restrictions on their use. The records of the Library of Congress Copyright Office indicate that the privately produced photographs are no longer under copyright.

Black-and-white reproductions of the pictures may be ordered from the National Archives. Prints and negatives in various sizes and slides are available. Send all requests for copies to the National Archives, Still Picture Branch (NNSP), Washington, DC 20408. Please cite the title of this guide and the photograph identification number. Ordering instructions and price lists will be sent in response to each request. All orders must be prepaid.

Part I

Federal Records

RG 3

RECORDS OF THE U.S. HOUSING CORPORATION
1918–21   2,000 items

3.1   Photographic negatives of blueprints, architectural drawings, and maps used to design housing and community structures for World War I workers, 1918 (BGP).

3.2   Photographs and lantern slides recording various stages in the construction of government housing projects and planned communities, 1918–21 (HC) (LS).

3.3   Photographic prints of slum housing in Chester, PA, 1918 (MCS). An album of photographic prints of trolley car track construction, interurban trains and street scenes, 1918–19 (MTF). Sketches for posters advertising war workers' housing in Washington, DC, 1918 (MPW). Photographic prints of dining and sleeping facilities at a factory cooperative in France, 1918–19 (MSF). Portfolios of architectural drawings of rural dwellings in France, ca. 1919 (MFB). Glass negatives of unidentified fields and houses, ca. 1919 (MFH).

3.4   Glass negatives from the Town Planning Division of a meeting of the American Association of Landscape Architects, 1918 (TP).

RG 4

RECORDS OF THE U.S. FOOD ADMINISTRATION
1917–20   5,812 items

4.1   Photographs taken or collected by the administration and used to document its activities and programs during World War I, including wartime conservation efforts. Subjects include agency buildings; billboards and posters used in campaigns in the United States and other countries; exhibits; sugar production in the United States, Cuba, and Puerto Rico; the activities of women's groups during the war; U.S. aid to Europe during and after the war; destruction in Europe from the war; prisoners of war; refugees; agency personnel; and several well-known individuals, such as Herbert Hoover. 1917–20 (G).

4.2   Posters used in U.S. and French Liberty Loan drives, Red Cross drives, war work and enlistment campaigns, and campaigns to promote food conservation and encourage production, 1917–19 (P).

4.3   Lantern slides used by the administration's Division of Education to illustrate lectures on the conservation, preservation, and preparation of food, 1917–19 (LS).

RG 5

RECORDS OF THE U.S. GRAIN CORPORATION
1919   20 items

5.1   Photographs showing the unloading of grain and cotton from U.S. merchant ships; the interior of warehouses in Hamburg, Germany, fully stocked with food; and corporation staff and offices in Hamburg and Berlin. 1919 (BH).

RG 7

RECORDS OF THE BUREAU OF ENTOMOLOGY AND PLANT QUARANTINE
1700–1954   13,961 items

7.1   From Leland O. Howard, chief of the bureau from 1894 to 1927, a collection of portraits of American and foreign scientists, with particular emphasis on Department of Agriculture entomologists, 1700–1936 (H).

7.2   Photographs of cotton insects and of a variety of cotton crop dusting practices, 1904–26 (CI). Photographic prints relating to fire ant infestations, 1950–51 (F).

7.3   Photographs of insects, insect infested plants, efforts to control and eradicate insects, and entomological experiments. Also included are portraits of bureau personnel. 1919–54 (EPQ).

7.4   Photographs—some of maps, graphs, and drawings— relating to pest control experiments at the bureau's Moorestown, NJ, research station, with particular emphasis on methods of controlling the Japanese beetle, 1920–54 (B).

7.5   Photographs of the cultivation and marketing of cotton, corn, blueberries, oranges, and tobacco, n.d. (T).

RG 8

RECORDS OF THE BUREAU OF AGRICULTURAL ENGINEERING
1913–47   3,679 items

8.1   Photographs relating to drainage, irrigation, and erosion control projects, 1913–47 (D) (N) (M). Photographs showing the terrain of El Rito, Rio Arriba County, NM, 1937 (NM).

RG 9

RECORDS OF THE NATIONAL RECOVERY ADMINISTRATION
ca. 1933   1 item

9.1   A photographic negative of Charles Toucey Coximer's drawing, ca. 1933, of the National Recovery Administration Blue Eagle. The original item is filed with the textual records of the administration. (X).

RG 12

RECORDS OF THE OFFICE OF EDUCATION
1913–65   1,737 items

12.1   Photographs, a few by Lewis Hine, collected for use as illustrations in the Bureau of Education's publications. The photographs show bureau offices, classroom scenes in schools, illustrations used in bulletins and exhibits, and participants in agricultural extension programs and the School Garden Army. 1913–23 (ED).

12-HE-118. *Los Angeles, California. Nursery in Elementary Schools.* n.d. (RG 12, Records of the Office of Education)

16-GA-125-N55700. *Horticulturist Henry Cathey of the U. S. Department of Agriculture's Agricultural Research Service places a ripe apple and a potted bromeliad houseplant in a plastic bag to make the plant bloom like the one in the foreground. As houseplants bromeliads rarely bloom but they can be made to flower and fruit by ethylene gas, which is given off naturally by ripe apples.* The Agricultural Research Center, Beltsville, MD. March 1965. Hermann Postlewaite. (RG 16, Records of the Office of the Secretary of Agriculture)

15-VR-2H-6. *Trainees in power plant operation at the State A.&E. College, West Raleigh, N.C.* Ca. 1921. (RG 15, Records of the Veterans Administration)

17-HD-3A-45327B. *Weight 121.7 lbs. Sarah born March 15, 1932, BW [birth weight] 97 lbs., fed from birth on a fortified cow's milk formula.* August 8, 1932. (RG 17, Records of the Bureau of Animal Industry)

12.2   Photographs collected by the Home Economics Section of the Service Division showing home economics instruction in elementary and junior high schools, 1925–30 (HE).

12.3   A collection of photographic prints from public and private school systems in the United States documenting vocational and academic training, and therapy and recreational activities for handicapped children, 1938–65 (HC).

12.4   Photographic prints of adult and youth forums organized under the Federal Forum Project, a program to provide employment and to encourage civic education, 1939–41 (PF).

12.5   Photographs showing enrollees at work and in training under the Civilian Conservation Corps Camp Education program, 1940 (CCC). Ink drawings by Marshall Davis that were printed in *Camp Life*, a series of elementary readers and workbooks used by the Civilian Conservation Corps, 1939–40 (CLR) (CLA) (CLM).

RG 15

RECORDS OF THE VETERANS ADMINISTRATION
1833–1968   7,582 items

15.1   Photographs of the Commissioners of the Pension Office who served from 1833 to 1925 (PC).

15.2   Photographic prints recording the construction of the U.S. Pension Bureau Building and showing pension examiners in 1909; a view of the Tomb of the Unknown Soldier of the Civil War; a photographic print by Mathew Brady of Gen. Winfield Scott and his staff; a U.S. Army recruiting poster featuring George Washington; a color lithograph of the 1862 Philadelphia Volunteer Refreshment Salon; and a drawing of the veterans of the Grand Army of the Republic. 1862–1909 (M).

15.3   Photographs showing veterans in rehabilitation programs instituted under the Federal Board for Vocational Education, 1918–28 (VR). Photographs (some in color) of Veterans Administration (VA) hospitals, regional offices, agency personnel, veterans undergoing therapy and rehabilitation, and VA beneficiaries receiving assistance, 1944–62 (MFS).

15.4   Photographs of VA facilities and construction projects, and microfilm of plans and architectural and landscape drawings for some hospitals, 1922–65 (HDC) (HDM). Two albums of photographic prints showing the construction of VA facilities, 1938 (WPA).

15.5   An album of photographic prints taken in 1931 of the staff of the VA center, Hines, IL, and a scrapbook documenting the Patient Evacuation and Fire Control Institute sponsored by the VA and held in 1959 in Minneapolis, MN. Photographs of Veterans Day ceremonies at Arlington Cemetery, VA, from 1961–68, including pictures of President John F. Kennedy at the 1961 and 1963 ceremonies. Photographs of members of the Veterans Advisory Council, council meetings, and the council's 1967 election observers trip to South Vietnam. Also photographs of dedication ceremonies for VA hospitals. 1931–68 (CVC).

RECORDS OF THE
OFFICE OF THE SECRETARY OF AGRICULTURE
1794–1975   205,913 items

16.1   Photographic prints of oil paintings of officials of the department and other individuals important in the history of U.S. agriculture. The images were made by the Office of Information. 1794–1933 (P).

16.2   The Erwin F. Smith collection of photographic prints of American and foreign scientists, department personnel, department buildings, and experimental farms; also a picture of the members of the National Academy of Sciences with President Warren G. Harding and Albert Einstein. Smith was head of the Laboratory of Plant Pathology, Bureau of Plant Industry. 1886–1937 (ES).

16.3   Joseph Abel, a scientist with the Bureau of Animal Industry, collected photographs of Washington, DC, its buildings, memorials, monuments, and street scenes; and pictures of Presidents Woodrow Wilson, Warren G. Harding, and Calvin Coolidge. 1899–1932 (AD). Hand-colored lantern slides collected by Abel and showing the department's exhibits at the 1915 Panama-Pacific International Exposition in San Francisco, CA, as well as views of the exteriors of some exhibition halls and outdoor sculpture at the exposition site, 1915 (SFX).

16.4   Photographic prints documenting rural life and agricultural activities from the Office of Information's "historical file" of images selected from the files of the Extension Service, Forest Service, Rural Electrification Administration, Biological Survey, Bureau of Entomology, Federal Crop Insurance Corporation, Agricultural Adjustment Administration, and other units of the department. Subjects include farmers and their families; soil conservation measures; planting and harvesting of crops, and marketing procedures; care and raising of livestock; farm equipment and farm buildings; pests and their control; research activities; food preparation and preservation; department officials and other personnel; agency buildings and experimental farms. 1900–75 (G) (GA).

16.5   Photographs collected by Frank Lamson-Scribner, a special agent in charge of department exhibits for many national and international expositions. Shown are exhibits at several expositions, including the Louisiana Purchase Exposition, the Brazilian International Exposition, and the Panama-Pacific International Exposition; cities where the expositions were held; botanical gardens; landscapes; plant varieties; buildings in Washington, DC; and the Lamson-Scribner family. 1901–34 (FLS).

16.6   Photographs taken primarily by E. C. Purdy and F. S. Knoblock for use in agency publications on a variety of subjects, including views of various expositions; scenic views in and around Washington, DC; markets; and the activities of Secretary H. A. Wallace. 1901–43 (PSA) (PSB) (PSC) (PSD).

16.7   Photographs from the Photography Division of the Department's Office of Information of agency officials and personnel, conferences, 4-H clubs, experiments and tests, agricultural practices, and animal husbandry. Also included are photographs of German prisoners of war working on farms in Georgia, and President Harry Truman signing the School Lunch Bill. 1939–75 (N) (ST).

16.8   Lantern slides documenting the activities of the War Hemp Industries, Inc., and showing the cultivation, harvesting, and processing of hemp, 1942–46 (WH).

RG 17

RECORDS OF THE BUREAU OF ANIMAL INDUSTRY
1864–1949   7,419 items

17.1   Photographic prints and some negatives of various breeds of dogs and horses; zebras; and mules and other equine cross breeds. Also included are views of the Beltsville Agriculture Center, MD, the U.S. Morgan Horse Farm, Middlebury, VT, and horse pens in Montana and Wyoming; and portraits of bureau officials and other personnel. 1864–1943 (N) (HD) (HDA) (HM).

17.2   Photographic prints of sheep and sheep pelts taken to illustrate the results of breeding Karakul rams with other breeds of sheep, 1928–49 (S).

17.3   Photographic prints of breeds of poultry and other birds, exhibits, and bureau facilities in Beltsville, MD, and Glendale, AZ, 1905–30 (P).

RG 18

RECORDS OF THE ARMY AIR FORCES
1903–64   ca. 118,700 items

18.1   Photographs of foreign and domestic aircraft taken or collected by the Engineering Division of Wright-Patterson Air Force Base, OH, and the Wright Air Development Center, OH, 1903–59 (WP).

18.2   Lantern slides documenting events, subjects, and individuals important to the history of military aviation, 1903–27 (AH).

18.3   Photographic prints of U.S. Army balloon and airship facilities and schools, 1908–20 (MA).

18.4   Photographs of early aircraft, activities, and personnel at the army-navy aviation school at Rockwell Field, CA, and of several individuals important to aviation history. The photographs were taken by H. A. Erickson and Harold R. Taylor and were purchased in 1941 by the Army Air Corps. 1914–18 (HE).

18.5   Photographs taken by the Air Service Photographic Section under the direction of Major Edward Steichen. Included are aerial views of towns and battlefields, and pictures of U.S. aviation activities, facilities, and personnel in Germany and France during World War I. 1918–19 (E).

18.6   Photographs documenting the activities of the Spruce Production Corporation, including views of timber stands, sawmills, camps, logging operations, and workers, 1918–20 (SPCA) (SPCB) (SPCC) (SPCD).

18.7   Portraits of people important to the history of aviation, ca. 1918–45 (HP). Flight personnel identification photographs, 1911–41 (P) (PU).

18.8 Aerial photographs of cities and communities, landmarks and historic sites, national parks, geographical features, the aftermath of natural disasters, ports, and airfields, 1917–64 (AA) (AN).

18.9 Photographs taken by photo squadrons stationed at Scott Field, IL, of facilities, equipment, and personnel at the field; and of cities and towns, airports, military bases and airfields, floods, and landscapes in Florida, Illinois, Indiana, Kentucky, Michigan, Missouri, and Wisconsin. 1923–39 (SF).

18.10 Transparencies of buildings and various facilities at March Field, CA, including several views of construction activities, 1928–34 (MRR) (MFC). Transparencies documenting a variety of aircraft accidents that occurred at or near March Field, 1928–34 (MFA). Transparencies of the Aircraft Supply Depot at Rockwell Field, CA, ca. 1930 (RFF).

18.11 Photographic negatives showing in-flight refueling operations, ca. 1923 (HER).

18.12 Photographs taken by observation squadrons stationed at three airfields, and showing municipal and military airfields, aircraft, cities, landmarks, and scenic views of the United States. Includes a 1929 photograph of the airship *Graf Zeppelin* over Oakland, CA, and views of earthquake damage to Santa Barbara, CA, in 1925 and to Long Beach, CA, in 1933. 1925–47 (LMU).

18.13 A filmstrip entitled "Round the World Flight" about aviators Harold Gatty and Wiley Post and their monoplane, the *Winnie Mae*, 1931 (FS).

18.14 Aerial and ground photographs taken by the Overseas Technical Unit of the Air Transport Command along air flight routes in the United States and other countries. Shown are command facilities, bases, military and civilian personnel; route maps and navigational beacons; people, scenery, and landmarks; and topographical features. Many of the pictures were taken by noted photographer Russell Lee. 1943–45 (AG) (AM) (AO) (MO) (ATC) (ZC).

18.15 Portraits of African-American flight training graduates of the Tuskegee Army Air Field, AL, 1943 (T).

RG 19

RECORDS OF THE BUREAU OF SHIPS
1776–1966   ca. 450,000 items

19.1 The general photographic file of the bureau documenting the history of the U.S. Navy including identification views of U.S. Navy vessels; pictures of the construction and launching of ships; and pictures of shipyards, drydocks, and equipment. Also included are photographs of sailors and officers, Navy Department officials, noted individuals, and works of art. Ca. 1776–1941 (N).

19.2 The Child Collection containing mounted photographic prints of ships selected from the general file, 1860–1922 (NC). Also from the general file, a selection of photographic prints primarily showing small boats and auxiliary vessels, ca. 1865–1941 (NS).

19.3 Photographs accumulated by the Bureau of Steam Engineering showing bureau buildings at the New York Navy Yard, steam turbines, coaling operations, coal mining, diving bells, radio installations, the Honda Point disaster, and other subjects; and photographic prints used to illustrate a report by Lt. W. H. Chambers on the "Corrodibility of Boiler Tubes." 1863–1929 (SEA) (SEB) (SEC) (SEE) (SEM).

19.4   Albums of photographic prints compiled or collected by the Bureau of Construction and Repair showing U.S. Navy vessels, including pictures of ships under construction; damage to and the repair of ships; ship fittings and interior furnishings; figureheads and ornaments; silver service gifts; crew and officers quarters; workshops and storerooms; deck scenes; radio installations; coaling operations; shops and facilities at New York and other navy yards; merchant vessels; and navy schools and classes. Also included are pictures of ships of the French and German navies; views of the ports of Brest and Cherbourg, France; and scenes in Samoa. 1883–1914 (A). An album of photographic prints showing damage to ships, and the salvage of the battleship *Maine* and other ships, 1898–1917 (AWD).

19.5   Photographic prints of the following: Ship fittings, equipment, and interiors; models of ships; tests and experiments; damage to ships; views of the navy yards in Boston, MA, and New York; the Department of the Navy exhibit at the 1926 Sesquicentennial International Exposition in Philadelphia; and other subjects. 1902–39 (E).

19.6   Photographic prints of the construction, launching, refitting, and sea trials of U.S. Navy vessels, 1902–65 (LC) (LCA) (LCM).

19.7   Oversize photographic prints of navy radio and communication installations and equipment, 1907–24 (RS).

19.8   Photographs of U.S. Navy ships at Veracruz, Mexico, in 1914, Mexican refugees, and Mexican and American dignitaries. Also photographs of ships on sea trials, in drydocks and fitting out wharves, and U.S. Navy midshipmen. 1914–20 (VC).

19.9   Photographs of a naval review of the Atlantic Fleet at Boston, MA, during a 1915 governors conference (BNR). Several undated photographic prints and diagrams of a motor buzzer transmitter (MBT). Photographic prints of Secretary of the Navy Josephus Daniels and bureau chiefs, ca. 1917 (NBC). Photographs of ships of the British Royal Navy, 1941–45 (SB). Albums of photographic prints of models and mock-ups of navy ships, 1941–46 (MM). Photographic negatives showing alterations to the carrier U.S.S *Lexington*, CV–2, 1942 (X). Photographic prints of the launching and commissioning of post-World War II ships, including nuclear submarines, ca. 1946–66 (NV).

RG 21

RECORDS OF
DISTRICT COURTS OF THE UNITED STATES
ca. 1840–1930   12 items

21.1   Photographs of paintings of jurists, the Justices of the 1894 Supreme Court, and of a bust of Justice Louis Brandeis, ca. 1840–1930 (PJ).

21.2   A photographic negative of an 1865 Mathew Brady portrait of President Andrew Johnson. The original image is filed with the textual records of the District Courts (X).

RG 22

RECORDS OF THE
U.S. FISH AND WILDLIFE SERVICE
1870–1962   ca. 42,900 items

22.1   Photographic prints, primarily cyanotypes, mounted in albums and documenting the hydrographic surveys conducted by the staff of the U.S. Fish Commission during voyages on the steamer *Albatross*. The steamer traveled to the Pacific Ocean, the Caribbean islands, South America, and various places in North America. Shown are scenery, communities, the seal and fish industries, fish hatcheries, fishing vessels, seal rookeries, and marine life. 1879–1922 (FA) (FFA) (FFB) (FFC). An album of photographic prints by F. M. Chamberlain, an assistant on the scientific staff of the *Albatross*, of seacoasts of the Hawaiian Islands, 1902 (FH). Two albums of prints photographed by Harry Clifford Fassett, captain's clerk on the *Albatross*, showing scenery, communities, and the populace of several islands in the South Pacific Ocean, including Tonga, Fiji, Guam, the Cook Islands, the Society Islands, the Ellice (Tuvalu) Islands, the Marshall Islands, the Caroline Islands, the Marquesas Islands, and the Gilbert (Kiribati) Islands, 1899–1900 (SS).

22.2   Photographic prints of paintings created in 1872 and 1890 by Henry Wood Elliott showing seals, seal rookeries, seal hunts, and the topography of St. George and St. Paul, Pribilof Islands, AK (HE). Panoramas of seal and sea otter rookeries in the Pribilof Islands photographed by C. H. Townsend and N. B. Miller with the steamer *Albatross*, 1892–97 (SR).

22.3   Cyanotypes from the Division of Statistics and Methods of the Bureau of Fisheries showing wharves, fishing vessels and fishing communities in California, Connecticut, Maine, Maryland, Massachusetts, New York, Rhode Island, Virginia, and the Great Lakes area, 1882–92 (CA) (CB) (CC) (CD) (CE) (CF) (CG) (CH) (CJ) (CK) (CL).

22.4   Photographs collected by the Division of Statistics and Methods showing activities of commercial fish, oyster and shrimp industries in the Chesapeake Bay, Hampton Roads, Roanoke River-Albermarle Sound and Great Lakes areas; and along the Pacific and Gulf of Mexico coasts. Ca. 1891 (FCB) (FCC) (FCD) (FCE) (FCF). Cyanotypes photographed by bureau employees W. T. Bowers, H. D. Chichester, G. D. Hanna, and C. H. Townsend showing commercial fishing and fur seal industries in Alaska, as well as lobster hatcheries in Florida, communities in Alaska, the mother-of-pearl button industry in Iowa, and marine specimens, 1904–18 (BF).

22.5   Photographs showing coastal and inland areas adjacent to Kiska Harbor, AK, 1904; sturgeon, ca. 1902; sponges, ca. 1908; interior views of a fish hatchery, the steamer *Albatross*, and Bureau of Fisheries railway cars, ca. 1910; foreign and domestic fishing vessels, 1894–1911; seal hunting in Alaska, 1882–89; and the mother-of-pearl button industry in Iowa, n.d. (MDF) (MFK) (MFM) (MFP) (MPB) (MSF) (MSP). Hand-colored stereographs of game birds and animals, 1870 (MSW).

18-AG-5671. *Hickam Field, Oahu, T.H. Putting patch on C54 with cherry rivets.* July 12, 1945. (RG 18, Records of the Army Air Forces)

19-LC-19A-23. *U.S.S.* Arizona *approaching end of ways, Navy Yard, New York.* June 19, 1915. (RG 19, Records of the Bureau of Ships)

22-CL-269. *Crew of New York bluefish fisherman.* Ca. 1882. (RG 22, Records of the U.S. Fish and Wildlife Service)

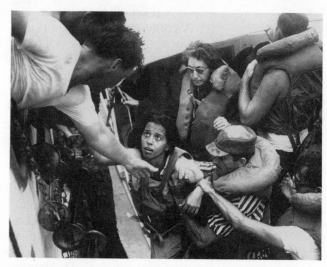

26-G-10-13-65(01). *Pickup of Cuban refugees aboard U.S.C.G.C.* Layman *on barrier patrol, Florida Straits.* October 1965. (RG 26, Records of the U.S. Coast Guard)

22.6 Glass negatives taken by C. G. Atkins, Superintendent of the Craig Brook National Fish Hatchery, of the buildings, equipment, personnel, hatcheries, fish eggs, and fish at the Craig Brook, Green Lake, and Bangor, ME, facilities, 1890–1900 (H).

22.7 Photographs created or acquired by the Bureau of Sport Fisheries and Wildlife and the earlier Biological Survey showing birds, mammals, reptiles, botanical specimens, wildlife, refuges, topographical features, natives of Alaska, scientists, and agency personnel and facilities, ca. 1899–1962 (WB) (WB-M) (WB-T) (WB-X) (WB-Z).

22.8 Photographs of wildlife collected for publicity purposes, ca. 1899–1922 (WBP).

22.9 Photographs from the Alaska Game Commission showing wildlife, communities, methods of transportation, and warden districts, 1927–40 (WA).

RG 23   RECORDS OF THE COAST AND GEODETIC SURVEY

1859–1965   29,500 items

23.1 Photographic prints, graphic art, and original art from the papers of Henry L. Whiting, a former assistant to the Coast and Geodetic Survey, showing areas along the Hudson River, NY, dredging operations, and machinery, 1859 (HW).

23.2 Photographs, including color slides, relating to the topographic, hydrographic, and physical observations undertaken by the survey. Includes photographs of personnel, equipment, survey activities, navigational aids, underwater views, Alaskan terrain, and disasters. 1860–1965 (G) (GS).

23.3 Photographs taken to illustrate activities associated with research in terrestrial magnetism and electricity, 1901–54 (Q).

RG 24   RECORDS OF THE BUREAU OF NAVAL PERSONNEL

ca. 1777–1944   ca. 11,400 items

24.1 Photographs of Navy and Marine Corps personnel, including commissioned, noncommissioned, and reserve officers; enlisted men; the families of some servicemen; men who were commended or died in World War I; and civilian employees. 1904–38 (P) (PA) (PB) (PC) (CD) (RP). Photographic prints of officers of the U.S.S. *Arethusa*, 1915 (RPA). Portraits of navy officers, ca. 1917–37 (PP).

24.2 Photographs—some of paintings and engravings—of navy chaplains who served from 1790 to 1941 (PNC) (NCP). Photographs of navy chapels, ca. 1940 (NRF).

24.3 An album of halftone prints from the Office of Naval Intelligence showing ships of the Spanish Navy and damages to Spanish ships during the Spanish-American War, 1895–98 (FS).

24.4   Photographic prints, some panoramas, of navy training camps, schools, and stations, ca. 1916–20 (TC) (PAN).

24.5   Photographic prints of Lt. Comdr. Albert Read, his crew, and their NC–4 aircraft during their historic transatlantic flight, 1919 (GC).

24.6   Photographs of various subjects, including navy ships and crews; navy chaplains; members of the 1917 Aeronautic Expedition; recruiting posters; a bronze relief, ca. 1930, of George Washington at Valley Forge; a painting and a statue of Revolutionary War hero John Paul Jones; and a 1933 painting of Franklin D. Roosevelt. Ca. 1777–1935 (PNCP) (PM) (PNA).

24.7   Lantern slides used by the New York City Navy Recruiting Bureau, 1925 (RS). Recruitment posters, some encouraging women to enlist in the WAVES or men to join the SEABEES, the Navy's construction battalions, 1943–44 (DP) (PO).

24.8   An oversize photographic print of President Herbert Hoover with the crews of the U.S.S. *Saratoga* and the U.S.S. *Mississippi*, 1930 (H).

RG 26

RECORDS OF THE U.S. COAST GUARD
1855–1974   ca. 52,627 items

26.1   A general photographic file documenting the history of the U.S. Coast Guard (U.S.C.G.) and relating to agency activities in the enforcement of customs and navigational laws, protection of life and property at sea, and the maintenance of aids to navigation. Included are photographs of U.S.C.G. personnel, crews, ships and boats, and aircraft; ice patrols and icebreaking activities; training programs; the Coast Guard Academy, New London, CT; the Coast Guard in action in Europe and the Pacific in World War II and during the Vietnam conflict; U.S.C.G. activities during the 1946–47 Antarctic expedition led by Adm. Richard Byrd; disasters; rescue operations; Coast Guard support during National Aeronautics and Space Administration's space programs; and several pictures of the Coast Guard aiding refugees fleeing Cuba in the 1960s. 1886–1967 (G).

26.2   Photographs, lantern slides, drawings, and engravings showing lighthouses, light stations, and other aids to navigation, 1855–1933 (LG) (LGA) (LGL). Photographs of lightships and lighthouse tenders, 1891–1935 (LS) (LSH) (LSON). Photographs of lifeboat stations and lighthouses, 1893–1974 (MLN) (CGS). Photographic prints showing discontinued lifeboat and light stations, 1945–61 (LB). Photographs taken as part of a survey and consisting primarily of aerial views of lighthouses; also including pictures of auxiliary structures and equipment. 1945 (S). Photographic prints of exhibition buildings at the World's Columbian Exposition, Chicago, IL, 1893, and nine certificates of award from several expositions, 1883–1930 (LH).

26.3   Three albums of photographic prints documenting the work of the Bureau of Marine Inspection and Navigation, 1938 (MA). Photographs of Coast Guard and merchant ships, ca. 1930–45 (MLS) (MS).

26.4   Albums containing portraits of commissioned officers of the U.S. Revenue Cutter Service and the Coast Guard, 1860–1945 (PC) (PR). Photographs

27-G-1A-1-1. *Peoria, Ill. (Illinois River) Flood of 1922.*
(RG 27, Records of the Weather Bureau)

of enrollees in training at U.S. Maritime Service and U.S.C.G. stations, 1938–41 (A). Photographs of recruits training aboard the U.S.C.G.C. *Unimak*, 1962 (U).

26.5 Photographic prints showing the U.S. Revenue Cutter *Nunivak* and its crew in Alaska and scenes of Alaska, 1899–1900 (RSN). Photographs of the U.S.C.G.C. *Kukui* during visits to loran stations in Alaska, the Philippine Islands, and a few Pacific Ocean islands. Shown are station buildings, transmission equipment, and personnel at work; 1952 inspection tour of several stations by the Appropriations Committee of the House of Representatives. 1948–53 (T). Photographic prints of Greenland taken or acquired by the U.S.C.G.C. *Duane* during a survey of the country and its ports, 1940 (H).

26.6 Photographic prints from the Office of Naval Intelligence showing pre-World War II Japanese merchant vessels and merchant vessels of neutral and Allied countries in San Francisco Bay, CA, 1937–43 (SAN) (SJ).

26.7 Photographs documenting the effects of the 1927 Mississippi River flood and Coast Guard relief efforts, (MF).

26.8 Photographs of Amelia Earhart taken during the 1930s (XC).

26.9 Filmstrips documenting the work of the Steamboat Inspection Service and showing vessels used by the Service, 1938 (MSB). Filmstrips on commercial whaling, ca. 1939 (FS).

26.10 Posters commemorating the 150th anniversaries of the U.S. Coast Guard and the U.S. Lighthouse Service, 1939–40 (P).

RG 27   RECORDS OF THE WEATHER BUREAU
ca. 1880–1968   ca. 19,000 items

27.1 Photographs and lantern slides of charts, maps, and graphs; meteorological instruments and apparatus; natural disasters and the resulting damage; cloud formations; atmospheric occurrences; expeditions; observatories, and weather stations; exhibits at expositions; and scientists and Weather Bureau personnel. Ca. 1880–1954 (G) (GO) (MP) (ND) (GS). Photographs of atmospheric conditions and natural disasters, 1916–68 (C).

27.2 An oversize photographic print showing delegates to the Weather Bureau Convention in Omaha, NE, 1898 (OP).

27.3 An album of photographic prints taken by J. Cecil Alter of cooperative weather stations in Utah, meteorological equipment, and Weather Bureau employees in Salt Lake City, UT, and Washington, DC, 1914 (A).

27.4 A volume of prints of cloud formations photographed at the Charleston, SC, municipal airport and assembled by R. C. Aldredge, 1939 (SC).

27.5 Photographic prints (some in albums) of the rehabilitation of weather stations in the Philippine Islands, 1947–50 (PH).

RG 28

RECORDS OF THE U.S. POSTAL SERVICE
1877–1960   ca. 11,700 items

28.1   Photographs and drawings of post office buildings; photographic prints of agency personnel; and two posters advertising mail service. 1877–1959 (M).

28.2   Photographs showing the development of airmail service. Subjects include the first transcontinental flight, airplanes, and airports; post offices and equipment; airmail pilots, notably, Charles Lindbergh; post office officials; ceremonies; and the operation of the Pan American (Airlines) Mail Service. 1916–60 (MS).

28.3   Photographs of post office facilities showing the interiors and exteriors of buildings, as well as unsafe and hazardous working areas, 1931–59 (F).

28.4   A filmstrip about processing mail for transport by sea, ca. 1920 (FS).

RG 29

RECORDS OF THE BUREAU OF THE CENSUS
1890–1959   155 items

29.1   Photographs and lantern slides of tabulating machinery, 1890–1950 (CM). Photographs relating to the Navajo Indian enumeration, 1930 (NR). Photographs of bureau activities during the 1940 census, 1940–41 (C).

29.2   Filmstrips used to train enumerators, 1959 (F).

RG 30

RECORDS OF THE BUREAU OF PUBLIC ROADS
B.C.–1963   ca. 43,100 items

30.1   Photographs, some of graphic arts, illustrating the evolution of transportation from ancient times to 1963. Also shown are cities and communities throughout the United States; trails, roads, highways, highway construction, roadside facilities, and traffic in the United States and other parts of the world; and of the construction of the Inter-American, Mount Vernon Memorial, and Alaska highways (N).

30.2   An album of photographic prints showing San Francisco after the 1906 earthquake (HH).

30.3   Color transparencies of a diorama exhibit illustrating the history and importance of trails, roads, and highways in the expansion and development of North America from 1539 to 1939 (HOH).

30.4   Lantern slides of road construction; equipment and techniques used in repairing roads; scenic views of the United States and a few foreign countries; railroads; convict labor camps; immigrants; and the 1915 Panama-Pacific International Exposition, San Francisco, CA. 1900–42 (R).

28-MS-3F-45. Jack Knight, pilot, Airmail Service, Omaha, Nebraska. n.d. Nathaniel L. Dewell, Dewell Photo. (RG 28, Records of the U.S. Postal Service)

29-CM-C-9. *This is a card puncher an integral part of the tabulation system used by the United States Census Bureau to compile the thousands of facts gathered by the Bureau. Holes are punched in the card according to a prearranged code transferring the facts from the census questionnaire into statistics.* Ca. 1920. (RG 29, Records of the Bureau of the Census)

32-RS-11. *Work that is play on a hot day sometimes falls to the lot of Merchant Marine apprentices being trained by the United States Shipping Board for service in the Merchant Marine. This picture shows a detail of apprentices testing a patent life raft to determine its capacity.* 1918. (RG 32, Records of the U.S. Shipping Board)

30-N-62-618. *Route 173/165, Los Angeles County.* February 17, 1962. California Division of Highways. (RG 30, Records of the Bureau of Public Roads)

RECORDS OF THE U.S. SHIPPING BOARD

1914–30   43,189 items

32.1   Photographic prints of shipyards and equipment, shipbuilders, progress views of the construction of ships, ship launchings, concrete barges, concrete tests, employee housing, and transportation facilities, 1917–29 (CV). Photographic prints of the construction of a plant in Bristol, PA, and the construction of housing and public utilities at a townsite in Harriman, PA, 1917–19 (PC). Photographic prints of housing projects submitted by the Passenger and Transportation and Housing Division, 1918–20 (H).

32.2   A photographic print of the members of the Emergency Fleet Corporation, 1917 (CV-P). Photographs showing storage conditions for board records in the Gulf District, 1920 (GD).

32.3   Photographic prints of fuel oil installations in Honolulu, HI, 1920 (HH). Glass negatives of the James River Bridge, VA, n.d. (JRB). Photographic prints showing workers at the Fore River, MA, shipyard, n.d. (FRS). Photographs and blueprints of shipyard construction and facilities in the Delaware River area near Philadelphia, PA, 1917–19 (SCF).

32.4   Photographs of merchant marine training and apprenticing programs, ca. 1918 (RS). Photographic prints of ships, cargo, ice patrols, icebergs, seal hunting, port facilities, board personnel, political personalities, and other subjects used as illustrations in the *Merchant Marine Bulletin*, 1920–30 (MMB).

32.5   Photographic prints taken by news bureaus to publicize events and people on board United States Lines ships, including pictures of aviators Amelia Earhart and Clarence Chamberlain, the 1928 U.S. Olympic team, and other notables, 1925–28 (PUS). Photographic prints showing the interior of the SS *America*, 1919 (PIA). Photographs of the SS *Republic*, SS *President Roosevelt*, SS *Manhattan*, and SS *President Hoover*, ca. 1919–30 (SS). Five posters advertising the ships and promoting travel on the vessels of the United States Lines: the SS *Leviathan*, the SS *President Harding*, the SS *President Roosevelt*, the SS *America*, and the SS *George Washington*, 1928–29 (P).

32.6   Albums of photographic prints of the Hamburg-American Line showing company vessels, harbor buildings, warehouses, offices and other properties; also photographs of emigration facilities in Hamburg and Emden, Germany. 1914–18 (SB).

RECORDS OF THE EXTENSION SERVICE

1910–54   ca. 29,600 items

33.1   Photographic negatives primarily of posters used in agency publications, ca. 1910–36 (B).

33.2   Photographs of agency personnel, program activities, and National 4-H Club camps, 1913–35 (C).

33.3   Photographic negatives, many taken by G. W. Ackerman and E. C. Hunton, showing rural life, farming, and the raising of livestock, with emphasis on the programs of the Federal Extension Service, 1920–54 (S)(SC).

33.4 Photographic negatives relating to the National 4-H Club Camp in Washington, DC, 1950 (CC).

RG 35

RECORDS OF THE
CIVILIAN CONSERVATION CORPS
1933–42   10,850 items

35.1 The general photographic file of the Civilian Conservation Corps (CCC) and its predecessor agency consisting of photographs by Wilfred J. Mead and others that record all aspects of the agency's programs, including those programs operated in conjunction with the Forest Service, the National Park Service, the Bureau of Reclamation, the Soil Conservation Service, the Fish and Wildlife Service, the Tennessee Valley Authority, and the Army Air Corps. Other activities of enrollees also are pictured. 1933–40 (GE) (G).

35.2 Photographs acquired from the Army Signal Corps, newspapers, and news agencies showing the recruitment and early activities of President Franklin D. Roosevelt's reforestation army, 1933 (EC). Photographs made by the Army to show enrollee activities in Army Air Corps area programs, 1936–38 (GC). Photographic negatives taken by Bluford W. Muir of the Forest Service and documenting civilian defense training, 1942 (CD).

35.3 Aerial oblique photographs made by the Connecticut National Guard of CCC camps in Connecticut, Massachusetts, and Rhode Island, 1933 (CA). Panoramas of camps and personnel in Arkansas, Colorado, Ohio, and Wyoming, 1934–40 (MOPB). Photographs of the interiors of buildings at Camp Ludington-Pere, MI, ca. 1938 (MOPA). Photographs of CCC companies, 1939–42 (SU). Composite photographic prints of CCC sites and personnel, 1939–40 (MOPD).

35.4 Camp superintendent reports containing photographic prints illustrating the work accomplished by the CCC at twelve camps supervised by the National Park Service, 1933–35 (MP). Color slides by Wilfred J. Mead of CCC enrollees working on soil conservation and road construction projects in Idaho, Oregon, and Washington, 1941 (K) (KI) (KO) (KW).

35.5 Three albums of photographic prints collected by Chaplain N. L. Linebaugh showing religious services in camps and nearby communities in Kentucky, 1935–42 (GK).

35.6 Photographic prints showing African-American enrollees in vocational, academic, and job training programs; performing conservation, reclamation, and reforestation duties; aiding in the restoration of historic buildings and sites; and pursuing recreational activities. 1936–39 (N).

35.7 Lantern slides obtained from the National Youth Administration (NYA) to show the need for and the results of NYA and CCC emergency conservation work, ca. 1938 (LS).

35.8 Photographic prints made by the Forest Service of Thlinget enrollees and others restoring Haida and Thlinget totem poles in the Tongass National Forest, AK, 1938–39 (TA).

35.9   Photographic negatives showing enrollees visiting memorials in Washington, DC, 1941 (WM). Photographic prints documenting the construction of a CCC camp at Bolling Field, Washington, DC, ca. 1940 (CCC).

RG 36

RECORDS OF THE U.S. CUSTOMS SERVICE
ca. 1875–1910   77 items

36.1   Portraits of special agents and other employees of the Bureau of Customs, ca. 1875–1910 (SA).

RG 37

RECORDS OF THE HYDROGRAPHIC OFFICE
1889–1920   168 items

37.1   Glass negatives taken by Lt. Charles Pond of the U.S.S. *Ranger* during a survey of Lower California and Mexico, 1889–90 (CSA) (CSB) (CSC).

37.2   Photographic prints and drawings of harbors and coastal areas in Uruguay, Cuba, Samoa, and California, the Great Lakes, and other areas in the United States, 1903; and photographic prints of a time ball in Japan, 1902, the U.S.S. *Paducah* and U.S.S. *Mahana*, 1920, and of delegates to the 1919 International Hydrographic Conference (M).

RG 38

RECORDS OF THE
OFFICE OF THE CHIEF OF NAVAL OPERATIONS
1891–1946   18,389 items

38.1   Photographs of military defenses at Valparaiso, Chile, 1897 (VAL). Aerial photographs of coastal defenses in the United States and its territories, 1914–23 (FCD). Aerial oblique photographic prints that were acquired by the U.S. naval attaché in Rome from the Italian naval aviation photographic section showing Italian ports and landmarks and aerial bombing tests, 1920 (IS). Halftone prints assembled by the Office of Naval Intelligence showing the defenses of Japanese-mandated Marshall, Caroline, and Mariana islands, ca. 1935 (SS).

38.2   Photographs submitted to the Department of the Navy by manufacturers detailing the design and construction of domestic, foreign, and experimental aircraft, 1914–43 (AC).

38.3   An album of photographic prints of armor tests at the naval facility in Indian Head, MD, 1891–92. Photographic prints of sailors at the Naval Training Station, Newport, RI, 1918; Veracruz and Tampico, Mexico, 1914; buildings in Haiti, ca. 1930; the construction of the German vessel *Kaiser Wilhelm II*; maps of the U.S.S.R., ca. 1919; medals and service ribbons, ca. 1900–20; and civilian and military personnel at the Navy Department during World War II. (HS).

38.4   Portraits of Allied military and political leaders photographed by Comdr. Maurice Constant, 1942–46 (MCN) (MCP).

38.5   Operational Readiness Section photographs of antimine and torpedo devices, and mine warfare tests, 1941–45 (MW).

38.6   An album of photographic prints relating to storage facilities at the Naval Supply Depot, Oakland, CA, ca. 1943. An album of photographic prints prepared by Comdr. C. S. McDowell, U.S.N., as a report on exterior and interior views of German U-boats, 1918. (NS).

38.7   An album of photostats recording the training program for advance base naval units staging in and near Hawaii, ca. 1944 (SNT). Photographic histories of Lion 2 and Lion 4, advance base naval units, ca. 1944 (LT).

GENERAL RECORDS OF THE
DEPARTMENT OF COMMERCE
1903–37 and 1959–64   742 items

40.1   Photographs of buildings and office spaces occupied by the department, and of the seals of the department's bureaus and services, 1903–37 (B).

40.2   Photographs of exhibits at the Sesquicentennial International Exposition in Philadelphia, PA, 1926 (EXA); at the International Exposition in Seville, Spain, 1929–30 (EXB); and at the Safety First Exhibit in Washington, DC, in 1916 (EXC).

40.3   Photographs of the Secretaries of Commerce and other officials including a portrait of President John F. Kennedy; and photographs of meetings, conferences, receptions, and exhibits. 1959–64 (G).

RG 41

RECORDS OF THE BUREAU OF
MARINE INSPECTION AND NAVIGATION
1886–1938   485 items

41.1   Photographic prints and an engraving of commissioners of the Bureau of Navigation, 1886–1927; photographic prints showing the American delegation to the 1929 International Conference on Safety of Life at Sea and a 1938 bureau banquet. (C).

41.2   A photographic print of the SS *Tarragon*, ca. 1917 (T).

41.3   Photographs of merchant marine instructors, officers, and sailors; merchant marine training vessels and classes; trainees involved in recreation and social activities; ceremonies; and members of the United States Shipping Board. 1918–19 (M).

RG 42

RECORDS OF THE OFFICE OF PUBLIC BUILDINGS AND PUBLIC PARKS OF THE NATIONAL CAPITAL
ca. 1776–1937   2,218 items

42.1 Photographs and lantern slides of Washington, DC, showing aerial views; pictures of monuments and memorials, statues, parks, gardens, bridges, and street scenes; and portraits of George Washington and Pierre L'Enfant. Ca. 1776–1930 (MS) (SPB).

42.2 Photographic prints showing views of public buildings and military facilities in Washington, DC; the placement of the statue of Abraham Lincoln in the Lincoln Memorial; the construction of the Washington Monument; White House rooms and china; officers of the Washington Monument Society; the U.S. Capitol Police in 1932; President Woodrow Wilson with Generals Leonard Wood and John Pershing; views of Paris, France; and various nongovernmental ceremonies. 1875–1932 (M).

42.3 Photographs of the White House buildings, gardens, and lawns; a 1903 Easter egg roll on the White House grounds; the State, War, and Navy buildings; and views of Washington, DC. 1900–03 (WH). Also, photographs recording repairs made to the White House in 1927 (WHA).

42.4 Photographs of models for statues and finished statues; landscaping of the Mount Vernon Memorial Highway; members of the Grant Memorial Commission and the dedication ceremony for a memorial to Ulysses S. Grant; and various dignitaries, including President William Howard Taft and his wife. 1921–37 (PR).

42.5 Photographs documenting the construction of the Arlington Memorial Bridge, VA, 1926–33 (AMB).

RG 43

RECORDS OF INTERNATIONAL CONFERENCES, COMMISSIONS, AND EXPOSITIONS
1888–1934   1,596 items

43.1 Photographs of U.S. exhibits at the following expositions: the Centennial International Exposition, Melbourne, Australia, 1888–90; the Universal Exposition, Antwerp, Belgium, 1894; the Louisiana Purchase Exposition, St. Louis, MO, 1904; the Sesquicentennial International Exposition, Philadelphia, PA., 1926; and the International Colonial and Overseas Exposition, Paris, France, 1931–32. Also included are photographs of government exhibits at the Chicago World's Fair Centennial Celebration, Chicago, IL, 1933–34. (EX).

43.2 Photographs taken during Intercontinental Railway Commission surveys of Central and South America, 1890–99 (IRC). Photographic negatives of triangulation stations on the upper Niagara River, ca. 1910 (NR).

43.3 A photographic print showing Henry White, chairman of the U.S. delegation to the Fourth International Conference of American States with President Augusto Bernardino Leguia of Peru and other dignitaries, and a photographic print of German Cisneros, Chief of Protocol, Peruvian Foreign Office, ca. 1910 (M).

RG 44

RECORDS OF THE
OFFICE OF GOVERNMENT REPORTS
1939–45   ca. 4,000 items

44.1   Posters from various federal agencies assembled by the Division of Public Inquiries, Office of War Information, and used to promote the war effort in World War II, ca. 1942–45 (PA). Black-and-white photographic prints of some of the posters in series PA, ca. 1942–45 (PAA).

44.2   Posters produced during World War II by foreign information offices and war relief associations located in the United States, ca. 1942–45 (PF).

44.3   "Newsmaps" portraying in chronological order U.S. military actions in World War II, 1942–45 (NM).

44.4   Production stills from the documentary film *Fight for Life* produced by Pare Lorentz for the United States Film Service, and from *The City*, a documentary film produced by the American Institute of Planners, 1939–40 (LF). Photographic prints apparently used in Office for Emergency Management (OEM) films; also pictures of Carl Sandburg at work on an OEM film. Ca. 1940–41 (F).

RG 45

NAVAL RECORDS COLLECTION OF THE
OFFICE OF NAVAL RECORDS AND LIBRARY
1914–18   783 items

45.1   Posters, some from foreign countries, used by the U.S. Navy during World War I in recruitment and as a means of involving civilian and navy personnel in the war effort. Besides encouraging enlistment in the military, the posters promote conservation and increased productivity, and advertise the work of the Red Cross. 1914–18 (WP).

RG 47

RECORDS OF THE
SOCIAL SECURITY ADMINISTRATION
1936–70   72,788 items

47.1   Photographs (some by famous photographers) from the Office of Information Service of the Social Security Administration (SSA). The photographs were used to publicize and to encourage participation in SSA public assistance and annuity programs. Featured are pictures of public service notices, posters, and exhibits; beneficiaries and annuitants; workers and the unemployed; and SSA personnel and offices. Also included is a photograph of President Franklin D. Roosevelt signing the Social Security Act. 1936–48 (N) (G) (GA).

47.2   Photographs showing the program activities of the Children's Bureau, the Office of Education, and the Public Health Service, 1936–48 (M).

47.3   Filmstrips used by the Social Security Board to illustrate lectures on benefits and to recruit war workers, 1936–42 (FS).

33-SC-17549. *Canning peas at a farm home (Townsend home), Multnomah County, Oregon.* August 1933. George W. Ackerman. (RG 33, Records of the Extension Service)

38-AC-9D-7. *Consolidated Aircraft Corp. Model XPBY-5A. Front view of aircraft on ramps.* December 7, 1939. (RG 38, Records of the Office of the Chief of Naval Operations)

44-F-1C-2. *Poet turns movie maker. Carl Sandburg, famous poet and Pulitizer prize winning historian has turned moviemaker. He has just written the commentary for* Bomber, *a national defense motion picture produced by the Office of Emergency Management Film Unit. He is shown here in the cutting room with Phillip Martin, film editor and technical supervisor of the Film Unit.* Ca. 1941. (RG 44, Records of the Office of Government Reports)

47.4   Photographs (some in color) of agency personnel and offices; Social Security beneficiaries; wage earners; social service program activities; conferences and conventions; views of rural and urban areas; photographs of Presidents John F. Kennedy, Dwight D. Eisenhower, and Harry S. Truman, and President Lyndon B. Johnson signing the 1965 Medicare amendment to the Social Security Act. 1953–70 (SSA) (SSB). Color slides documenting a 1958 trip by Social Security personnel to the U.S.S.R., Sweden, Finland, Scotland, West Germany, and Berlin (SSC).

47.5   A set of color slides about African-American children, 1968 (SSD).

RG 48

RECORDS OF THE
OFFICE OF THE SECRETARY OF THE INTERIOR
1858–1978   1,200 items

48.1   Engravings used to illustrate a report by the Pacific Railway Expedition and Survey on its exploration in 1858 of areas along the 41st parallel (PR).

48.2   Photographic prints and crayon photographic prints of the secretaries, assistant secretaries, assistant attorneys general, and solicitors of the Department of the Interior, 1862–1953 (PO) (PLS).

48.3   Photographic prints of the Columbia Institution for the Deaf and Dumb (Gallaudet College), Washington, DC, 1878 (RSD); and the Hospital for the Insane (St. Elizabeths), Washington, DC, 1898 (RSI). Photographs showing the construction of a U.S. House of Representatives office building, n.d. (RSH); construction of Freedmen's Hospital, Washington, DC, 1906 (RSF); and a construction project at Howard University, Washington, DC, 1924 (RSP). Photographic prints used to illustrate an 1899 report to the Architect of the Capitol on damage to the U.S. Capitol (RSC).

48.4   Photographs submitted with reports from the territorial governors showing national parks, industries, agriculture, and towns in Arizona, Oklahoma, and Hawaii; scenes of California's Imperial Valley and the Wind and Crystal Caves in South Dakota; American Indians and their schools; the Oklahoma land rush; logging operations in Tennessee; views of Hot Springs, AR; and exhibits at the Milwaukee Public Museum, Milwaukee, WI. Ca. 1880–1907 and 1930 (RST).

48.5   Photographic prints on a variety of subjects, including John Wesley Powell and Zachariah Chandler; Department of the Interior officials and other personnel; American Indians; Yosemite; the battleship U.S.S. *Maine*; oil wells in the Los Angeles, CA, area, 1927; the Alaska exhibit building at the Louisiana Purchase Exposition, St. Louis, MO, 1904; and a chart showing the original boundary stones for the District of Columbia. 1892–1954 (M).

48.6   Photographic prints of the department's exhibits at the International Exposition, Seville, Spain, 1928–29 (EXS).

48.7   Color slides of earthquake and flood damage to the Alaska Railroad, 1964 (ARR).

48.8   Color transparencies of works of art commissioned by the Visual Arts Program of the Office of the Secretary of the Interior for the exhibit "America '76," the department's Bicentennial Arts Program, 1974–78 (BA).

RG 49 · RECORDS OF THE BUREAU OF LAND MANAGEMENT
1814–1946   721 items

49.1   Photographs, some of paintings and engravings, of Commissioners of the General Land Office, 1814–1933 (CP).

49.2   Albums containing prints, some photographed by Frank C. Ashton. The albums were used in a General Land Office investigation, and show oil fields, oil derricks, equipment, people, and communities in several districts in California. 1898–1900 (KRA).

49.3   Card photographs showing settlers at the 1893 opening of the Cherokee Strip in the Oklahoma Territory. The photographs were taken by W. A. Flowers of Guthrie, OK, and collected by Anthony Rice, Chief of the Homestead Division (AR).

49.4   Photographs taken as part of a survey of the ecology of Ferry Lake, LA, 1914 (FL). Photographs of geological formations and conditions in California that were used in a U.S. District Court civil case, 1916 (DC). Photographs of War Relocation Authority Centers in Manzanar and Tule Lake, CA, 1946 (RC).

RG 51 · RECORDS OF THE OFFICE OF MANAGEMENT AND BUDGET
1921–77   331 items

51.1   Portraits of directors, assistant directors, and staff members of the Bureau of the Budget and its successor, the Office of Management and Budget; photographs of Presidents Harry S. Truman, Lyndon B. Johnson, Richard M. Nixon, Gerald R. Ford, and Jimmy Carter, and of Ronald Reagan before he became President. Also photographs of ceremonies marking the 30th anniversary of the Executive Office of the President. 1921–77 (P).

RG 52 · RECORDS OF THE BUREAU OF MEDICINE AND SURGERY
1900–70   1,434 items

52.1   Photographic prints of the old Navy Corps hospitals at Norfolk, VA, and Washington, DC; and of graduates of Navy Hospital Corps schools. 1900–10 (C). Photographic prints documenting the construction of the U.S. Navy Hospital, Portsmouth, VA, 1918–19 (H).

52.2   Photographs (some in color) of Navy Nurse Corps uniforms, 1908–70 (NNU). Lantern slides showing World War I gas-warfare equipment, first-aid treatment for gas contamination, and other related subjects, 1918–19 (S).

52.3 Photographs of Navy hospitals and dispensaries in Normandy, France, and southern England, and showing medical treatment for World War II casualties, 1944 (G).

52.4 Black-and-white and color photographs showing Navy dispensaries, hospitals, hospital ships, medical equipment and instruments, and research activities. Also included are photographs showing evacuation of the wounded and battlefield surgical techniques, postoperative care, and medical personnel and patients during the Korean conflict. 1952–56 (KST) (NMB) (NMF).

RG 53 | RECORDS OF THE BUREAU OF THE PUBLIC DEBT
1917–46   524 items

53.1 Drawings and paintings collected for use in war bond drives during World War I, 1917–18 (DP). Photographic prints of motion picture stars and other prominent persons participating in bond campaigns and lantern slides of Liberty Loan posters, 1917–18 (LL).

53.2 Posters promoting war bonds, War Savings Stamps, and U.S. Savings Bonds, 1917–46 (WP).

RG 54 | RECORDS OF THE BUREAU OF PLANT INDUSTRY, SOILS, AND AGRICULTURAL ENGINEERING
1883–1955   ca. 60,000 items

54.1 Photographic prints mounted in albums showing the cultivation, harvesting, and processing of fruits, vegetables, and nuts. Also includes pictures of types of plants; orchards, groves, and gardens; diseased plants; farm and factory workers; equipment; and fairs, exhibits, memorials, and ceremonies. 1883–1941 (F). Mounted photographic prints relating to the growing and marketing of fruits showing fruit trees and orchards, home gardens, canneries, packing houses, storage facilities, and markets, 1903–24 (FM).

54.2 Lantern slides used in culture studies of fruits, vegetables, flowers, plants, and trees that grow in the United States, India, China, Italy, France, the Philippine Islands, and several countries in South America. Included are pictures of charts; maps; types of equipment; farms; markets; storage facilities; processing plants; bureau exhibits; exhibits at expositions; various fruits, flowers, trees, and vegetables; and farm workers. 1902–41 (LS) (LSF).

54.3 Photographic prints documenting research on varieties of vegetables; the cultivation of vegetables, agricultural equipment, farm workers; views of rural areas in Brazil, the Philippine Islands, and Denmark; and Covent Garden, London, England. 1897–1953 (VV). Photographic prints and a few drawings documenting research on the effects of vegetable diseases; cultivated fields, irrigation methods, markets, and farm workers. 1901–34 (VD).

54.4 Mounted photographic prints showing landscape gardening in the United States and some foreign countries, 1892–1933 (L). Mounted photographic prints showing the use of ornamental plants and trees in landscape gardening in the United States; also pictures of children and teachers involved in school gardening projects, and some of the exhibit halls at the 1900 Paris Universal Exposition. 1892–1940 (HP). Mounted photographic prints taken by the Office of Horticultural and Pomological Investigations and its successors to illustrate landscape design projects, 1902–41 (PD). Mounted photographic prints showing the buildings and grounds at the bureau's Arlington Experimental Farm, VA, the results of landscape gardening in rural and urban areas, and types of farmsteads, 1902–29 (FT).

54.5 Photographic prints in albums, from the Office of Corn Investigations, documenting various aspects of corn culture, 1892–1941 (CI). Albums of photographic prints apparently assembled under the direction of Dr. Frederick D. Richey at the University of Tennessee Experiment Station to show the cultivation and processing of corn. The photographs relate primarily to the cultivation of corn in the United States; also in Mexico and other locations in Latin America. 1920–42 (CC).

54.6 Photographic prints taken by J. E. McMurtrey and others and mounted in albums to record various stages in the cultivation of tobacco and to document light and nutrition experiments on various plants, including tobacco. The photographs are from the bureau's Division of Tobacco and Plant Nutrition Investigations. 1908–36 (TI) (TIA).

54.7 Photographic negatives recording sights at the Panama-Pacific International Exposition, San Francisco, CA; parks in California, Pennsylvania, New York, and Washington, DC; and various trees and flowers. 1913–16 (SN).

54.8 Photographs either taken or acquired by Peter A. Yoder, a sugar cane technologist, while investigating the cultivation, harvesting, and processing of sugar cane in the southeastern United States. Included are a few photographs concerning the sugar cane industry in the Philippine Islands and pictures of other crops and animals. 1913–28 (Y). Photographs documenting the work of sugar plant field laboratories, including pictures relating to experimental and research projects and sugar cane cultivation programs, 1920–50 (B).

54.9 Photographs of types of machinery used in harvesting sweet potatoes and sugar beets, 1931–55 (DA). Lantern slides, color slides, and black-and-white prints and negatives showing sugar beet machinery and sugar beet farming operations in Davis, CA, and Fort Collins, CO, 1931–55 (LSB) (LSDa) (Kd) (Kf) (SB).

54.10 Photographs of bureau facilities and personnel, 1928–41 (C). Photographs taken by Wilfred J. Mead, a bureau photographer, to record various types of plants and document the work of the bureau, 1941–53 (M).

54.11 Photographs showing machinery (some experimental) used in the cultivation of the kok-saghyz rubber plant, 1942–44 (RR) (RRK). Photographs and color slides, relating to the Guayule Emergency Rubber Plant Project, Salinas, CA, 1942–43 (SA) (SK). An album of photographic prints documenting a guayule rubber production project in Texas, 1951 (TX).

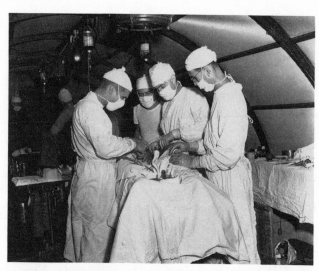

52-NMB-9. *Typical scene in the major surgery operating room at a Medical Company, 1st Medical Battalion, 1st Marine Division, FMF.* Munsan-ni, Korea. October 20, 1952. Sgt. W. G. Landers. (RG 52, Records of the Bureau of Medicine and Surgery)

57-HS-78. *Tower Falls 115 Feet.* Yellowstone National Park. 1871. William Henry Jackson. (RG 57, Records of the Geological Survey)

59-VPT-50-149-1. *Vice President and Mrs. Nixon with the President of Burma and niece.* December 10, 1953. U.S. Air Force. (RG 59, Records of the Department of State)

64-D-7-1. *This is an old photograph which attempts to illustrate space saving which can be achieved through disposal filming. The mound of bundled papers comprises a portion of some seven million cross reference or index sheets. The two film file cabinets, one of them only half full, contained the film reels which now constitute the index to some 300 file cabinets of paper records.* Departmental Records Branch, Department of the Army. Ca. 1957. (RG 64, Records of the National Archives and Records Administration)

65-H-376-1. *Vice-President John Nance Garner being fingerprinted by J. Edgar Hoover.* March 15, 1939. (RG 65, Records of the Federal Bureau of Investigation)

69-TC-NYC-93-12. Rex Ingram as General Christophe in the play *Haiti.* The Federal Theater Project. New York, NY. February 3, 1938. (RG 69, Records of the Work Projects Administration)

75-ID-71a. *Many Horns - Hatona.* 1872. Alexander Gardner. (RG 75, Records of the Bureau of Indian Affairs)

RG 55

RECORDS OF THE
GOVERNMENT OF THE VIRGIN ISLANDS
1931–43   ca. 1,000 items

55.1   Photographs of projects sponsored by the Civil Works Administration, the Public Works Administration, the Work Projects Administration, and the Civilian Conservation Corps concerning improvements to housing, public buildings, parks, and roads in the U.S. Virgin Islands. Also included are scenic views of the islands; photographs of schools, jails, and a leper colony; and a picture taken of Secretary of the Interior Harold Ickes during a visit to the islands. 1931–43 (FRP).

RG 56

GENERAL RECORDS OF THE
DEPARTMENT OF THE TREASURY
1804–1917 and 1941–77   900 items

56.1   Lantern slides illustrating the history and activities of various branches of the Department of the Treasury, including photographs of officials, other personnel, and buildings, 1804–1917 (AT) (AE).

56.2   Lantern slides documenting the work of the Lifesaving Service and the Revenue-Cutter Service, ca. 1915 (AL) (AR).

56.3   Photographs of American Indian delegates to an 1875 conference in Washington, DC (ID).

56.4   Photographs of Civil War generals, ca. 1875 (PR).

56.5   Portraits of officials of the Treasury Department taken by W. H. Slater, ca. 1895 (P).

56.6   Filmstrips promoting the sale of World War II war bonds, 1941–45 (FS). Posters used in war bond and U.S. Savings Bond campaigns, 1942–77 (SP).

RG 57

RECORDS OF THE GEOLOGICAL SURVEY
1869–1941   3,140 items

57.1   Photographs taken by William Henry Jackson during the U.S. Geological and Geographical Survey of the Territories. The survey, under the direction of Ferdinand V. Hayden, explored areas in Colorado, Idaho, Montana, Nebraska, Utah, and Wyoming. Images record physical features of the land in those areas, particularly in the Yellowstone, Grand Teton, and Bad Lands areas. Also included are pictures of survey members and equipment, American Indians, military posts, communities, mining operations, and railroads. 1869–78 (HS). Albumen prints by Jackson of areas of Colorado, including Indian ruins, 1874 (HSA). Mounted photographic prints of Lake Tahoe, CA, and vicinity published by Jackson's photo company, ca. 1885 (HSB). Drawings created by Henry Wood Elliott and William Henry Holmes during the Hayden Survey illustrating land features in Montana, Utah, and Wyoming, 1869–72 (HAA) (HAB) (HAC).

57.2   Photographs taken by E. O. Beaman, James Fennemore, and John K. Hillers of areas in Arizona, Utah, and Wyoming adjacent to the Colorado River and its tributaries. The photographs were taken during the U.S. Geographical and Geological Survey of the Rocky Mountain Region led by John Wesley Powell, 1871–78, and show land features, survey members, surveying equipment, American Indians, and Indian ruins. Also included are photographs unrelated to the Powell Survey taken by John K. Hillers and others showing earthquake damage to Charleston, SC, 1886, and geological formations in North Carolina, Georgia, Tennessee, New York, Florida, California, and the Chesapeake Bay area. Ca. 1886–1900 (PS).

57.3   Albums assembled by Maj. Joseph Wheat, an agency topographer. The albums contain stereograph halves by Beaman, Hillers, and Fennemore showing areas along the Colorado and Green Rivers, and various American Indian groups who lived along the Colorado River, including Utes and Paiutes, 1871–75 (PR) (PL) (PM) (PE). An album of photographic prints showing landscapes, towns, farms, mines, and railroads, ca. 1880–1900 (MA).

57.4   Early film base negatives, stripping film negatives, glass negatives, and albumen prints taken by F. A. Nims and others to document areas explored during a 1889–90 survey of the Colorado River and its tributaries by Robert B. Stanton, chief engineer of the Denver, Colorado Canyon and Pacific Railroad (RS) (RSA) (RSB).

57.5   Photographs of geological formations and landscapes apparently assembled for use in agency publications, 1881–1941 (ISA) (ISB) (ISC).

RG 59

GENERAL RECORDS OF THE
DEPARTMENT OF STATE
ca. 1774–1956   ca. 13,100 items

59.1   Portraits of colonial legislators; members of conventions, the Continental Congress, and the Confederation Congress; signers of the Declaration of Independence, Articles of Confederation, and the Constitution; and other statesmen. Many of the portraits are engravings. Ca. 1774–1876 (LP) (SP).

59.2   Photographic prints, drawings, lithographs, and daguerreotypes relating to diplomacy and international relations. Included are pictures of department officials, early American statesmen, foreign dignitaries, treaty ceremonies, international conferences, U.S. consulates, and U.S. exhibits at several expositions. Ca. 1783–1955 (DA) (M).

59.3   Portraits of presiding officers (Vice Presidents and presidents pro tempore) of the U.S. Senate, 1789–1901 and U.S. Presidents from George Washington to Herbert Hoover, 1789–1933 (PS) (PP). Photographic prints of federal buildings in Washington, DC; pictures of Carpenters' Hall in Philadelphia, PA; a suspension bridge and a hospital in Cincinnati, OH; Chicago, IL, after the 1871 fire; scenes of Quebec, Canada; a statue of Andrew Jackson; and the interior of an Ohio Railroad car. 1870–80 (HB).

59.4   Photographic prints that were submitted to the department by U.S. diplomats or presented by foreign officials. Included are pictures of U.S. consulates in several cities; businesses in Ecuador, Panama, and Rumania; and the German battleship *Graf Spee* in 1939 in Montevideo, Uruguay. 1915–48 (BF). Photographic prints relating to the Balkans obtained from U.S. consulates abroad by the Office of the Counselor. The pictures were apparently used for propaganda purposes by the Germans. Ca. 1916 (GP). Photographs, drawings, posters, and newspaper clippings concerning economic and social conditions abroad that were submitted with consular trade reports, 1943–48 (CTR).

59.5   World War I posters displayed during the Second and Third Liberty Loan drives, 1918 (WP).

59.6   Photographs of U.S. and foreign officials, including President Harry S. Truman, Cordell Hull, Edward Stettinius, Dean Acheson, Dean Rusk, George Kennan, John Foster Dulles, John Kenneth Galbraith, Sam Rayburn, Ellsworth Bunker, Alger Hiss, Konrad Adenauer, and Marshal Tito, 1943–56 (JB).

59.7   Photographic prints of President Warren G. Harding, his wife, and members of his cabinet and their wives, ca. 1921 (PC).

59.8   Photographs of World War II war surplus and lend-lease materials, and of the activities of the department's Office of Foreign Liquidation Commissioner, 1945–49 (TLC).

59.9   Photographs of officials, guests, and representatives at seminars, conferences, and committee meetings of the United Nations Educational, Scientific, and Cultural Organization (UNESCO), 1945–51 (UNP).

59.10   Photographs from the Special War Problems Division documenting the care given to German, Japanese, American, and Canadian repatriates while on the SS *Gripsholm*, a Swedish-American ship; also photographs of Japanese internees at Camp Kenedy, TX, a reception and holding area for enemy aliens. 1943–44 (RAG) .

59.11   Posters produced by the Office of International Information for distribution to foreign information centers. The posters were used to publicize the U.S. standard of living and relate to a variety of subjects, including agriculture, industry, education, health, and politics. 1946–51 (FNL).

59.12   Photographs of U.S. housing projects used in the *Guide to Study Collection on Housing Planning and Construction Techniques* prepared under the direction of Harold Sandbank, housing consultant for the department, for distribution to foreign information centers, 1949 (HP).

59.13   Photographs (some in color) taken during Vice-President Richard M. Nixon's goodwill tour to Korea, Iran, Indonesia, Burma, Ceylon (Sri Lanka), India, Pakistan, Afghanistan, Taiwan, Libya, and Australia, 1953 (VPT).

RG 63

RECORDS OF THE
COMMITTEE ON PUBLIC INFORMATION
1917–18   87 items

63.1   Photographic prints taken by the U.S. Signal Corps showing U.S. aviators in France during World War I. Also included are photographic prints apparently used for propaganda purposes by the Germans and obtained by the U.S. naval attaché at The Hague, Netherlands. These images show agricultural production, sports events, dignitaries, ceremonies, and views of Russia. Ca. 1917–18 (CPI).

RG 64

RECORDS OF THE NATIONAL ARCHIVES AND RECORDS ADMINISTRATION

ca. 1860–1969   ca. 6,000 items

64.1   Photographic prints copied from the *United States Military Railroad Photographic Album* by Andrew J. Russell in the custody of the Virginia Historical Society. The photographs show a variety of Civil War subjects, including railroads, bridges, fortifications, battle sites, artillery, and ruins in Virginia; and buildings in Washington, DC. Ca. 1861–65 (CV). Photographic prints of Washington, DC, copied by the National Archives from issues of *Harper's Weekly*, *Frank Leslie's Illustrated Newspaper*, *The Illustrated London News*, and *Gleason's Pictorial Drawing Room Companion* in the custody of the Historical Society of Washington, DC, 1861–65 (CC).

64.2   Photographs copied by the National Archives from material in other institutions, private collections, and from publications on a variety of subjects. Featured are pictures of Presidents of the United States and other persons, Civil War views, public buildings, and historical events. Ca. 1860–1963 (M). Photographs of buildings and monuments in Washington, DC, reproduced by the National Archives from images held by the Architect of the Capitol, ca. 1900–63 (AC).

64.3   Photographs of Abraham Lincoln copied by the National Archives from the 1933 publication, *Engraved and Lithographed Portraits of Abraham Lincoln*, ca. 1860–65 (CT). Photographs showing President Franklin D. Roosevelt and his family reproduced by the agency from materials at the Franklin D. Roosevelt Library in Hyde Park, NY, ca. 1882–1945 (FDRL).

64.4   Copies of photographs taken by contractors recording the construction of the National Archives building, 1932–42 (NAC). Publicity photographs created by the agency to document administrative activities in the National Archives building, including visits by prominent individuals, special exhibits, and commemorative ceremonies; and to show interior and exterior views of the National Archives building and pictures of other agency buildings. 1935–69 (NA). Photographs taken by agency photographer Harry J. Baudu to document storage conditions for federal records held in buildings in the Washington, DC, area and show some state and foreign archives, ca. 1936–45 (NAD).

64.5   Photographs of Archives microfilming activities and experiments, 1936–47 (NAX). Photographs from a 1959 ceremony in honor of the inventor of the Dagron microfilm camera, Rene Prudent Patrice Dagron. The photographs were copied from items borrowed from the Musée de l'Histoire de France, Paris, France (RD).

64.6   Photographic prints showing types of data processing machines. The images were collected by the Archives Information Technology Division. 1879–1959 (K).

64.7   An album of photographic prints recording the records management operations of the Departmental Records Branch, the Adjutant General's Office, Department of the Army, 1957 (D).

RG 65

RECORDS OF THE
FEDERAL BUREAU OF INVESTIGATION
ca. 1900–84   ca. 9,400 items

65.1   Photographs, drawings, cartoons, and posters collected by J. Edgar Hoover, director of the Federal Bureau of Investigation (FBI). The collections document Hoover's life and career and feature pictures on a wide range of subjects including Hoover at various ages, his family, his friends, and at work and relaxing. Also included are photographs of notorious criminals and relating to famous crimes. The majority of the pictures, however, relate to Hoover receiving gifts, awards, and honoraria; meeting with Presidents from Herbert Hoover to Richard Nixon, various members of Congress, attorneys general, and FBI staff; and greeting foreign police officials and numerous celebrities. Ca. 1900–72 (H) (HM).

65.2   Original cartoons, many autographed by the artists, apparently given to and collected by J. Edgar Hoover because they relate to the bureau, crime, and political events. Among the artists represented are Herbert Block (Herblock), Rube Goldberg, Charles Schulz, Ding Darling, and Hy Rosen. 1934–72 (HC) (HCA). A presentation album commemorating Hoover's 25th anniversary as the FBI director. The album contains original cartoons autographed by the artists. 1949 (HA).

65.3   Posters promoting crime prevention and safety measures produced by the Crime Resistance Section, ca. 1984 (P).

RG 66

RECORDS OF THE COMMISSION OF FINE ARTS
B.C.–1950   ca. 7,500 items

66.1   Lantern slides, glass negatives, photographic prints, and graphic materials collected by the commission. The images are quite varied, reflecting the agency's interest and involvement in art, architecture, and design. There are pictures documenting projects undertaken by the commission; and pictures showing ancient ruins; Roman, Greek, and European architecture; colonial homes; public buildings; parks and arboretums; memorials and monuments; and national cemeteries. Much of the coverage is of places in Washington, DC. Also included are several panoramas showing construction of the Panama Canal. B.C.–1950 (G) (M).

66.2   Photographic prints, original art, and maps assembled ca. 1948 for use in a pictorial history of Washington, DC, that the commission planned to publish in celebration of the sesquicentennial of the U.S. Capitol. Included are pictures of early meeting halls and State capitols. Ca. 1774–1948 (HW). Photographic prints of the capitol buildings of all of the states, except Hawaii and Alaska, 1950 (USC).

66.3   Folios containing photographic prints of sculptures submitted to the commission by artists as examples of their work, 1920–40 (SS).

RECORDS OF THE U.S. FUEL ADMINISTRATION
1917–19   55 items

67.1   Photographic prints of administration buildings, offices, and personnel, 1917–19 (A).

67.2   Panoramas showing the West Virginia Coal & Coke Company and the Hitcham Coal & Coke Company installations in West Virginia, and an unidentified community, 1917–19 (FAP).

RECORDS OF THE WORK PROJECTS ADMINISTRATION
1922–44   ca. 94,300 items

69.1   Publicity photographs documenting the programs, activities, and personnel of the agency; its predecessors, the Civil Works Administration and the Federal Emergency Relief Administration; and its successor, the Federal Works Agency. Included are pictures taken during "area studies" of Alabama, Iowa, Ohio, and Pennsylvania; photographs showing exhibits, construction projects, conservation activities, and health and sanitation efforts; pictures of the employed and unemployed; Work Projects Administration (WPA) art, music, theater, and writing programs; photographs of posters advertising WPA *American Guide* publications; New Deal and WPA officials, including Florence Kerr; and other well-known personages. 1934–42 (MP) (N) (NN) (NS).

69.2   Photographic prints of Federal Emergency Relief Administration projects in various States, Puerto Rico, and the Virgin Islands. Included are pictures from the North Carolina Emergency Relief Administration. 1934–35 (FERANC) (FERA).

69.3   Photographs documenting Civil Works Administration projects in Wisconsin, primarily showing the construction and/or repair of public facilities, 1933–34 (CWA) (CM). Photographic prints showing WPA defense and defense-related projects, such as the construction of airports, bridges, roads, armories, military training camps, and navy yards, ca. 1935–42 (DC).

69.4   Photographs collected for use in state guide books prepared by the Federal Writers' Project for its *American Guide* series. Illustrated are the scenic, historical, cultural, and economic aspects of each state, Washington, DC, Puerto Rico, and the Virgin Islands. Also included is a photo of Simon Bolivar, the Venezuelan statesman. 1936–42 (GU).

69.5   Photographic prints taken or acquired by the National Research Project to illustrate its reports. Shown are workers engaged in agricultural, manufacturing, mining, and transportation occupations. 1936–40 (RH). Photo studies undertaken by Lewis Hine, the chief photographer for the National Research Project, to document workers, working conditions, and housing in 14 industrial communities, 1936–37 (RP) (RPA) (RPM) (RPR).

69.6   Vertical and oblique aerial photographs of airports and airport sites collected by the Airport and Airways Section of WPA to document its work and serve as a historical survey of airport systems in the United States, 1922–40 (AAA) (AAB) (AAC) (AAN).

69.7 Photographs from the Federal Theater Project showing production scenes, sets, theaters, audiences, performers, playwrights, WPA officials, and politicians, 1935–39 (TC) (TS) (TMP). Photographs and original drawings and paintings of costume and set designs for the Federal Theater Project, 1935–39 (TSR). Posters and broadsheets advertising Federal Theater Project productions, 1935–39 (TP).

69.8 The general photographic file and the state file of the Federal Art Project (FAP), documenting its programs in the fine arts, practical arts, and art education, including photographs of artists and their work; exhibits; art centers; and FAP officials and other notable persons, such as Eleanor Roosevelt and Holger Cahill, FAP director. 1936–43 (AG) (AS).

69.9 Photographs of the activities of the New York City FAP, including pictures of project artists and their works, 1935–43 (AN) (ANM) (ANS).

69.10 Photographs depicting life in New York City taken as part of creative assignments by photographers working for the New York City FAP Photographic Division. Among the photographers represented are Sol Liebsohn, David Robbins, and Helen Levitt. Ca. 1935–39 (ANP).

69.11 Photographic prints showing professionals in New York City working on WPA library and museum service projects, and in other white-collar positions, 1935–39 (NY).

69.12 Photographs documenting projects funded by the Public Works Administration, such as the construction of highways, public buildings, bridges, dams, schools, sewer systems, and power plants, 1936–42 (PWA). Photographic negatives of the program activities of the Public Building Administration, the U.S. Housing Authority, the Public Roads Administration, and the Federal Works Agency, 1939–44 (B) (H) (R) (F). Color transparencies showing various activities and projects of the Federal Works Agency, the Work Projects Administration, the Public Roads Administration, the U.S. Housing Authority, the Office of Civil Defense, and the Office of Price Administration, such as, a housing project in Key West, FL, a nursery school in Middle River, MD, and a school in San Diego, CA. Ca. 1940–42 (C).

69.13 Photographic prints used in the periodic issuance, *Report on Progress of the Works Program*, 1935–41 (PS). Photographic prints collected from state WPA administrators for use in a planned pictorial report highlighting accomplishments in 46 states, Washington, DC, and Puerto Rico, ca. 1935–43 (PR). Photographic prints of WPA projects and activities in Texas, and other states, ca. 1937–41 (PT). Reports and accompanying photographs relating to the Survey of Federal Archives cosponsored by the National Archives, ca. 1936–41 (SFA).

69.14 Photographic prints of hurricane and flood damage in the New England states of Connecticut, Massachusetts, New Hampshire, Rhode Island, and Vermont, 1938 (MPH).

RG 70

RECORDS OF THE BUREAU OF MINES

ca. 1910–78   97,453 items

70.1   General photographic files showing bureau equipment, buildings, research and experimental projects, and personnel. Also included are pictures of mines, mining operations, types of mining equipment, types of minerals, safety techniques, mine communities, and miners. Ca. 1910–78 (G) (GP).

70.2   An album of photographic prints documenting research during World War I by the Chemical Warfare Service, American University Experiment Station, Washington, DC. The research involved gases, gas masks and other equipment, methods to combat gas contamination, and the production of gas. 1917–18 (CW).

70.3   Albums of photographic prints showing helium plants in Texas and New Mexico, including pictures of plant operations, buildings, equipment, and machinery; and employee housing. 1919–53 (H).

RG 71

RECORDS OF THE BUREAU OF YARDS AND DOCKS

1876–1944   178,895 items

71.1   Photographs, including lantern slides, documenting the construction of U.S. naval shore establishments, including navy yards, air stations, submarine bases, coaling stations, and training stations. 1896–1944 (CA) (CB) (CC) (CCF) (MB) (CR) (TDM) (BH) (GS). An album of photographic prints showing construction projects of the Work Projects Administration and the Public Works Administration at several naval facilities, 1935–43 (CF). Photographic negatives recording the construction of the U.S. Naval Training Station, Sampson, NY, ca. 1942–43 and construction at a James River, VA, shipyard, 1942 (SA) (JRS).

71.2   Photographic prints, some in albums, showing navy yards at Mare Island, CA, and New York, NY; drydocks in Charleston, SC; shipways at Newport News, VA; and buildings at Balboa, Canal Zone, Panama. 1876–1935 (SY) (NYA). Panoramas of training facilities in Pelham Bay, NY, and Parris Island, SC; and pictures of yeomen in the U.S. Navy during World War I. Ca. 1917–19 (PA). Aerial photographic prints of naval facilities, ca. 1942–44 (NS).

71.3   Photographic prints of floating drydocks, lighters, barges, cranes, bridges, piers, docks, and breakwaters, 1891–1944 (CDD) (CD) (MA) (BW) (NB). Blueprints recording navy yard power plant data, 1909–15 (PPD). Photographic prints included in a 1926 report on damage to a depot at Lake Denmark, NY, resulting from an ammunition explosion. (LD). An album of photographic prints showing the Risdon plant, Union Iron Works, San Francisco, CA, 1918 (UI). Photographic prints recording improvements to facilities at the Naval Fuel Depot, Pearl Harbor, HI, 1933–34. (PH).

71.4   Photographic prints representing the training and work of navy construction battalions (SEABEES), 1941–44 (SB) (SBE).

RECORDS OF THE BUREAU OF AERONAUTICS
1918–54   ca. 100,950 items

72.1   Photographs taken at the Naval Aircraft Factory, Philadelphia, PA, to document the construction and testing of dirigibles, balloons, airplanes, parachutes, component parts, and other equipment. There are also pictures of navy and civilian personnel at the factory. 1918–41 (AF) (AFC) (PE).

72.2   Photographic prints of U.S. Navy and Marine Corps aerial photography trainees, 1917–20 (NTP).

72.3   Lantern slides used in the training of aviators and photographers, and showing ships, aircraft, equipment, navy yards and stations, aerial charts and maps, and historic flights, 1916–26 (GS).

72.4   Photographic prints showing the construction of balloons and airships, including the dirigibles *Shenandoah*, *Los Angeles*, and *Akron*; and the progress of construction at the U.S. Naval Flying Field, Akron, OH. 1917–38 (DW) (CP) (DC) (DG) (BA).

72.5   Photographic prints supplied by manufacturers as a contract requirement to document tests, designs, structural details, and completion views of airplanes manufactured for the U.S. Navy, 1930–54 (AC).

72.6   Photographic prints of aircraft parts used to illustrate a technical inspection manual, n.d. (AFM).

RECORDS OF THE BUREAU OF ORDNANCE
1863–1946   11,465 items

74.1   Photographic prints of U.S. and foreign ordnance and testing of armaments such as armor plating, guns, shells, torpedoes, and mines; also includes photographs of naval bases and other facilities, factories and machine shops, trains, ships and boats, machinery, instruments used in manufacturing guns, factory workers, and Navy Department and bureau officials. 1863–1922 (B) (BB).

74.2   Mounted photographic prints of artillery and carriages made in the Creusot works of Schneider and Company, France, 1874–81 (CS).

74.3   Glass negatives and lantern slides showing ordnance tools; smoke bomb tests; graphs and charts; the construction of the Fort Defiance Machinery Co., Defiance, OH; machinery at the Russell Motor Company, Ontario, Canada; the Allied fleet at Scapa Flow, Scotland; mine laying; guns; ships; machines; naval railway batteries; and Secretary of the Navy Josephus Daniels during his trip to Europe. 1917–21 (M) (LS).

74.4   Photographs showing naval ordnance and ships used in atomic bomb tests during Operation Crossroads at Bikini, Marshall Islands, and resultant damage from the explosions, 1946 (BO) (BU) (BN) (BT).

RECORDS OF THE BUREAU OF INDIAN AFFAIRS

1868–1979   ca. 130,000 items

75.1   Photographic prints taken by William S. Soule, Ben Wittick, and John K. Hillers showing Arapaho, Cheyenne, Kiowa, Comanche, Navajo, and Apache Indians, 1868–75 (BAE). Portraits of members of Indian tribal delegations during their visits to Washington, DC, photographed by Alexander Gardner, 1872 (ID). Portraits of American Indian chiefs and warriors, including Geronimo and Sitting Bull, 1880–1910 (IC). Studio portraits of unidentified American Indians from southeastern Idaho reservations, 1897 (SEI).

75.2   Four albums of photographic prints showing agency buildings, personnel, and American Indians at 40 Indian agencies and schools. Also portraits of Algonquin, Kiowa, and Sioux leaders taken by William Dinwiddie of the Bureau of Ethnology. 1876–96 (IP). Photographic prints of Cheyenne and Arapaho students, mission employees, school buildings, and homes at Seger Colony, OK. The pictures apparently were used to illustrate annual reports. 1886–1913 (SE). Photographic prints primarily showing life among the Pueblo Indians and Indians who served in the Armed Forces during World War II, 1890–1961 (PU). Lantern slides showing life among the Seminole Indians, ca. 1913 (SS). Two albums of photographic prints showing activities and facilities at the Sacaton Indian Agency, Pima, AZ, ca. 1918 (PAM).

75.3   Photographs acquired or created by the Information Office of the Bureau of Indian Affairs (BIA) to document the functions, interests, and activities of BIA. Included are photographs of BIA offices and personnel, Indian agencies and reservations, schools, hospitals, farms, houses, and arts and crafts, as well as photographs on other subjects pertaining to American Indian culture and life. 1900–74 (N) (TLA).

75.4   Photographic prints relating to the life and career of Charles H. Burke, Commissioner of Indian Affairs, and including pictures of Burke at conferences, on tours, and with American Indians. There are also images relating to the sale of oil leases on Osage land in Oklahoma, pictures of Secretary of the Interior Hubert Work, and panoramas of Presidents Warren G. Harding and Calvin Coolidge with American Indians. 1894–1928 (BK). Photographic prints, glass negatives, and lantern slides showing a variety of subjects, including irrigation projects on Indian lands, oil drilling on the Osage Reservation, and the Phoenix Tuberculosis Sanitarium. Included are group portraits of U.S. Indian Service Special Officers. Ca. 1900–27 (M) (GIR).

75.5   Photographs taken by the BIA's Division of Forestry and its predecessors recording the care and management of forests on approximately 70 reservations. Included are views of tree nurseries, lumber mills, reforestation activities, grazing lands, fire damage, and land erosion. 1900–44 (FA) (FB) (FC).

75.6   Panoramas used to illustrate conditions at Indian schools and U.S. Public Health Service hospitals. Shown are BIA personnel; schools, grounds, and students; and hospitals and sanitariums. Also shown are pictures of the Indian Congress held in 1926 at the Sesquicentennial International Exposition, Philadelphia, PA, and a celebration at Tulalip Agency, WA, in honor of the 60th anniversary of Treaty Day. Ca. 1904–31 (PA). Photographs depicting Navajo life in Arizona and New Mexico, including photographs of a delegation of Navajo and Pueblo Indians with President Franklin D. Roosevelt and Eleanor Roosevelt; elderly Indian scouts who fought against Geronimo; and a reenactment of the signing of the Treaty of 1868 at Window Rock, AZ. 1936–56 (NG).

75.7   Exhibit panels containing photographic prints created by BIA primarily to illustrate activities at several Indian schools, including pictures of the schools and students; academic and vocational classes; athletics and recreational activities; 4-H clubs; Indians in tribal dress; and Indians at work on farms, in lumber mills, and on an irrigation project. 1904–36 (L) (EXA) (EXB) (EXC) (EXD) (EXE) (EXF) (EXH) (EXJ) (EXN) (EXP) (EXQ) (EXS) (EXT) (EXU) (EXPM).

75.8   Photographic negatives copied by the National Archives from photographs in BIA textual records. Shown are the 1912 Olympic Games medalist Jim Thorpe at Carlisle Indian Industrial School, PA, 1904–13; and students at the Salt River and Lehi Indian Day Schools, 1917–19 (X) (XC). Commercially produced lantern and stereopticon slides used by the Carlisle Indian Industrial School, PA, for recreational and teaching-aid purposes. The slides show scenes of Japan, landmarks in France, England, and the United States, and demonstrate the uses of concrete in farming operations. Ca. 1900–20 (SL) (SJ) (SEN) (SC).

75.9   An album of photographic prints taken by Louis R. Bostwick of Omaha, NE, showing vocational training and educational facilities at the Genoa Industrial School for Indian Youth in Nebraska, ca. 1910 (GS). Photographic prints used in a study of Indian schools and homes in rural areas of northeast and northwest Oklahoma, 1935 (RS).

75.10   Photographic prints depicting American Indians suffering from various illnesses, ca. 1915 (SW). Lantern slides that were used to illustrate prevention and treatment programs for diseases prevalent among American Indians, ca. 1915 (SD).

75.11   Photographs used in detailed surveys of reservation farms conducted by the Industries Section of the Education Division, 1922 (MN). Albums of photographic prints received from Indian agencies and reservations to demonstrate the effects of emergency conservation and relief efforts, 1927–40 (RA).

75.12   Photographs maintained by BIA's Branch of Land operations relating primarily to water and land conservation projects. Also included are photographs showing agricultural operations, forestry activities, educational programs, housing, tribal councils, fairs, recreation, tourism, and Indian arts and crafts. 1948–61 (CP).

75.13   Photographs (some in color) submitted by BIA area offices to illustrate their activities and operations. Included are photographs showing BIA personnel and tribal leaders; living and working conditions for American Indians; Indians involved in a variety of jobs; Indian art; and educational programs. 1950–76 (AO). Photographic prints documenting a wide variety of BIA activities, and including photographs of BIA personnel and offices; Presidents and congressmen; scenes of the 1972 takeover of the BIA building by Indian dissidents; educational programs for American Indians; industrial development on or near reservations; arts and crafts; housing; and council meetings. 1955–77 (CL). Black-and-white and color photographs taken by BIA photographers showing the activities and programs of the Bureau's Education Services Center, and documenting Indian life on reservations in Alaska and several western states, 1947–72 (ED) (CED) (CS).

75.14   Black-and-white slides, showing types of housing, churches, parks, and transportation systems in Chicago, IL, Cleveland, OH, Denver, CO, and San Francisco, San Jose, Los Angeles, and Oakland, CA. The slides apparently were used to familiarize reservation Indians with opportunities in the cities. Ca. 1955 (UOS).

75.15   Black-and-white and color photographs used in the BIA monthly publication, *Indian Record*, 1967–79 (IR).

RG 76

RECORDS OF BOUNDARY AND CLAIMS COMMISSIONS AND ARBITRATIONS
1849–1942   4,373 items

76.1   Seven photographic prints of boundary sites and markers erected in the northwestern United States under the 1846 treaty between the United States and Great Britain, 1860–61 (NW). Photographic prints credited to Alexander Gardner and printed graphics showing forts and trading posts in Idaho and Washington. The images were collected by a commission established to settle the claims of the Puget's Sound Agricultural Company and the Hudson's Bay Company. Ca. 1849–1860s (PS).

76.2   Eighteen albums of photographic prints showing areas along the Alaska-British Columbia boundary, taken by photographers with the British Section of the Alaska Boundary Commission, 1893–94 (BC). An oversize album of photographic prints showing mountains along the eastern borders of Alaska, taken by the British Section of the Alaska Boundary Commission, 1903 (AB).

76.3   Photographs of Alaska taken by E. C. Barnard, chief U.S. topographer of the United States-Canada boundary survey, 1898 (BA) (BB). Photographic prints of Mounts Logan and Fairweather, and adjacent mountains and glaciers along the borders between Alaska and British Columbia and the Yukon Territory, 1926 (AA).

76.4   Mounted photographic prints (some credited to photographer Orrin E. Dunlop) showing Niagara Falls and vicinity, collected by the U.S. Section of the International Waterways Commission, 1903–05 (C). An album of photographic prints from the U.S. Section of the International Waterways Commission documenting boundary markers along the St. Lawrence River, n.d. (WC).

76.5   Photographic prints and lantern slides taken of boundary markers and areas along the United States and Canada borders, 1893–1942 (AL) (CB).

76.6   Glass negatives of old boundary monuments and markers, and scenic views along the United States-Mexico border, taken by D. R. Payne of Albuquerque, NM, for the U.S. Section of the International Boundary Commission. Prints for most of the negatives are in the records of the Office of the Chief of Engineers, RG 77. 1892–94 (OM) (MB).

76.7   Photographs relating to the Costa Rica-Panama Boundary Arbitration, including an album entitled "Report of the Commission of Engineers," 1910–12 (CR) (CP).

RECORDS OF THE
OFFICE OF THE CHIEF OF ENGINEERS
1783–1948   ca. 115,600 items

77.1   Photographic prints of paintings of the Chiefs of the Corps of Engineers (COE), 1789–1884 (PC). Photographic prints of COE officers, 1927–38 (P).

77.2   Lantern slides, photographic prints, and negatives of various subjects, including COE engineers and other personages, engineering equipment, bridges, fortifications, power stations, and the Illinois and Mississippi Canal, 1783–1935 (X) (M) (CE).

77.3   Photographic prints, lithographs, engravings, and drawings withdrawn from the COE Headquarters, Fortifications Map File by the National Archives. The images relate primarily to fortifications and coastal defenses in the United States and overseas but also include pictures of civil works projects; military training camps; COE uniforms; ordnance; Civil War subjects; views of China during the China Relief Expedition; and COE exhibits at the 1893 World's Columbian Exposition, Chicago, IL. The file also contains photographs taken by Andrew J. Russell used to illustrate Gen. Herman Haupt's 1863 report on construction and transportation operations. Ca. 1830–1920 (F).

77.4   Photographs documenting the various activities of the COE. Much of the documentation relates to bridge-building training and the construction of land defenses, including pictures of tools and equipment; construction materials; training facilities, buildings, and grounds at Washington Barracks, Washington, DC, and Willets Point, NY; maneuvers; reconnaissance maps; forts and harbor defenses; weapons and explosives; engineers in the Philippine Islands; and COE insignia. There are also pictures of San Francisco, CA, after the 1906 earthquake, and Johnstown, PA, after the 1889 flood. 1861–1912 (A) (AA) (AB) (AC) (AD) (AE) (AF) (AH) (AI) (AJ) (AK) (AL).

77.5   Photographic prints from the COE Headquarters, Civil Works Map File documenting projects of the COE, including photographs of river and harbor improvements; the construction and repair of canals; flood control projects; dredges and dredging operations; the construction of bridges, breakwaters, dams, and locks; engineering equipment; and civil works projects in the United States, Canada, France, Panama, and the Philippine Islands. 1863–1927. The records also contain stereographs by W. H. Illingworth of Lt. Col. George Custer's Black Hills reconnaissance expedition, 1874; stereographs and albumen prints taken by John Moran and Timothy O'Sullivan during the U.S. Naval Expedition and Survey of the Isthmus of Darien (Panama), 1870–71; and mounted photographic prints of the Yellowstone region taken by William Henry Jackson in 1872 during the Hayden Survey (H).

77.6   Photographic prints probably obtained from the U.S. Signal Corps as examples of Civil War fortification techniques. The prints were made from Mathew Brady negatives. Ca. 1864 (MF).

77.7   Photographs taken by Timothy O'Sullivan, staff photographer, for the Geological Exploration of the Fortieth Parallel (King Survey) headed by Clarence King. The images record the physical features of areas of California, Colorado, Idaho, Nevada, Utah, and Wyoming; and also show members of the expedition and their campsites, mining towns and mining operations, and military posts. 1867–72 (KN) (KS) (KSP) (KS-LCV) (KW).

77.8   Glass negatives and prints, most of which are stereographs, photographed by William Bell and Timothy O'Sullivan during the U.S. Geographical Surveys West of the 100th Meridian (the Wheeler Survey). The surveys were led by Lt. George M. Wheeler. Recorded are geological formations, landscapes, and American Indians in Arizona, California, Colorado, New Mexico, Nevada, and Utah. 1871–74 (WA) (WB) (WC) (WD) (WE) (WF).

77.9   An album of photographic prints transferred to the COE from the U.S. Army Quartermaster General showing various army posts and government steamers, 1871–1910 (CA). Photographic prints in albums showing construction work at The Presidio, Fort Mason, Fort Winfield Scott, and Fort Baker in San Francisco, CA, 1911–16 (SFA). An album of photographic prints showing military installations in the U.S. Army Southern Department, 1920 (SD). Albums containing photographic prints recording the construction of military installations in the Philippine Islands, 1920–21 (PIA). Albums of photographic prints showing the completed construction of military housing at several installations, 1927–36 (CC). Two albums of photographic prints depicting the construction of Albrook Field, Canal Zone, Panama, 1931 (CZ). Albums of photographic prints showing aerial views of U.S. Army and Army Air Force installations, 1934 (AFF). Two albums of photographic prints showing military installations in Puerto Rico and scenic views of San Juan, 1939 (TPR).

77.10   Photographs and a few halftone prints of equipment, facilities, and construction techniques used by the COE in its efforts to improve the United States' rivers and harbors, 1897–1948 (RF) (RH) (RHEO) (DP). Reports and pamphlets containing photographic prints and halftone prints documenting the progress of civil works projects undertaken by the Engineering Department, as well as some National Defense and Public Works Administration projects, 1934–41 (CP) (PR).

77.11   Photographic prints taken by Capt. C. F. O'Keefe of the 36th U.S. Volunteers of the Philippine Islands from 1899–1900, and U.S.troops with the China Relief Expedition in and around Peking (Beijing) during the Boxer Rebellion, 1900–1901 (CR-P) (CR).

77.12   Four albums of photographic prints showing old and new boundary markers along the United States-Mexico border and views of areas along the border. Negatives for most of these prints are in the records of Boundary and Claims Commissions and Arbitrations, RG 76. 1892–94 (OM) (MB).

77.13   Photographic prints submitted to the COE with annual reports from the Office of Public Buildings and Grounds showing interior and exterior views of the White House, 1899–1900, 1903–04, 1910 (WH).

77.14   Glass negatives recording the techniques and equipment used by the U.S. Lake Survey in its water-level observations of northern and northwestern lakes, ca. 1898–1902 (LS). Glass negatives documenting the efforts of the U.S. Lake Survey to take discharge measurements on the Niagara River, 1906–11 (NHD). Lantern slides taken by Oscar Hagenjos of the U.S. Lake Survey for a COE report comparing the effects of water diversion on the Niagara River and Niagara Falls. The slides indicate the flow and water levels of the Niagara River and show cataracts, rapids, Horseshoe Falls, American Falls, the Whirlpool, and Goat Island. 1906, 1917, and 1927 (BW). Glass negatives from the same study. Some of the

76-AL-37-16. *Camp at S.E. foot of Mt. Bertha.* Alaska. 1940. Bradford Washburn. (RG 76, Records of the Boundary and Claims Commission and Arbitrations)

79-OC-62. *Cape Sebastian from south. Oregon. Picture is taken from a point just north of Pistol River mouth.* December 1938. George Alexander Grant. (RG 79, Records of the National Park Service)

77-HQ-695F-30. *Kansas City Reach. Pile sinker used on K. C. Division for sinking piles for 3 row dike.* 1889. Kansas City View Co. (RG 77, Records of the Office of the Chief of Engineers)

80-G-469319. *A SB2C approaching the U.S.S.* Hornet *(CV-12) after an attack on Japanese shipping in the China Sea.* February 1945. LCDR Charles Kerlee. (RG 80, General Records of the Department of the Navy, 1798-1947)

images were printed in Senate Document No. 105–62–1. 1906 (NSD). Glass negatives for images used in a report by Col. J. G. Warren, Division Engineer of the Lakes Division, on his investigation into the effects of water diversion on the flow of the Niagara River and Niagara Falls, 1917 (CW).

77.15   Photographs showing in detail the damage to the U.S.S. *Maine*, and equipment and engineering techniques used to salvage the ship, ca. 1910–12 (RM) (RMN) (RMP).

77.16   Photographs, drawings, and blueprints of coastal defense equipment and searchlights in the United States, Puerto Rico, the Philippine Islands, and the Panama Canal Zone, 1912–35 (CD). Photographic prints of types of searchlights and related equipment, 1917–31 (SE).

77.17   Photographic prints showing flood conditions in urban and rural areas, and documenting flood control methods undertaken by the COE, 1913–47 (FC).

77.18   Photographic negatives recording drills and other methods used to train engineers. Also included are portraits of U.S. generals and other prominent individuals, and maps of military campaigns. Ca. 1917 (ED).

77.19   Lantern slides used as visual aids in ordnance and engineering classes, ca. 1917–25 (OT). Mounted photographic prints used for instructional purposes to illustrate aerial photography, assault boats, types of bridges, camouflage, demolition, engineering equipment, the use of obstacles, construction techniques and other COE activities, particularly during World War I, 1918–41 (AQ).

77.20   Photographic prints documenting the World War I occupation of Vladivostok, Siberia, by American Expeditionary Forces (AEF), including views of the city and Siberia, the U.S. base and headquarters, Russian troops and citizens, Bolsheviks, AEF personnel, units of the Allies, and naval forces, 1918–20 (VE). Photomechanical reproductions showing panoramic views of Russia and Italy, 1915–26 (PF).

77.21   Posters used to recruit for service in the Engineer, Ordnance, and Transportation Corps, 1918–20 (EP).

77.22   Photographic prints taken or acquired by the Mississippi River Commission to document civil work projects along the southern portion of the Mississippi River. Also included are pictures relating to the 1927 flooding of the river. 1922–39 (MRC). Photographic prints documenting the 1927 flood of the Mississippi River. Shown are rescue workers, flood victims, refugee camps, and property damage (MRF) (IC).

77.23   Albums of photographic prints apparently used to accompany reports from the Kansas City district office on civil works projects along the Missouri River and its tributaries. Also included are pictures showing the terrain of areas along the basins of the Cheyenne, Niobrara, Platte, and Yellowstone Rivers. Ca. 1932–40 (OED). Photographic reports from the COE district office in Omaha, NE, documenting the progress of civil works projects along the Missouri River, 1934–39 (QR).

77.24   Photographs from an engineering survey of the Orinoco, Casiquiare, and Negro Rivers in Venezuela, Colombia, and Brazil. The survey was led by Lt. Col. Gerdes. 1943 (OCN).

77.25 Atomic Energy Commission photographs collected by the COE Manhattan District. The images document the destruction to Hiroshima and Nagasaki, Japan, and the injuries caused by the World War II atomic bomb explosions. Some of the pictures were used as illustrations in the 1948 unpublished "Manhattan District History" prepared by the Adjutant General's Office, Department of the Army. 1945 (AEC) (MDH).

RG 78

RECORDS OF THE U.S. NAVAL OBSERVATORY
1878–1905   90 items

78.1 Photographs, glass transparencies, and drawings from U.S. naval expeditions studying solar eclipses in 1878, 1889, 1897, and 1905 showing the various phases of eclipses, equipment, buildings, personnel, and panoramas of several European cities, 1878–1905 (AE).

RG 79

RECORDS OF THE NATIONAL PARK SERVICE
1815–1989   ca. 59,200 items

79.1 The general photographic file of the National Park Service (NPS) covers historic sites, national parks, recreational areas, battlefields, monuments, parkways, and NPS employees. The file is comprised of the following eight collections: the Charles Porter Collection, the Retired TV File, the T. J. Hileman Collection, the Frank J. Haynes Collection, the James E. Thompson Collection, the Stephen T. Mather Collection, the Freelance Photographers Collection, and the Miscellaneous Collection. Ca. 1880–1962 (G).

79.2 Lantern slides (many are hand colored) depicting views of Washington, DC, plans for the city, federal buildings, monuments, and statues; and picturing Presidents William G. Harding and Calvin Coolidge addressing crowds. The slides were maintained by the National Park Service, National Capital Parks office. 1815–1936 (LS).

79.3 A collection of photographs of Civil War sites at Gettysburg, PA, Antietam, MD, and Harpers Ferry, WV, that was purchased from the W. H. Tipton Company of Gettysburg, 1863–1925 (T) (TM).

79.4 The Louisa Bellinger Collection of albumen prints photographed by Timothy O'Sullivan, William Bell, Carleton Watkins, and William Henry Jackson. The majority of this collection consists of images taken by O'Sullivan and Bell during the King and Wheeler surveys of Arizona, Colorado, Nevada, New Mexico, and Utah. There are also photographs by Jackson of railroads, and several Watkins images taken at California locations: Yosemite, Mount Shasta, San Francisco, and Monterey. Ca. 1866–80 (BC).

79.5 Portraits of Maj. John Wesley Powell and his family, 1859–68 (JWP).

79.6 Albertypes made from negatives taken by William Henry Jackson during the Hayden Survey of areas in Idaho, Montana, Utah, and Wyoming, 1871–72 (JAG) (JAH).

79.7 Photographic prints, negatives, transparencies, and lantern slides taken by Pasadena, CA, photographer Henry G. Peabody to illustrate lectures. The images primarily show scenic views of national parks and also include pictures of monuments; historic sites and landmarks; cities and villages; California missions; the natural features of land in several states, Canada and Mexico; and American Indians. 1890–1937 (HPA) (HPM) (HPP) (HPS).

79.8 Photographic prints of buildings, monuments, and parks in Washington, DC, ca. 1900–18 (PB).

79.9 Glass negatives showing artifacts and depicting individuals and events associated with the Revolutionary War that were taken ca. 1930 of items displayed at the Yorktown Sesquicentennial Commission and the George Washington Bicentennial Commission exhibits (PGHN).

79.10 Lantern slides from the Branch of Engineering Activities recording construction and engineering projects at national parks and historic sites, 1928–39 (EA).

79.11 Glass negatives taken by NPS personnel of scenes in national parks, historic sites, monuments, wildlife, park officials, American Indians, and tourists, 1887–1932 (PGN). Two albums of prints photographed by NPS photographers George Alexander Grant and H. E. Stork showing areas of Zion and Bryce Canyon National Parks, 1929 (ZBC). Photographs from several NPS parks and the office of NPS Director Horace Albright showing activities at several national parks. Also included are postcards picturing Barcelona and Cardonna, Spain, and park areas in Zaire (the Belgian Congo); lithographs of the American buffalo; and photographs of U.S. Army Ski Troops, World War II soldiers and sailors convalescing at the parks, Gen. Dwight D. Eisenhower at the Grand Canyon National Park, King Albert of Belgium at Glacier National Park, William "Buffalo Bill" Cody, Secretary of the Interior Albert B. Fall, and NPS personnel (M).

79.12 Photographic prints showing scenic views of national parks and monuments taken by Ansel Adams for an NPS-commissioned photo mural. Several of the images relate to American Indians of the southwestern United States and show views of Boulder (Hoover) Dam. 1933–42 (AA through AAW).

79.13 Photographic prints showing Civilian Conservation Corps enrollees performing emergency conservation work in Washington, DC, 1933–37 (CCC). Photographs of Civilian Conservation Corps, National Youth Administration, Public Works Administration, and Work Projects Administration artists, draftsmen, and engineers preparing museum displays for national parks at the NPS Western Museum Laboratories in California, 1934–41 (ML).

79.14 Photographs of recreational facilities in 29 state parks throughout the United States, 1935–36 (SP). Photographs of state and national parks, 1900–45 (NP) (HB) (MI).

79.15 Photographic prints credited to Ansel Hall and taken during surveys of the Monument Valley area of Arizona and Utah, 1933–34 (MV). An album of photographic prints showing Mt. Baker and the nearby Washington State recreational facilities, 1934 (MB).

79.16 A photographic report by the Committee to Investigate the Oregon Coastal Areas that surveyed the coast for possible recreational development. The photographs were taken by NPS photographer George Alexander Grant. 1938 (OC).

79.17 Photographs taken by J. Diederich for a survey of areas adjacent to the Alaska Highway, 1943 (AH).

79.18 Photographs taken by Abbie Rowe, NPS photographer for the White House Press Office, showing the daily activities of Presidents Franklin D. Roosevelt, Harry S. Truman, Dwight D. Eisenhower, John F. Kennedy, and Lyndon B. Johnson, including bill signings and other ceremonies, Cabinet meetings, visits from dignitaries, and the Presidential families, 1941–67 (AR). Photographs by photographers H. H. (Harry) Rideout and Abbie Rowe relating to President Franklin D. Roosevelt, 1940–41 (XAR).

79.19 Photographic prints acquired by the John Marshall Bicentennial Commission to commemorate the anniversary of the birth of the Supreme Court justice, including portraits of Marshall, his family, and Supreme Court judges; pictures of Marshall's home and grave site; and several historic buildings. 1955 (JM).

79.20 Photographic prints accumulated by the Civil War Centennial Commission to document its functions, and to record various events commemorating the 100th anniversary of the war. Included are pictures of commission members, meetings, and ceremonies; exhibits; battle reenactments; copies of works of art; and well-known persons such as John F. Kennedy, Robert F. Kennedy, Lyndon B. Johnson, Eleanor Roosevelt, and Richard M. Nixon. 1957–66 (CWC).

79.21 Posters advertising national parks, monuments, historic sites, and recreation areas, 1968–89 (P).

RG 80

GENERAL RECORDS OF THE DEPARTMENT OF THE NAVY, 1798–1947

1798–1958   ca. 785,600 items

80.1 Color transparencies made by the navy in 1943 of the official portraits of Secretaries of the Navy from 1798–1939. Also included are photographs of Secretary Frank Knox attending an awards ceremony. n.d. (PS). Photographic prints of U.S. Navy officers and enlisted personnel, 1917–45 (PA) (PB).

80.2 Photographic prints on a variety of subjects pertaining primarily to the early years of navy aviation. Included are pictures of historic flights, types of aircraft, air races, expeditions, trophies, aviators, secretaries and assistant secretaries of the department, and U.S. Presidents. 1903–41 (HAN) (HAP) (HAS) (HAT).

80.3 Photographs (some in color) of U.S. Navy officers and enlisted men; Navy Department personnel; aircraft, ships, and boats; ordnance and other equipment; training activities and facilities; air stations, bases, and navy yards; harbors and docks; foreign navies and dignitaries; geographical areas; navy operations during World War II and the Korean war; expeditions and surveys; tests, including nuclear bomb tests; and various other subjects relating to U.S. Navy history. Ca. 1900–58 (G) (GK) (CF).

80.4 Stereographs produced by the Rose Stereograph Company documenting the visit of the Great White Fleet to Australia, 1908 (AA). Photographs showing the wreckage of the dirigible *Shenandoah* (ZR–1), 1925 (MS). Photographic prints relating to the U.S.S. *Casablanca*, 1943–45 (CASA). Photographic prints from the 7th Naval District, Miami, FL, showing a variety of subjects, 1943–46 (MF).

80.5 Photographs showing exterior views of the Naval Powder Factory, Indian Head, MD, ca. 1912 (IH). Photographic prints of artifacts displayed in a U.S. Navy and Marine Corps exhibit at the Navy Yard in Philadelphia, PA, 1926 (ME). Photographic prints documenting activities at the naval air stations at Lambert Field, St. Louis, MO, and Hitchcock, TX, including views of personnel and aircraft, 1943–45 (LSM) (HT). Aerial photographs of Houma, LA, and the nearby naval air station, housing, and drydocks at Morgan City, LA, and views of the ruins of Fort Livingston, LA, 1943–44 (HL).

80.6 Photographic prints showing U.S. Navy and Marine Corps personnel, and navy air fields and bases in several foreign countries, including the Panama Canal Zone, 1903–40 (HAG). Photographs of navy personnel, ships, aircraft, and activities used for publicity purposes, 1921–43 (PR).

80.7 Photographic prints of navy admirals and commodores. Also included are several pictures of Col. Charles A. Lindbergh and activities relating to his 1927 flight to France. 1920–44 (PC). Photographic prints of women in the Army Air Forces, U.S. Navy, and Marine Corps during World War II, 1943–45 (PSW).

80.8 An album of panoramas showing the naval oil reserve fields in the Teapot Dome area of Wyoming, 1922 (TD). Photographic prints showing the operations and facilities of businesses under contract to supply materiel to the Navy during World War II, 1943 (PM) (PII).

80.9 Photographic prints documenting the burning and sinking of the French military transport *Vinh Long*, 1922 (VL).

80.10 Photographic prints recording the Japanese surrender ceremonies at the end of World War II on board the U.S.S. *Missouri*, 1945 (GJS).

RG 83

RECORDS OF THE
BUREAU OF AGRICULTURAL ECONOMICS
1896–1947   26,600 items

83.1 Photographs from the Office of Farm Management and Farm Economics, a predecessor of the Bureau of Agricultural Economics (BAE), taken as part of studies of agricultural methods in the United States. Shown are land features; types of crops; cultivating, harvesting, and marketing of crops; farm animals; farmsteads and ranches; farm machinery and equipment; irrigation and conservation methods; and farmers and their families. 1896–1922 (F) (FA) (FB) (FC).

83.2 Photographic prints illustrating the efforts of the BAE to study and promote standardization of agricultural products and to improve the processing and marketing of products. Included are pictures of agricultural products, marketing cooperatives, marketing methods, rural homes and industries, transportation facilities, and people engaged in processing and marketing agricultural products. 1902–38 (ML).

83.3 Glass negatives from the Office of Farm Management and Farm Economics relating to the care and breeding of livestock, 1900–22 (L).

83.4 Photographs documenting efficient farming and marketing techniques throughout the United States and showing farming operations, land utilization methods, crops, livestock, markets, farm equipment, landscapes, climatic conditions, and rural industries and social institutions. Also featured are photographs taken by Dorothea Lange and Irving Rusinow for "Community Stability and Instability," a ca. 1941 study documenting rural living and working conditions in Arizona, California, Georgia, Iowa, Kansas, New Hampshire, New Mexico, Pennsylvania, and South Carolina. 1911–47 (G).

83.5 Photographs by D. S. Bullock, Agricultural Trade Commissioner, depicting farming operations in Argentina, Chile, and Peru, 1921–23 (ACP).

83.6 Photographic negatives of illustrations on such subjects as land economics, production and marketing, farm conditions, acreage, and agricultural finance prepared by BAE for use in the Department of Agriculture yearbooks, 1921–34 (YB).

83.7 Filmstrips on general and World War II-related agricultural subjects, 1939–44 (FS). Glass negatives made from selected frames of the motion picture *The Battle is in Our Hands*, 1942 (BHM).

RG 84

RECORDS OF THE FOREIGN SERVICE POSTS OF THE DEPARTMENT OF STATE
1942–47   126 items

84.1 Photographs collected by Walter A. Foote, U.S. consul general, Batavia, Java, showing the remains of victims of atrocities committed by the Japanese during their World War II occupation of Indonesia, 1942–46; Japanese political indoctrination programs in Indonesia, 1943–45; and homes and businesses damaged by saboteurs during the Indonesian war for national independence. 1946–47 (IA) (IJ) (IS).

RG 86

RECORDS OF THE WOMEN'S BUREAU
1892–1945   3,625 items

86.1 Photographs showing women at work in factories and other jobs during World War I and the 1920s. The images document the evolution of working conditions for women and the struggle for women's rights. Included are pictures of several notable women. 1892–1945 (G).

86.2 Photographs of women working in various occupations, including the military, during World War II, 1940–45 (WWT).

86-WWT-14-13. *Mrs. Max Hartl, only G-E engineer at the General Electric Flight Test Center, dressed in gear for high altitude flying checking instrument panel board for flight data on the operation of the jet engine.* Ca. 1944. General News Bureau, General Electric Company. (RG 86, Records of the Women's Bureau)

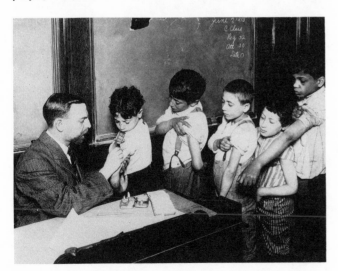

90-G-5-6. *Vaccinating school children.* June 7, 1910. (RG 90, Records of the Public Health Service)

88-GP-3-C389. *Inspector D. F. Angier (Post Office Dept) and Dr. L. F. Kebler (formerly of Food and Drug Admin.) are trying out a stretching device, alleged to effect an increase in height from 2 to 6 inches.* February 4, 1931. (RG 88, Records of the Food and Drug Administration)

RECORDS OF THE
FOOD AND DRUG ADMINISTRATION
1885–1977   30,520 items

88.1   Photographs, including lantern slides, illustrating the functions of the Food and Drug Administration (FDA) and its predecessor agencies in the enforcement of the pure food and drug acts. Shown are agency personnel engaged in the chemical analyses of drugs; investigations into fraudulent labeling of drugs, inspections of milk, fish, and other foods; and seizures and destructions of contaminated foods. Included are pictures depicting the manufacture of sugar candy, liquors, and other commodities. 1885–1944 (GP) (GB) (GS) (GN).

88.2   Photographs, including color slides, recording the administrative, experimental, and investigative activities of the Food and Drug Administration, 1962–77 (A). Identification and public relations photographs of FDA personnel, 1968–77 (P).

RECORDS OF THE PUBLIC HEALTH SERVICE
ca. 1862–1985   ca. 10,573 items

90.1   Photographic prints of lithographs showing Civil War hospitals. Photographic prints of Civil War subjects taken by Alexander Gardner and Mathew Brady. Ca. 1862–65 (CM).

90.2   Photographs of hospitals, quarantine stations, and other facilities of the Public Health Service; and administrative and scientific personnel. Included are photographs pertaining to the treatment of malaria, yellow fever, and other diseases as well as research in communicable and epidemic diseases. Some of the images relate to nutrition, narcotics, sanitation and personal hygiene, and immigrants in the early 20th century. 1898–1934 (G).

90.3   An album of photographic prints showing views of Panama, Costa Rica, Nicaragua, Honduras, and Guatemala. The album was presented to the Surgeon General by the United Fruit Company following a tour of the areas by U.S. federal and state health authorities. 1906 (WW).

90.4   Posters describing hookworm, typhoid, and other diseases and urging better sanitation as a preventative measure, ca. 1920 (SP). Posters promoting the treatment of high blood pressure from the National Heart, Lung, and Blood Institute of the National Institute of Health, ca. 1979–85 (HP).

90.5   Photographic prints and filmstrips taken or acquired by the Emergency Health Services showing disasters and medical assistance programs, 1953–74 (M).

92-F-6-3. *Commanding Officers Quarters*. Fort Barrancas, FL. Ca. 1890.
(RG 92, Records of the Office of the Quartermaster General)

RECORDS OF THE
OFFICE OF THE QUARTERMASTER GENERAL
ca. 1776–1938   ca. 20,355 items

92.1   Photographic prints, including some cartes de visite, of quartermaster officers. Also included are drawings of Revolutionary War figures: Gen. Morgan Lewis, Col. Stephen Moylan, and Timothy Pickering. Ca. 1776–1906 (P). Color lithographs of paintings by H. A. Ogden illustrating U.S. Army uniforms for 1779–1907. The lithographs were printed ca. 1885–1907 (HO).

92.2   Photographic prints of U.S. Army forts and other installations; uniforms; flags and insignia; horse and mule tack and other equipment; wagons, carts, motor vehicles, and emergency vehicles; and food service operations. 1861–1920 (PS) (UF) (FL) (WC) (MA) (S) (M). Color lithographs illustrating U.S. Army installations at Point Lookout, MD; Camp Hill, Harpers Ferry, WV; Camp Dennison, OH; and Johnson's Island, OH. Also included is a lithograph illustrating details of Moseley bridges manufactured by the American Iron Bridge and Manufacturing Company, Chester, PA. Ca. 1865 (AI). Photographic prints taken or acquired by the Quartermaster General showing U.S. Army forts and installations in the United States, Cuba, and the Philippine Islands, ca. 1890–99 (F). Glass negatives showing Fort Egbert, Fort St. Michaels, and nearby areas in Alaska, 1899–1900 (FA). Photographic prints (many are panoramas) showing the construction of forts, hospitals, depots, coast defenses, and other U.S. Army facilities and the work of the Spruce Production Corporation in Portland, OR, during World War I, 1909–36 (CD).

92.3   Photographic prints showing U.S. Army exhibits at the World's Columbian Exposition, Chicago, IL, 1893; the Louisiana Purchase Exposition, St. Louis, MO, 1904; and the 1925 Alabama State Fair (EX).

92.4   Photographic prints acquired by the Army Transport Service to show boats and ships used by the Service to convey servicemen and equipment, 1898–1912 (AT).

92.5   Photographic prints of national cemeteries, 1881–1907 (CA). Panoramas of U.S. cemeteries for World War I servicemen, located in France, England, Belgium, and Scotland, 1919–22 (CAP). Glass negatives showing memorials in Maryland and Illinois dedicated to the Confederate Civil War dead, 1910–11 (CMG).

92.6   Photographic prints by *San Francisco Chronicle* photographer George W. Haley showing relief efforts following the 1906 San Francisco, CA, earthquake (ER). An album of photographic prints recording Mississippi River flood conditions in Tennessee and Kentucky, 1912 (MRF). Three albums of photographic prints used in investigations relating to a flood of the Rhine river at Coblenz (Koblenz), Germany, and to the damages sustained by U.S. Army motor vehicles parked in the flooded area, 1920 (CG).

92.7   Panoramas showing quartermaster military personnel at remount depots, camps, schools, and other facilities. A few of the images relate to events held in celebration of the 148th and 149th anniversaries of the Quartermaster Corps. 1918–24 (PN). Photographic prints made by the U.S. Signal Corps and the Army Air Forces of activities commemorating the 75th anniversary of the Battle of Gettysburg, 1938 (GA).

RECORDS OF THE
ADJUTANT GENERAL'S OFFICE, 1780's–1917

1861–1916   1,981 items

94.1   Lithographs and albumen prints showing Union and Confederate fortifications in Georgia, South Carolina, Tennessee, and Virginia. The lithographs were printed in the *Atlas to Accompany the Official Records of the Union and Confederate Armies, 1861–65*. Also, two stereographs of Lookout Mountain in Tennessee. 1861–66 (AUC).

94.2   Two albums of cartes de visite of employees of the U.S. Christian Commission, 1864–65 (CC). Cartes de visite of Civil War-era personages, ca. 1862–74 (BC).

94.3   Albumen prints credited to Lt. William R. Abercrombie that were enclosed in a report by Lt. Henry T. Allen on the 1885 Alaskan Expedition, also known as the Miles Expedition; shown are glaciers and geological formations near the Copper, Tanana, and Koyukul Rivers in Alaska (CR).

94.4   Glass negatives showing various ways to position the body while firing a rifle, ca. 1900 (R).

94.5   An album of photographic prints originally belonging to Col. Charles A. Dempsey relating to the Spanish-American War in Cuba and the Philippine Insurrection, 1898–1900 (SAW).

94.6   Photographic prints of military and aviation activities at Texas City, TX, and Fort Crockett, TX, 1913 (TM).

94.7   Photographic prints, many of which were taken by William Fox, staff photographer for Underwood and Underwood, showing U.S. military activities during the Mexican Punitive Expedition, including scenes of camp life, equipment, aviators, troops, and officers. Also shown are several news service correspondents. 1916 (UM) (UMA).

94.8   Military recruitment posters, ca. 1908–16 (WP).

RECORDS OF THE FOREST SERVICE

1897–1989   ca. 166,000 items

95.1   Photographs taken by Forest Service employees and others during the course of field work on such subjects as land features, types of trees and other plants, wildlife, the effects of plant diseases, research activities, forestry techniques, and forest and land management. Also included are images relating to the recreational and commercial uses of forest lands, and images of rural life. 1897–1965 (G).

95.2   Albums of photographic prints taken by George B. Sudworth, John G. Jack, H. B. Ayres, John B. Leiberg and others of forest reserve areas in Arizona, California, Colorado, Idaho, Montana, Oregon, South Dakota, and Wyoming. The images document the effects of fires, mining, soil erosion, and other hazards on forests. 1898–1900 (FRA) (FRB) (FRC) (FRD) (FRE) (FRF) (FRG) (FRH).

94-UM-195403. *Brigade Headquarters near Casas Grande, Mexico - General Pershing.* March 26, 1916. William Fox, Underwood and Underwood. (RG 94, Records of the Adjutant General's Office, 1780's-1917)

95-G-233418. *Marking virgin Douglas fir timber.* Lincoln National Forest, New Mexico. June 26, 1928. E. S. Shipp. (RG 95, Records of the Forest Service)

96-FHA-1232-377. *Blaine L. Bingham shocking barley. Dopey standing nearby.* Spanish Fork, UT. August 1946. William J. Forsythe. (RG 96, Records of the Farmers Home Administration)

97-G-115-1. *Airplane view of Fleischmann Malting Co. plant at Minneapolis, Minn. during the fire explosion. Two were killed, 6 injured and the loss $250,000*. March 22, 1938. (RG 97, Records of the Bureau of Agricultural and Industrial Chemistry)

102-LH-564. *Young cigarmakers in Engelhart & Co. Three boys looked under 14. Work was slack and youngsters were not being employed much. Labor leaders told me in busy times many small boys and girls were employed. Youngsters all smoke*. Tampa, FL. January 27, 1909. Lewis W. Hine. (RG 102, Records of the Children's Bureau)

106-WB-602. *Headlands north of Colorado River plateau*. 1872. William Bell. (RG 106, Records of the Smithsonian Institution)

95.3 Charts and lithographs relating to forestry, 1898–1941 (L).

95.4 Albums of photographic prints documenting the activities of Forest Service field parties. The images were taken by Stanton G. Smith. 1904–31 (FP). Photographic prints relating to national forests from the Forest Service's Permanent Image Collection, 1915–33 (GRA).

95.5 An album of photographic prints documenting research on the properties of wood, conducted for the military by the Forest Products Laboratory at the University of Wisconsin, 1917–18 (WR).

95.6 Four albums of photographic prints showing scenes in national forests. Included are images relating to types of forest cover, trees, streams, lookout stations, forest fires, erosion, reforestation efforts, communities, wildlife, and activities of the Civilian Conservation Corps. 1933–39 (VNF).

95.7 Photographs and color slides documenting the work of the Forest Service in connection with the Guayule Emergency Rubber Program, 1942–45 (GK) (RP).

95.8 Fire prevention posters from the Forest Service and several foreign countries. Most of the U.S. posters feature Smokey Bear, the symbol of the Forest Service's fire prevention programs. Ca. 1939–89 (SB) (SBF).

RG 96

RECORDS OF THE FARMERS HOME ADMINISTRATION
ca. 1935–46   621 items

96.1 Photographic negatives showing farmers and their families at work, ca. 1946 (FHA).

96.2 Production stills from the Documentary Film Section, Information Division, Farm Security Administration of two films by Pare Lorentz: *The Plow That Broke the Plains* and *The River*. Photographic prints made by the Historical Section of the Resettlement Administration to show land use, farms, and farmers. Some of the photographs were taken by Arthur Rothstein, Carl Mydans, Dorothea Lange, and Ben Shahn. Ca. 1935–43 (LF).

96.3 A poster advertising the Pare Lorentz film, *The River*, 1938 (P).

RG 97

RECORDS OF THE BUREAU OF AGRICULTURAL AND INDUSTRIAL CHEMISTRY
ca. 1878–1942   ca. 4,993 items

97.1 Photographs collected or produced by the Bureau of Chemistry and the Bureau of Chemistry and Soils showing agency personnel; dust explosions, including explosions at grain elevators, mills, and manufacturing plants; fires and fire prevention activities; laboratory tests; and exhibits, including exhibits at the 1927 Philadelphia Sesquicentennial International Exposition. Ca. 1878–1942 (G) (M) (C) (D).

97.2   Photographs relating to Bureau of Chemistry and Soils research activities and investigations of dust explosions, boll weevils, effects of smelter fumes, and methods of constructing safe turpentine stills. Also pictured are bureau personnel, laboratories, and field stations. Ca. 1908–37 (MS).

97.3   Lantern slides (some hand colored) used to illustrate lectures given by Dr. Charles A. Browne and other personnel of the Bureau of Chemistry and the Bureau of Chemistry and Soils. Among the subjects shown are eminent chemists, the early United States chemical industry, the development of the sugar cane industry, various industries in Europe and the Middle East, agricultural research, explosions and fires, and the New Harmony movement. Ca. 1913–41 (CB) (LS).

97.4   Photographic negatives of images collected for use in publications of the Bureau of Chemistry, the Bureau of Chemistry and Soils, and the Bureau of Agricultural Chemistry and Engineering. The agencies are predecessors of the Bureau of Agricultural and Industrial Chemistry. Some of the negatives show charts and graphs. Ca. 1908–40 (NP).

RG 102   RECORDS OF THE CHILDREN'S BUREAU

1908–26   488 items

102.1   Photographs of children working taken by Lewis Hine for the National Child Labor Committee, 1908–12 (LH).

102.2   Filmstrips relating to prenatal, infant, and child care and to children's diseases, 1919–26 (FS).

RG 106   RECORDS OF THE SMITHSONIAN INSTITUTION

1871–1934   3,300 items

106.1   Glass negatives, including stereographs, taken by photographers Timothy O'Sullivan and William Bell during the U.S. Geographical Surveys West of the 100th Meridian (the Wheeler Survey). Shown are landscapes, geological formations, military posts, archaeological ruins, mining operations, survey members, and American Indians. 1871–74 (WA) (WB).

106.2   Stereograph glass negatives taken by William R. Pywell during the Yellowstone Expedition of 1873. The expedition was organized by the War Department to escort and protect the Northern Pacific Railroad Survey. Most of the images are of views along the survey route (YX).

106.3   Photographs of American Indians, including chiefs and delegations, and Indian villages. Many of the images were taken by John K. Hillers. 1871–1907 (IN) (INE). Watercolor sketches by Matilda Coxe Stevenson of Acoma, Cochiti, and Laguna pueblos in New Mexico, and Pueblo pottery, 1882 (MCS). Photographic prints by F. A. Ames showing Indians, the reservation at Moqui, AZ, ranch life in Arizona, and Arizona landscape, 1887–89 (FAA).

106.4   Photographic prints, negatives, and lantern slides collected by Hugh M. Smith, an associate curator at the Smithsonian, showing types of fish and marine life, and the fishing industry around the world. Some of the images record everyday life in several foreign countries as well as the United States. 1886–1934 (HSA) (HSB) (HSC) (HSD) (HSE).

106.5 Lantern slides taken or collected by Nathaniel L. Dewell, a U.S. military and commercial photographer. Subjects pictured include the construction of the Panama Canal, 1900–14; historic sites in Europe and the Middle East and scenic views of the Philippine Islands, 1911–18; views of Philadelphia, PA, and the Delaware River area, ca. 1900; and Belgium and France during World War I (RC) (RM) (RP) (RW).

RG 107

RECORDS OF THE
OFFICE OF THE SECRETARY OF WAR
1943   117 items

107.1 Photographs of Undersecretary of War Robert P. Patterson's visit to the Pacific Theater (Hawaii, New Zealand, Australia, the Fiji Islands, Guadalcanal, and other areas) during World War II, 1943 (T).

RG 109

WAR DEPARTMENT COLLECTION
OF CONFEDERATE RECORDS
1861–63   3 items

109.1 Photographic negatives of an embossed seal of the Confederate States of America, a Confederate States recruitment broadside, and an 1863 broadside from the Chief Quartermaster, Trans-Mississippi Department. The original items are filed with the collection's textual records (X).

RG 111

RECORDS OF THE
OFFICE OF THE CHIEF SIGNAL OFFICER
1754–1981   ca. 1,038,800 items

111.1 Photographs (some in color) illustrating the history of the U.S. Army from the French and Indian War through the Vietnam years, including pictures relating to the Revolutionary War, the War of 1812, the Mexican War, the Indian wars, the Spanish-American War, the Philippine Insurrection, the China Relief Expedition, the Mexican Punitive Expedition, World War I, World War II, and the Korean conflict. Additional subjects pictured include civilian and military personages, significant historical events, the Old West, military installations, military training, maneuvers, ceremonies, U.S. Army uniforms and equipment, military engineering projects, expeditions, foreign armies, battle destruction and casualties, medical services, military recreation, and civilian wartime production activities. Those photographs pertaining to early military activity are reproductions of paintings, sketches, and artifacts. 1754–1981 (SC) (SCA) (MP) (O) (P) (PC) (C) (CC) (CCA).

111-B-36. Gen. Ulysses S. Grant at Cold Harbor. Virginia. 1864. Mathew Brady. Mathew Brady Collection. (RG 111, Records of the Office of the Chief Signal Officer)

111-SC-253415. *As the 2nd Battalion, 473rd Inf. Regt. reached the northern edge of Massa, Italy, a German machine gun opened up and wounded this man, who, after receiving first aid, is being taken by his comrade to a jeep evacuation.* April 10, 1945. (RG 111, Records of the Office of the Chief Signal Officer)

111.2 Photographs taken during the Civil War as well as some earlier and later coverage. Many of the pictures were taken by or under the direction of Mathew B. Brady. Included are pictures covering military land and naval engagements; Union and Confederate fortifications; weapons; military transport; officers, soldiers, and sailors from both armies; and prominent civilians. 1861–70 (B) (BA).

111.3 Photographs relating to aviation, including pictures of balloons, airplanes, aviators, and airfields. Also included are photographs of the Sino-Japanese War in 1894; U.S. troops during the Boxer Rebellion, the Spanish-American War and the Philippine Insurrection; and Cuba and Puerto Rico. Additionally, there are photographs documenting U.S. Signal Corps activities in Alaska, army camps and Signal Corps headquarters and other installations; Signal Corps personnel and equipment, and War Department exhibits at the 1893 World's Columbian Exposition. 1893–1918 (RB).

111.4 Photographs showing exhibits at the Louisiana Purchase Exposition, 1904; the Alaska-Yukon-Pacific Exposition, 1909; the Pan-American Exposition, 1901; the Jamestown Tercentennial Exposition, 1907; and the Panama-Pacific International Exposition, 1915 (EV).

111.5 Photographic prints relating to the Japanese capture of the German treaty port of Tsingtao, China, 1914 (J).

111.6 Photographs of World War I battlefields in France, 1919 (WM).

111.7 Photographic prints pertaining to Harry S. Truman while a soldier and as President, 1918–56 (T).

111.8 Photographic prints collected by Maj. Gen. Adolphus W. Greeley during his military career as Chief Signal Officer from 1882–1906. A few of the images pertain directly to Greeley including portraits, group pictures with noted persons, pictures relating to his receipt of the Medal of Honor, and views of his home. The majority of the images relate to U.S. military activities in the Philippine Islands from 1899 to 1905. There are also photographs showing U.S. Army balloon operations at Point Judith, RI, 1902; scenes of Valdez, AK, 1902; and views of San Francisco, CA, during and after the 1906 earthquake, including U.S. Army relief operations (AGA) (AGB) (AGC) (AGD) (AGE) (AGF) (AGG) (AGH) (AGI) (AGJ).

111.9 Photographic negatives relating to Signal Corps photography techniques and equipment, 1929–34 (L). Filmstrips used for training and other informational purposes, 1939–45 (FS).

111.10 Photographic prints showing federal buildings and monuments in Washington, DC, 1943–53 (WDC).

111.11 Scrapbooks containing newspaper clippings with photographs taken or transmitted by the Signal Corps for news agencies and released for publicity purposes, 1943–44 (NC).

RG 112

RECORDS OF THE
OFFICE OF THE SURGEON GENERAL (ARMY)

ca. 1799, 1918–24, and 1942–49   2,770 items

112.1   A variety of photographs relating to army medical training and therapeutic treatment for troops. Included are photographs of military medical facilities at Fort McPherson, GA, and images used in a report on dental equipment for field use. Ca. 1918–24 (SG).

112.2   Photographic prints and lantern slides documenting the work of the United States of America Typhus Commission in Europe, Africa, and other areas. Pictured are typhus patients, methods of controlling the disease, mosquito-infested areas, mosquito eradication programs, laboratory tests, hospitals, and other subjects. Also included are photographs of U.S. and British officers, Secretary of War Robert P. Patterson, and Surgeon General Norman T. Kirk. 1942–46 (T) (TS).

112.3   Photographic prints of Army Medical Corps activities in Europe during and after World War II showing wounded soldiers and civilians, transportation for the injured, hospitals, therapy programs, and medical personnel. Some of the notables pictured are Gen. Dwight D. Eisenhower, Secretary of War Henry Stimson, and Lt. Gen. George S. Patton. 1943–46 (SGA).

112.4   Photographic prints showing U.S. Army nurses, and army celebrations commemorating the 48th anniversary of the Army Nurse Corps, 1949 (SGN).

112.5   Lantern slides relating to the life of surgeon Valentine Seaman, who introduced the use of the cow pox vaccination in New York City in 1799 (TSA).

RG 114

RECORDS OF THE SOIL CONSERVATION SERVICE

1933–77   ca. 58,000 items

114.1   The general photographic files of the Soil Conservation Service (SCS) relating to the land utilization and conservation projects, and SCS research activities. Some of the subjects pictured are soil erosion, irrigation and drainage projects, the effects of floods and dust storms, farming operations, and Civilian Conservation Corps and Work Projects Administration programs. Many of the images were taken by SCS photographers Glenn L. Fuller and Charles W. Collier. 1933–77 (G) (P).

114.2   Photographs documenting the research projects of the Hill Culture Division of SCS in all regions of the United States. Most of the images, however, pertain to the mid-Atlantic region. The photographs show the division's efforts to develop and propagate erosion-inhibiting plants that would also produce commercially valuable commodities. 1933–48 (HC).

114.3   Photographs used in sedimentation studies. Shown are rivers, dams, reservoirs, floods, and topographical features throughout the United States. 1935–46 (SS) (WR).

114.4   Photographic prints accumulated by the SCS Rapid City, SD, regional office to illustrate soil conservation operations and dry land agriculture in North

Dakota, South Dakota, Montana, and Wyoming. Included are pictures showing soil erosion, farmlands, cultivation methods, and irrigation systems. 1935–39 (DL).

114.5   Photographs taken by Walter C. Lowdermilk, chief of the SCS Research Division, showing land utilization projects, and soil conservation and flood control practices in China, Europe, and the Middle East, 1938–43. Also, photographic prints by Lowdermilk documenting the experimental research in erosion control conducted by SCS in Puerto Rico, 1937–38 (L) (WCLM).

114.6   Lantern slides showing soil conservation activities, 1933–77; documenting reservoir surveys, 1941; and relating to stream and valley aggradation projects, 1937–40 (S) (SRS) (SSV).

RG 115

RECORDS OF THE BUREAU OF RECLAMATION
1899–1958   ca. 50,268 items

115.1   Photographs documenting activities of the bureau in the development and construction of irrigation projects. Included are pictures of dams, hydroelectric power plants, canals, reservoirs, and tunnels. Also shown are the physical and economic benefits of the projects as reflected in the towns, farms, recreation areas, transportation facilities, and industries in adjacent areas. 1902–36 (JA through JY) (JAA through JAJ).

115.2   Photographs of U.S. national parks, 1918–31 (PA through PJ). Photographic prints of bureau; U.S. Geological Survey, Division of Hydrography; Civilian Conservation Corps; and the Department of the Interior personnel; members of the U.S. Congress; and U.S. Presidents. 1900–33 (P) (GP) (HDP). Photographs of bureau exhibits and displays, 1922–32 (EX).

115.3   Photographs of maps and diagrams relating to bureau projects, 1902–33 (MD). Photographs showing irrigation projects in foreign countries, 1920–27 (FB through FM). Photographs of small irrigation projects, unfinished projects, and unsuccessful projects, 1904–31 (NA through NU). Photographs documenting irrigation projects in the western and southern United States, 1914–34 (SA through ST).

115.4   Photographic prints showing the construction and economic results of irrigation projects, including an album of prints on the construction of the Coolidge Dam in Arizona, 1927–29 (DE). Photographs of the official seal of the Department of the Interior and other subjects, 1905–33 (MS).

115.5   Photographic prints of Civilian Conservation Corps activities at Bureau of Reclamation projects in the western United States, 1934–42 (C) (CP).

115.6   Lantern slides of Indian tribes of the western United States illustrating their customs and cultures. The slides were apparently used to illustrate bureau lectures. 1899–1915 (L).

115.7   Lantern slides of bureau projects, ca. 1930 (LS). Color slides of water resource projects undertaken by the bureau in the western United States, 1946– (KS).

114-DL-SD5000. *View of back of farm buildings, showing dust piled up on one of them, which has been caved in by the weight of the drifts. The house is still furnished but not in use.* South Dakota. Ca. 1939. (RG 114, Records of the Soil Conservation Service)

119-G-14-4208D. *Auto mechanics shop - repairing the engine of a gov't official car.* Charleston, WV. Ca. 1940. Attributed to Barbara Wright. (RG 119, Records of the National Youth Administration)

115-JAJ-823. *Laguna dam - telephoto view of headworks, California side:* May 8, 1910. Walter J. Lubken. (RG 115, Records of the Bureau of Reclamation)

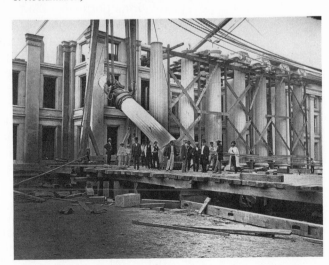

121-BC-9A. *North Front.* Construction of the Treasury Building. September 16, 1867. Lewis Emery Walker. (RG 121, Records of the Public Buildings Service)

RG 117

RECORDS OF THE
AMERICAN BATTLE MONUMENTS COMMISSION
1923–37   3,317 items

117.1   Photographic prints of World War I cemeteries and memorials in Europe built by the commission, other American sponsors, and European governments; also views of memorials in San Francisco, CA, New York, NY, and Honolulu, HI, 1924–35 (MC) (CM) (MP).

117.2   Albums containing photographic prints and corresponding maps showing battlefields in France and Belgium where several U.S. infantry divisions fought in World War I, 1923–25 (TPB).

117.3   Original drawings depicting designs for World War I monuments and memorials, 1923–30 (SK).

117.4   Photographic prints recording dedication ceremonies at U.S. cemeteries and memorials in Europe, 1937 (MM).

RG 119

RECORDS OF THE
NATIONAL YOUTH ADMINISTRATION
1935–43   ca. 22,115 items

119.1   Nine albums of photographic prints documenting activities at the National Youth Administration (NYA) resident training centers, educational camps, and work centers in Florida, Illinois, Kansas, Nebraska, South Dakota, Utah, Wisconsin, and Wyoming, 1935–43 (SCA).

119.2   Lantern slides showing NYA youth engaged in various projects, 1936–40 (LS). Photographs maintained by the NYA Office of Information for public relations purposes. Many of the photographs were taken by Barbara Wright and F. B. Hyde and show NYA youth engaged in a number of projects, including arts and crafts, aeronautics, clerical work, child care, construction, domestic science, health instruction, and immigration and naturalization assistance. Also included are photographs of NYA offices, exhibits, personnel, and government officials. 1936–42 (G) (S).

119.3   Photographic prints used to illustrate NYA publications. Subjects pictured include highways and roads, electricity and the light bulb, weather conditions and meteorological equipment, agricultural production, methods for establishing uniform measurements, and high school students involved in NYA projects. 1936–42 (M).

119.4   Photographs taken by Ron Partridge for an NYA pictorial essay on the need and benefits of youth programs. Shown are student antiwar activities, unemployed or underemployed youth, and job training programs in California. 1940 (CAL).

RG 120	RECORDS OF THE AMERICAN EXPEDITIONARY FORCES (WORLD WAR I), 1917–23

RECORDS OF THE AMERICAN EXPEDITIONARY FORCES (WORLD WAR I), 1917–23

1915–20   5,123 items

120.1   Photographic prints, maps, diagrams, and drawings relating to Army Air Service facilities and units, primarily in France, during World War I, 1917–19 (AS).

120.2   Portraits of recipients of the Croix de Guerre, 1917–19 (AC).

120.3   An album of photographic prints assembled by Capt. H. B. Boies, Chief of the Training Sections, to document training program activities of the 116th Engineers, 1918 (HB). Three albums showing the work of the Camouflage, Bridging and Mining Sections of the Army Engineer School, ca. 1918 (ESC) (ESB) (ESM). An album of photographic prints showing Quartermaster Corps oil and gasoline storage facilities in France and Belgium, 1918–19 (GO).

120.4   Photographic prints showing areas in France and Belgium occupied by American troops. The photographs were taken under the coordination of Maj. T. H. Griffin, Intelligence Section. 1918–19 (G). Photographic prints documenting the effects of Allied bombing, 1915–18 (AB).

120.5   Glass negatives of an inter-Allied marksmanship competition in Belgium, 1919 (RPM). Photographic prints of Memorial Day services at U.S. cemeteries in France, 1920 (AEFC).

120.6   Recruitment, conservation, and propaganda posters from the World War I period, ca. 1915–19 (WP).

RG 121   RECORDS OF THE PUBLIC BUILDINGS SERVICE

1855–1967   120,200 items

121.1   Photographs documenting the construction or alteration of post offices, customhouses, courthouses, hospitals, and other public buildings; and showing monuments and memorials around the United States. Some of the photographs show floor plans and sketches for various designs. Also included are a few photographs of public officials and their families, and government employees at work. 1855–1967 (BA) (BB) (BC) (BD) (BE) (BF) (BCP) (BS) (C).

121.2   An album of photographic prints compiled by the Office of the Supervising Architect of the Treasury Department documenting the construction of the Department of the Treasury Building and subsequent repairs to the building. The 19th-century photographs were taken by Lewis Emery Walker. 1857–67 and 1909 (TB).

121.3   Glass negatives made of paintings by Henry Wood Elliott depicting the fur seal industry in Alaska, ca. 1872–90 (HE).

121.4   Photographic prints and engravings of President Rutherford B. Hayes, members of his cabinet, postmasters, and architects, ca. 1877 (RBH). Portraits of President Grover Cleveland's children, ca. 1897 (BAC).

121.5   Photographs of federal government buildings and exhibits at the New York World's Fair (New York, NY), and the following expositions: World's Columbian (Chicago, IL); Cotton States and International (Atlanta, GA); Tennessee Centennial (Nashville, TN); Trans-Mississippi (Omaha, NE); Pan-American (Buffalo, NY); Louisiana Purchase (St. Louis, MO); Lewis and Clark Centennial (Portland, OR); Jamestown Tercentennial (Hampton Roads, VA); and Alaska-Yukon-Pacific (Seattle, WA). 1892–1939 (EX).

121.6   An album of photographic prints showing Department of the Treasury employees at work and interior and exterior views of the Treasury Department building, Washington, DC; the Mint, Philadelphia, PA; and the Sub-Treasury Building, New York, NY. 1910 (RT).

121.7   Photographic prints of public buildings and memorials in Washington, DC, ca. 1914 and 1931 (CJT) (MBW). Photographic prints of sites for federal buildings in 44 states and Puerto Rico, 1930–39 (SB).

121.8   Photographic prints documenting the construction of stairs, walkways, and terraces at the Lincoln Memorial. Also two photographic prints showing early phases in the construction of the Arlington National Cemetery amphitheater. 1916–19 (LM).

121.9   Photographic prints submitted by contractors to show the progress of construction of Veterans Administration buildings, 1922–29 (VA).

121.10   Lantern slides showing federal buildings in the United States and historic buildings in other countries, 1927–36 (LSB). Lantern slides from the Section of Fine Arts showing paintings, murals, and sculptures in federal buildings, 1933–43 (LSA).

121.11   Photographs of works of art created by artists employed under the Public Works of Art Project, 1933–34 (PWAP) (PWD). Photographs of works of art produced under the Treasury Relief Art Project (TRAP) for federal offices, and pictures of preliminary design sketches and several artists, 1935–39 (TR).

121.12   Photographs arranged by location or by name of artist, showing murals, sketches, sculptures, and paintings commissioned by the Section of Fine Arts for post offices, hospitals, courthouses and customhouses, and other federal buildings. Also included is some original art. 1934–43 (CMS) (PS) (GA).

121.13   Photographic prints of murals, paintings, and sculptures submitted by artists to various design competitions sponsored by the Section of Fine Arts, including the "48 States Competition," 1934–43 (MS) (FES).

121.14   Photographic prints recording construction progress of nonfederal public facilities—mostly schools—built under the auspices of the Emergency Operations Unit, 1942–46 (SHR).

121.15   Photographic prints of art purchased or selected by the Office of Emergency Management for various exhibits, including "Art in War" and "Soldiers in Production." The exhibits were designed to inform the public about war and defense activities. 1941–42 (WTE) (WDAE) (WSP). Photographic prints of paintings, drawings, and watercolors used in an exhibit about the American Red Cross, 1942 (WRC).

121.16   Photographs documenting the activities of the Public Buildings Administration in the construction and maintenance of public buildings. Pictured are buildings, the emblems of various federal agencies, and several members of Congress. 1943–51 (PB).

RG 126

RECORDS OF THE OFFICE OF TERRITORIES
1908–57   16,149 items

126.1   Photographs and lantern slides from the Alaska Engineering Commission showing the Copper River Railroad and the survey, construction, and operation of the Alaska Railroad. Also pictured are views of rural areas and cities and towns in Alaska; wildlife; mining operations; native Alaskans and settlers; government officials; and a 1920 inspection trip by Secretary of the Interior J. B. Payne and others. 1908–33 (AR) (ARS) (ARA).

126.2   Photographic prints collected from various sources showing Alaskan natives, settlers, agricultural and industrial activities, art and cultural activities, transportation facilities, and the construction of the Alaska Railroad. Also included are pictures documenting the Matanuska Colonization Project. 1915–45 (AG).

126.3   Photographic prints showing President Warren G. Harding touring Alaska. Photographs of Harding's funeral are also included. 1923 (ARB).

126.4   Photographs documenting the activities of the Puerto Rico Reconstruction Administration. Among the images are scenic views of Puerto Rico; pictures of farms, industries, hospitals, schools, government buildings, historic sites, and urban and rural housing conditions; pictures of government officials; and photographs of a 1948 visit to the island by President Harry S. Truman. 1935–48 (PG) (PRA).

126.5   Photographic prints of Hawaii from nongovernment sources showing agricultural and industrial development; educational, transportation, health services, and public officials; a 1938 labor demonstration in Hilo; and scenic views of the islands. 1936–57 (HG).

126.6   Photographs from the U.S. Antarctic Service (USAS) documenting a 1939–41 expedition to Antarctica. The expedition was under the command of Adm. Richard Byrd. Among the subjects pictured are USAS personnel, equipment, and vehicles; research activities; USAS buildings; various animals; and the Antarctic landscape (AS). Ground-level photographs by Finn Ronne showing the topography of Antarctica, 1940 (FR). Two photographic prints of Cape Eielson, Antarctica, donated by Adm. Richard Black of the USAS, 1940 (CE). Photographs of Donald Hilton's sledging expedition, 1940–41 (DH). Photographs transmitted by means of radio waves by the U.S. Antarctic Service showing expedition personnel and activities, 1940–41 (RP). Color slides and filmstrips showing people, animals, and scenic views of Antarctica, 1939–41 (CS).

RG 127

RECORDS OF THE U.S. MARINE CORPS
ca. 1775–1981   ca. 216,000 items

127.1   Photographs (some of art) used in exhibits on the history of the U.S. Marine Corps (USMC), ca. 1775–1941 (EX). The general photographic files of the

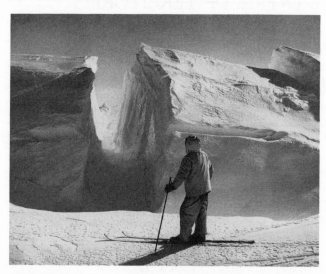

126-AS-5483. *Dr. Frazier inspecting a large pressure ridge broken in cross sections in the Bay of Whales*. Antarctica. October 25, 1940. P1/c. C. C. Shirley. (RG 126, Records of the Office of Territories)

129-G-174-10. *Alcatraz - ground floor cell in D block with attached fixtures before inmate moves in with personal possessions*. Ca. 1947. (RG 129, Records of the Bureau of Prisons)

127-G-126S-524676. *Privates R. F. and T. C. Seitzinger (brothers), U.S. Marine Corps Rifle Team*. Wakefield, MA. August 1927. (RG 127, Records of the U.S. Marine Corps)

Marine Corps, including images of historic events, battles, U.S. involvement in Central America and the Caribbean, USMC units, formal and informal pictures of USMC officers and enlisted men, USMC uniforms, weapons, training programs, aircraft, transportation equipment, and USMC bands. The Revolutionary War, the Civil War, World War I, World War II, the Korean conflict, and the Vietnam war are among the wars covered. Ca. 1775–1981 (G) (GC) (GK) (GR) (GS) (GW) (N).

127.2   Photographs covering Marine Corps participation in ceremonial functions during Presidential administrations from Theodore Roosevelt to Lyndon B. Johnson, including pictures of Marine bands at Presidential inaugurations and award ceremonies. Also included are pictures of Presidents George Washington, John Adams, Thomas Jefferson, James Monroe, James Polk, Zachary Taylor, James Buchanan, Andrew Jackson, Abraham Lincoln, and Ulysses S. Grant. Ca. 1789–1968 (PR).

127.3   Photographic prints showing aerial views of landing fields in Haiti and Santo Domingo (Dominican Republic), 1923, and activities of the Third Marine Brigade in China, 1927–29. Also included are a number of pictures of USMC personnel with various civilian government officials, 1870–1941 (M). Photographic prints of USMC aviators and aircraft, ca. 1931–37 (MA).

127.4   Portraits of USMC commandants and other officers, 1776–1945 (PC) (PG).

RG 129

RECORDS OF THE BUREAU OF PRISONS
ca. 1930–70   ca. 11,000 items

129.1   Photographs of Bureau of Prisons and Department of Justice personnel, including Attorneys General Robert F. Kennedy, Ramsey Clark, Nicholas Katzenbach, and John Mitchell; bureau directors Sanford Bates, James Bennett, Myrl Alexander and Norman Carlson; and Presidents John F. Kennedy and Lyndon B. Johnson, 1930–70 (P).

129.2   Photographs of federal penal institutions, including pictures of prison buildings, personnel, prisoners, and recreational and educational activities for the incarcerated, ca. 1930–70 (G).

RG 131

RECORDS OF THE OFFICE OF ALIEN PROPERTY
1910–43   44,813 items

131.1   Albums of photographic prints relating to the Hamburg-American Line (HAL), including pictures of ships, passengers, advertisements, and a Hamburg, Germany, facility operated by HAL for passengers in transit, 1910–30 (MA). Photographic prints of some of the vessels owned and operated by HAL. Also images showing the world ports and tourist attractions visited by ships of the Hamburg-American and North German Lloyd Steamship Lines, 1920–39 (SS) (WP). Photographic prints taken by news agencies showing passengers on board ships of the Hamburg-American Line; included are pictures of William R. Hearst, H. L. Mencken, Winston Churchill, Andrew Mellon, Eleanor Roosevelt, and other celebrities. 1920–39 (P).

131.2   Photographs of Nazi officials; German military operations; German cities, industries, festivals, and art; the 1936 Olympics; and other subjects relating to German life and culture. The photographs were collected and maintained by the German Railroads Information Offices in the United States. 1930–41 (GR) (N).

131.3   Lantern slides showing ports, cities, and tourist attractions around the world. The slides were probably used by the German Railroads Information Offices for promotional purposes. 1930–39 (LSC).

131.4   Photographic prints of Adolf Hitler and other Nazis, German military parades and ceremonies, activities of the Hitler youth and the Nazis, various conferences, views of Germany, and pictures of the German American Bund in the United States. The photographs were obtained from the files of a German Railroads Information Office and apparently used for propaganda purposes. 1933–41 (NO).

131.5   Still pictures, primarily militaristic in nature, produced from German motion pictures and newsreels, 1936–40 (UFA).

131.6   Photographic prints made from items in series WP(131.1) and GR(131.2) that were loaned to the Office of Strategic Services by the Office of Alien Property, 1942–43 (OSS) (OSSA) (OSSG) (OSSM).

RG 135

RECORDS OF THE
PUBLIC WORKS ADMINISTRATION
1939   ca. 11,000 items

135.1   The eight-album report, "Survey of the Architecture of Completed Projects of the Public Works Administration, 1939" contains mounted photographic prints and textual materials. The photographs, assembled for use in the report, show Public Works Administration projects in all the states, the District of Columbia, and Puerto Rico (SAA) (SAP) (SAR). Photographic negatives of the floor plans and pictures of buildings that were published in *Public Buildings: A Survey of Architecture* by C. W. Short and R. Stanley-Brown, 1939 (PB).

RG 136

RECORDS OF THE
AGRICULTURAL MARKETING SERVICE
1909–19   1,285 items

136.1   Photographs documenting cooperative studies of the egg and poultry industry undertaken by the Bureau of Chemistry, Bureau of Animal Industry, and the Bureau of Markets, 1909–19 (M).

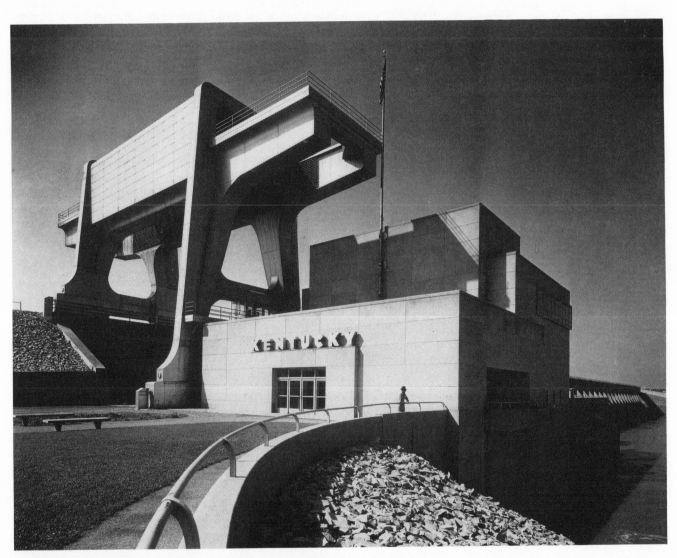

142-RS-2F-2. *TVA's* Kentucky Dam *(1938-1944) is of tremendous value for flood regulation purposes to the lower Ohio and Mississippi Rivers. Located on the Tennessee River near its mouth in Kentucky, the dam creates a reservoir 184 miles long, with a capacity of more than 6,000,000 acre-feet, two-thirds of which is useful storage. By regulating the flow of the Tennessee River at the* Kentucky Dam, *crests on the Ohio and Mississippi Rivers can be lowered as much as four feet. The dam has a generating capacity of 160,000 kw.* Ca. 1944. (RG 142, Records of the Tennessee Valley Authority)

Records of the
Tennessee Valley Authority
1918–41   2,191 items

142.1   Glass negatives documenting the progress of construction of plants and support facilities at the U.S. Nitrate Plant No. 2, Muscle Shoals, AL. Images showing plant employees and their families, and community services for workers are also included. 1918–19 (MS).

142.2   Photographs taken or collected by the Recreation and Conservation Section of the Tennessee Valley Authority (TVA) of areas affected by TVA's construction of hydroelectric and power plants, and reservoirs. Included are images of forests, lakes, mountains, rivers, parks and recreational areas, and TVA projects. 1933–41 (RS).

142.3   Photographic negatives of east Tennessee taken for TVA by Lewis Hine showing several families who were forced to vacate their homes and lands, industries in Kingsport, examples of local crafts and culture, applicants for TVA jobs, construction activities at the Norris Dam, and Civilian Conservation Corps enrollees, 1933 (H).

Records of the Agricultural Stabilization
and Conservation Service
1904–53 and 1977–83   ca. 20,100 items

145.1   Photographs created or accumulated by the Production and Marketing Administration (PMA) on a wide range of subjects, including commodity production and marketing, food preservation, surplus commodity disposal, soil conservation, grades and standards for products, and PMA officials, 1904–53 (PMA).

145.2   Agricultural Adjustment Administration (AAA) photographs showing farms and ranches, crops and livestock, farm equipment, farmers and their families, and farm laborers and migrant workers. There are also pictures of AAA agents and exhibits. A significant portion of the images are of U.S. Army and National Guard units training, and military food service operations. A few of the pictures show military units at the 1941 inaugural parade for President Franklin Roosevelt, and Roosevelt visiting troops. 1939–46 (AAA) (AAA-A).

145.3   Photographs made for the Consumer Council of the Agricultural Adjustment Administration showing the growing, processing, and merchandising of agricultural products; federal inspection of farm products; and consumer education programs. 1934–39 (CC). Photographs collected for use in the Agricultural Adjustment Administration publication, *Consumers' Guide*, 1937–42 (CG).

145.4   Filmstrips on soil conservation, grain production, and marketing, 1935–41 (FS). Color slides illustrating the history and programs of the Agricultural Stabilization and Conservation Service, 1977–83 (TA).

RG 148

RECORDS OF EXPOSITION, ANNIVERSARY AND MEMORIAL COMMISSIONS
ca. 1771–1939   2,130 items

148.1   Photographs of works of art pertaining to the life and career of George Washington that were collected by the George Washington Bicentennial Commission from 1931 through 1932. Pictured are Revolutionary War leaders, battles, maps, flags, documents, historic sites, and commission-sponsored bicentennial parades, reenactments, and exhibits. Ca. 1776–1932 (GW).

148.2   Photographs of the art and memorabilia exhibited at the Corcoran Gallery in Washington, DC, from 1937 through 1939. The exhibit was sponsored by the U.S. Constitution Sesquicentennial Commission to commemorate the ratification of the Constitution. Pictured are portraits of deputies to the Constitutional Convention, the signers of the Constitution, and the signers of the Declaration of Independence. Portraits of the families of some of the delegates are also included. Ca. 1771–87 (CP). Portraits of the delegates to the Constitutional Convention and the signers of the Declaration of Independence; some of the images were used in the Corcoran Gallery exhibit. Ca. 1776–87 (CC) (CD).

148.3   Photographs of historic buildings and famous individuals of the Revolutionary and pre-Constitutional period collected during the period 1935–39 by the U.S. Constitution Sesquicentennial Commission. Also included are a few photographs relating to commemorative ceremonies held at the U.S. Congress and the Library of Congress (CCD).

RG 151

RECORDS OF THE BUREAU OF FOREIGN AND DOMESTIC COMMERCE AND SUCCESSOR AGENCIES
1899–1939 and 1954–63   ca. 10,850 items

151.1   Photographs collected by the bureau to show industries, agricultural practices, and transportation services in the United States and almost a hundred foreign countries. Included are pictures of people, cities, agricultural and industrial products, markets and stores, shipping activities, transportation equipment, machinery, and international trade fairs. 1899–1939 and 1954–63 (FC) (K) (M) (F).

151.2   Photographic prints of bureau personnel, U.S. government officials, and other dignitaries, including photographs of President John F. Kennedy, 1913–30 and 1954–63 (P) (PA).

RG 153

RECORDS OF THE OFFICE OF THE JUDGE ADVOCATE GENERAL (ARMY)
1912–46   798 items

153.1   Two albums of photographic prints used as an exhibit in the war crimes trial of Ilse Koch, wife of the commandant of the Buchenwald concentration camp. The prints show Koch's friends and family, Koch's quarters at Buchenwald, World War I destruction, and pre–World War II scenes of Germany. 1912–41 (IK).

153.2　　Six albums of photographic prints from the law library of the Judge Advocate General showing German and Nazi atrocities, war crimes trials, and looted property recovered by the Allies, 1942–46 (WC).

RG 155

RECORDS OF THE WAGE AND HOUR DIVISION
1930–60　　246 items

155.1　　Photographs collected by the Branch of Child Labor to document concern for children working in industry and agriculture, 1930–60 (CL).

RG 156

RECORDS OF THE OFFICE OF THE CHIEF OF ORDNANCE
1816–1967　　64,983 items

156.1　　An album of photographic prints showing officers' quarters at the arsenal at Fort Monroe, VA, and shops, offices, and buildings at the Frankford, PA, arsenal, ca. 1870 (AB). An album of photographic prints showing small arms and light artillery at the Washington Arsenal, Washington, DC, ca. 1866–79 (AA).

156.2　　Two albums of printed illustrations depicting armaments built by the Grunsonwerk company of Germany, 1877–89 (GRA).

156.3　　Photographic prints collected by the Historical Branch to document various weapons, vehicles, and ordnance plants primarily in Nitro and Charleston, WV, 1917–19 (H).

156.4　　Photographs, drawings, and textual material on mobile machine guns and quick-fire cannons, 1917–19 (MG).

156.5　　One album of photographic prints recording the construction of buildings at Edgewood Arsenal, MD, including views of various chemical plants at the arsenal, 1918 (EA).

156.6　　Two albums of photographic prints showing production activities at the Wisconsin Gun Company Plant in Milwaukee, WI, 1917–19, and at the New York Air Brake Company in Watertown, NY, ca. 1917 (OP).

156.7　　Albums of photographic prints documenting plant construction and operations, employees at work and relaxing, and housing for workers at the Muscle Shoals, AL, nitrate plant, 1917–19 (MS) (B).

156.8　　Panoramas of the Old Hickory, TN, munitions plant and other buildings, 1918 (PMP).

156.9　　An album of photographic prints recording the first transcontinental motor convoy (Washington, DC, to San Francisco, CA), 1919 (TMC). Glass negatives relating to personnel and activities of the Bureau of Ordnance, n.d. (GN).

156.10   An album of photographic prints documenting activities at the Fort Morgan, AL, firing range, 1916 (FM).

156.11   Photographs relating to the manufacture of ordnance materials, the transcontinental motor convoy, and proving grounds, ca. 1917 (PA) (PB).

156.12   Photographic prints of small arms, 1917–41 (SAD). Photographic prints from the Small Arms Division documenting research and development of small arms and accessories at arsenals in Frankford, PA; Raritan, NJ; Rock Island, IL; and Springfield, MA; and Aberdeen Proving Ground, MD, 1911–49 (RD) (RDA) (RDI) (RDL) (RDV). An album of photographic prints showing German World War II small arms (ESA). Oversized photographic prints showing various types of small arms, ca. 1900–43 (RDO).

156.13   Cyanotypes of guns and gun carriages; bombs and airplanes; anti-aircraft equipment; armor plate; oblique and vertical cameras obscura; miscellaneous equipment, personnel, and activities at Aberdeen Proving Ground, MD; and types of vehicles, 1917–41 (GGC) (GBA) (GAP) (GMP) (GAV) (GAA) (GCO) (GAM) (GLS) (GIM) (GBS) (GMO) (GMI) (GKF) (N).

156.14   Photographs of buildings, equipment, employees, tests and experiments, and weapons at the Springfield Arsenal, MA, 1965–67; the Watertown Arsenal, MA, 1816–1967; the Rock Island Arsenal, IL, 1878–1963; and the Benecia, CA, facility, 1899–1906 (SA) (WA) (WAA) (WAC) (WAN) (WAP) (WAM) (WAS) (WAOL) (WAHM) (WAVP) (RA) (RAW) (RIV) (BE).

156.15   Photographic prints from Wright Air Development Center, OH, relating to aerial ordnance research, ca. 1920 (ASW). Three albums of photographic prints showing antiaircraft and mobile artillery guns and equipment at various arsenals, 1927–36 (MA).

156.16   World War II posters and broadsides primarily encouraging the correct use of camouflage, ca. 1942 (WPC) (WPOD). Two original drawings for World War I-era posters, n.d. (WP).

RG 162

RECORDS OF THE FEDERAL WORKS AGENCY
1936–49   5,998 items

162.1   Photographs relating to Federal Works Agency (FWA) supervised projects, including the construction of war industries, defense housing, highways, and airports; and the construction of schools, health, and other municipal facilities in communities affected by wartime industrial growth. Included are photographs relating to FWA relief work following natural disasters, Public Roads Administration activities in the construction of the Alaska Highway, and exhibits by the United States Housing Authority. Also recorded are selective service lotteries and FWA support for the construction and operation of recreational facilities for servicemen. Some of the important individuals pictured are Presidents Franklin Roosevelt and Harry S. Truman, Eleanor Roosevelt, and FWA officials. 1936–49 (FWA) (G).

162.2   Photographic prints showing the construction, operation, and maintenance of public buildings by the Public Buildings Administration, 1939–43 (PBA). Photographic prints relating to the construction and operation of public services in communities impacted by defense projects. Included are photographs of schools, post-World War II housing for veterans, hospitals, and municipal facilities. 1941–44 (WP).

RECORDS OF THE
WAR DEPARTMENT GENERAL AND SPECIAL STAFFS
1774–1947   95,780 items

165.1   War Department collections of Civil War-era photographs. Included are images of Union and Confederate fortifications; Union camps, barracks, hospitals, prisons, and other facilities; battlefields; artillery; military railroads; gunboats and other ships; and Union and Confederate troops. Also pictured are individual and group portraits of generals and other military officers; prominent civilians; and Union government officials, including President Abraham Lincoln. Many of the photographs were taken by Mathew Brady, Andrew J. Russell, Sam A. Cooley, George N. Barnard, and S. R. Seibert. 1861–70 (A) (B) (C) (CA) (CO) (CS) (PR) (PV). Photographic prints from Alexander Gardner's 1866 *Photographic Sketch Book of the War* showing Union Army activities in Virginia, Maryland, and Pennsylvania, 1862–65 (SB). Photographs taken by George N. Barnard during General William T. Sherman's campaign through Georgia, Tennessee, and South Carolina, 1863–64 (SC). Cartes de visite of U.S. military and civilian notables collected by photographer John Taylor, ca. 1861–65 (JT). Stereographs of military activities and installations, including some photographs by Sam A. Cooley, 1865–86 (S). Original watercolors of Civil War views painted by Herbert E. Valentine, ca. 1861–65 (HV). Lantern slides collected by J. M. Moon relating to President Lincoln's life and career, 1809–65 (JM).

165.2   Stereographs showing U.S. soldiers, American Indians, forts, geological formations, ships, railroads, and factories in the United States, ca. 1865–1909 (XS). Photographic prints of U.S. forts, 1860–1914 (FF). Individual and group portraits of U.S. Army officers, ca. 1860–1918 (P) (PF) (PS). An album of photographic prints showing buildings, grounds, and cadets at the Michigan Military Academy, Orchard Lake, MI, 1877–1908 (MMA).

165.3   Photographic prints of American Indians, ca. 1881–85 (AI). Stereographs showing Captain Jack and other Modoc Indians, an army camp, and the lava bed area of California where the U.S. Army and the Modocs fought. Some of the images were taken by Eadweard Muybridge. 1873 (MH) (MM) (MS). The William H. Carter collection of photographic prints of American Indians, U.S. military personnel, and frontier forts, 1860–1900 (WHC).

165.4   Photographic prints of types of U.S. and foreign artillery, 1877–95 (ORD). Photographic prints showing U.S. military exhibits and displays at the Centennial International Exhibition in Philadelphia, PA, 1876, and the World's Columbian Exposition, Chicago, IL, 1893 (EP) (EC). Color lithographs of paintings by H. A. Ogden showing U.S. Army uniforms from 1774–1908 (HOA) (HOB) (HOC).

165.5   Photographic prints taken during the Spanish-American War, including pictures of U.S. troops, weapons and equipment, fortifications and campsites, transport vessels, naval scenes, and battles. Also shown are views of Puerto Rico, the Philippine Islands, and Cuba. 1898–99 (SW) (SWS) (SWR). Photographic prints showing ships used to transport troops and equipment during the Spanish-American War, 1898–1900 (SS). Issues of *Leslie's Illustrated Weekly* and *Harper's Weekly* containing photographic coverage of the Spanish-American War, 1898 (IWN). Panoramas of Santiago and Havana, Cuba, and of St. Thomas, Virgin Islands, ca. 1908 (PCW). Photographic negatives apparently made by the Corps of Engineers to document railroads in Cuba, ca. 1900 (RRC).

165.6   An album containing photographic prints and maps showing harbors, railroads, and bridges in Canada. The album is part of an 1890 reconnaissance report by Lt. A. S. Rowan, 15th U.S. Infantry, on areas in Canada between Lake of the Woods and Calgary. A few other areas in Canada are also pictured. 1889–90 (CPM). Stereographs with scenic views of countries in Europe, the Middle East, Cuba, and the Philippine Islands, ca. 1867–1900 (FS).

165.7   Photographic prints showing fortifications, U.S. troops, and insurgents during the Philippine Insurrection, 1899–1903 (PW). An album of photographic prints assembled by Capt. Archibald W. Butt showing military and civilian activities in the Philippine Islands, including pictures of William H. Taft. There are also a few photographs relating to Hawaii. Ca. 1900 (AB). Photographic prints of unidentified military maneuvers, 1904 (UMM). Aerial oblique photographs of U.S. Army maneuvers at Fort William McKinley, Philippine Islands, 1925 (MC).

165.8   Photographic prints taken or collected by Brig. Gen. Frederick King Ward during his tours of duty with the U.S. 1st Cavalry and other units. Many of the images are of Ward and his family, but there are also pictures of U.S. military activities in the United States, the Philippine Islands, and Panama. Also included are scenic views of the Philippine Islands, Japan, and China. 1899–1922 (FKW).

165.9   Photographic prints of U.S. and foreign troops in China during the Boxer Rebellion (China Relief Expedition), 1900–1901 (CR).

165.10   Photographic prints of Mexican Army maneuvers, 1901 (MA). Six albums of photographic prints showing Mexican villages and transportation facilities, including roads, bridges, railroads, and tunnels. The albums accompanied reconnaissance reports from Army officers. 1904–11 (MR). Photographic prints showing Mexican Pacific Railway bridges, 1907–8 (MPR). Photographic prints relating to U.S. military forces in Veracruz, Mexico, and during the Mexican Punitive Expedition. The pictures were taken by various newspaper correspondents, the Underwood and Underwood studio, C. Tucker Beckett, and Col. George H. McMaster. 1914–17 (MP) (UM) (CB) (CM). Aerial photographs of civilian and military airfields in Mexico, ca. 1930–35 (APM). Photographic prints taken by H. D. McLean showing Gulf Oil Company camps and towns in Mexico, 1921 (GOC).

165.11   Photographic prints of U.S. Army installations in Hawaii. Pictured are military buildings at Camp Leilehua; and buildings and activities at Forts Shafter, Armstrong, DeRussy, Ruger, and Kamehameha; and Luke Field and Schofield Barracks. 1909 and 1914–29 (HHD).

165.12   *The Russo-Japanese War: A Photographic and Descriptive Review of the Great Conflict in the Far East* published by P. F. Collier and Son in 1905, (RJC). Photographic prints taken by Capt. P. C. March, U.S. military attaché to the Japanese Army, during the Russo-Japanese War, 1904 (RJ). An album of photographic prints showing the Japanese Army during maneuvers. The album was submitted by Col. James A. Irons, military attaché at the U.S. Embassy in Japan. 1909 (JAM). Photographic prints taken during Chinese Army maneuvers, 1909 (CAM). Photographic prints recording Spanish military operations in Morocco, 1924–25 (LZ). Photographic prints showing Czechoslovakian Army troops, 1923 (CAP).

153-WC-12-24. *Vice Admiral D. Okoochi of the Imperial Japanese Navy, testifies against Lt. Gen. Tomoyuki Yamashita during the war crimes trial, Manila, P.I.* November 16, 1945. Kramer. (RG 153, Records of the Office of the Judge Advocate General [Army])

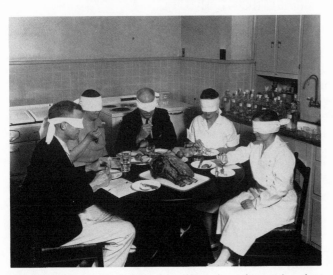

176-HE-33096c. *Meat Judging.* Lucy Alexander and group in palatability study. July 30, 1936. (RG 176, Records of the Bureau of Human Nutrition and Home Economics)

165-WW-127-8. *Some of the colored men of the 369th (15th N.Y.) who won the Croix de Guerre for galantry in action.* Left to right. Front row: Pvt. Ed. Williams, Herbert Taylor, Pvt. Leon Fraitor, Pvt. Ralph Hawkins. Back row: Sgt. H. D. Prinas, Sgt. Dan Storms, Pvt. Joe Williams, Pvt. Alfred Hanley, and Cpl. T. W. Taylor. 1919. International Film Service Co. (RG 165, Records of the War Department General and Special Staffs)

185-G-1892. *Gatun upper locks. Looking north from lighthouse on centerwall. Atlantic entrance in distance.* January 24, 1914. (RG 185, Records of the Panama Canal)

165.13 Photographic prints known as the "American Unofficial Collection of World War I Photographs" assembled by the Committee on Public Information from private, state, and federal government sources for publication in a history of World War I. Included are images on a variety of subjects primarily reflecting life on the homefront. Among the subjects pictured are wartime industries; bond, stamps, and loan drives; demonstrations and parades; volunteer and war relief organizations; military training at universities and colleges; women's suffrage; and the flu epidemic of 1918. The majority of the military-related subjects show training camps and programs. 1914–19 (WW). Panoramas of U.S. military camps and units in the United States and Europe, 1917–21 (PP) (PPO). Panoramas showing areas in Italy, Poland, the U.S.S.R., and Austria, 1915–26 (ARC). Photographic prints from the War Industries Board showing industries involved in the manufacture of ordnance, women working in industries and U.S. arsenals, and views of Quincy, MA, during the war, 1917–19 (EO). Photographic prints submitted to the Committee on Education and Special Training by various educational institutions to show the activities of Students' Army Training Corps, 1917–21 (EI). Lithographs created by artist Joseph Pennell depicting U.S. war industries, 1916–18 (LIT) (LIH). Issues of the *New York Herald Tribune* and the *New York Times* containing World War I photographic coverage, 1917–18 (NYT). Photographic prints on a variety of World War I subjects, including war industries, U.S. forts and camps, U.S. and foreign troops, battlefields, and artillery, ca. 1914–19 (WCF) (WGZ) (WLS) (WOW) (WPA). Photographic prints documenting community activities in Springfield, MA, during World War I, 1917–18 (WAR).

165.14 Postcards by French printers showing views of France before and after World War I, ca. 1914–18 (FC). Photographic prints of Allied and German military activities in Belgium, 1914–16 (BW). Photographic prints taken by British photographers to document British military activities in England and in the European theaters of operation, 1914–18 (BO). Photographic prints showing Italian troops and equipment, 1918 (WIT). Photographic prints showing the Romanian Army during World War I and the occupation of Hungary. Also included are pictures of Russian soldiers engaged in peace demonstrations in Romania. 1917–19 (RA). Aerial prints of German and Allied positions along the Belgian coast, 1917 (BEA). Photographic prints from German photographers showing German and Austrian military activities during World War I, 1917–18 (GB) (GK). Postcards by German printers showing ships of the German Navy and German military activities during the First World War, 1914–18 (GP) (GPC) (GPO). Lantern slides relating to German military activities, 1918–19 and 1939–41 (GS). Photographic prints showing Austrian troops on the Isonzo and Dalmatian fronts (Yugoslavia), ca. 1914–18 (AO). Photographic prints by U.S. military attaché Maj. F. T. Colby showing military personnel and activities, civilians, and villages in Belgium and the Balkan States, 1915–19 (BC).

165.15 Photographic prints taken by a Major Griffiths of areas in France where the 36th Division fought, 1919 (GG). The Louis J. Cohen Collection of photographic prints showing U.S. cemeteries in France, 1920–21 (BCT). Photographic prints of the American Forces in Germany and the Inter-Allied Rhineland High Commission in Koblenz, Germany, 1920–21 (AEF). Photographic prints of ceremonies marking the embarkation from France of the Unknown Soldier on October 24, 1921. (K).

165.16 Photographic prints relating to activities in the IX Corps area of California, ca. 1921 (WBA). Panoramas (some by E.O. Goldbeck) of U.S. Army units, forts, and airfields, 1936–38 (PX). Fifteen photographic prints showing U.S. World War II-era aircraft, n.d. (XA).

165.17   Photographic prints and newspaper clippings relating to visits to aircraft factories during World War II by the U.S. Army B–17 bomber *Hell's Angels* and the B–24 liberator *Boomerang* (HE) (BBL). Photographs of German, Russian, and Japanese military equipment, 1921–46 (MID). Photographic prints showing Japanese atrocities in the Philippine Islands during World War II (JA). A photographic print showing a military parade in Texas, n.d. (TX). Photographic prints recording an "Industry-Army Day" celebration at Fort Lewis, WA, 1947 (WA). Photographic prints recording a simulated combat war show in San Diego, CA, during World War II, n.d. (WS). Photographic prints relating to military activities during World War II, n.d. (XX).

RG 166

RECORDS OF THE
FOREIGN AGRICULTURAL SERVICE
1942–53   5,880 items

166.1   Photographic negatives showing agricultural practices in Central and South America, the Caribbean, west and east Asia, and Africa, 1942–52 (G) (M). Photographic negatives relating to agricultural practices and products in Thailand, including pictures of rural and urban areas, Thai culture, ethnic groups, trade, commercial and industrial activities, and transportation facilities, 1951–53 (T).

RG 167

RECORDS OF THE NATIONAL INSTITUTE OF
STANDARDS AND TECHNOLOGY
1920–59   1,395 items

167.1   Lantern slides made by several National Bureau of Standards (NBS) divisions to show their equipment, and to document tests and experiments conducted by the bureau, 1920–50 (RS). Lantern slides of bureau buildings and grounds, ceremonies, and portraits of bureau officials, ca. 1942 (GS).

167.2   A collection of lantern slides named in honor of Lyman J. Briggs, former director of the NBS, documenting various experiments undertaken by the bureau. Also included are slides relating to a 1935 National Geographic Society stratosphere balloon flight. 1933–59 (LBC).

167.3   The Wallace R. Brode Collection of lantern slides showing scientific equipment and machinery used in various tests conducted by the bureau, research activities, bureau buildings, and personnel. From 1947 to 1957 Mr. Brode was the Associate Director of Chemistry at the National Bureau of Standards. 1940–54 (WBC).

RG 168

RECORDS OF THE NATIONAL GUARD BUREAU
1898–1935   609 items

168.1   Photographic prints, drawings, and printed graphics of the crests and coats-of-arms of state National Guard units. Photographic prints of state militia personnel, camps, and equipment including the Oklahoma National Guard in 1924, the activities of the California National Guard in Santa Ana and Long Beach following a 1933 earthquake, and patrolling in 1934 during civil disturbances in San Francisco. Also included are photographs of U.S. Army personnel in Cuba during the Spanish-American War and views of Puerto Rico following a 1933 cyclone. 1898–1935 (G).

RG 169

RECORDS OF THE
FOREIGN ECONOMIC ADMINISTRATION
1941–45   2,528 items

169.1 Photographic prints relating to the procurement and development of agricultural and mineral commodities; aerial views of forested areas near Finca El Porvenir, Guatemala; photographic prints showing cinchona production in Guatemala; and pictures of agency personnel at work in Morocco, Tunisia, and Algeria. 1941–45 (GA) (AP) (C) (GP).

RG 170

RECORDS OF THE
BUREAU OF NARCOTICS AND DANGEROUS DRUGS
1973–80   14,000

170.1 Color and black-and-white slides documenting the activities of the Drug Enforcement Administration (DEA) in the enforcement of substance laws and regulations. Included are pictures of U.S. Border Patrol, U.S. Customs Service, and Bureau of Alcohol, Tobacco, and Firearms agents at work; types of drug-producing plants; types of drugs; plant eradication programs; and drug abusers. There are also photographs of Presidents John F. Kennedy and Jimmy Carter, DEA officials, and some retrospective material relating to alcohol prohibition. 1973–80 (S).

RG 171

RECORDS OF THE OFFICE OF CIVILIAN DEFENSE
1930–45   4,376 items

171.1 Photographs, aerial photographs, drawings, blueprints, and maps relating to camouflage plans for industrial, military, and municipal sites in California, 1930–43 (T). Photographs, including lantern slides, illustrating methods for industrial and military camouflage and techniques for constructing and installing types of camouflage; and aerial photographs of industrial sites and aerial oblique views of camouflaged areas in England. Ca. 1939–45 (CMT) (CDI) (EC) (PI).

171.2 Photographs documenting World War II civilian defense activities relating to emergencies, air raid drills, and rescue operations. Pictured are Office of Civilian Defense (OCD) communication systems, uniforms, insignia, equipment, and personnel. Also included are photographs recording the activities of the Citizens Service Corps, the Civil Air Patrol, and the Forest Fire Fighters Service. There are also a few photographs relating to civil defense programs in other countries. 1940–44 (G) (N) (OCD).

171.3 Lantern slides used to record bomb detonation tests at the Aberdeen Proving Ground in Maryland, 1940–42; to provide information on civilian defense activities in Detroit, MI, ca. 1941; to illustrate rescue operation lectures, ca. 1941; and to show U.S. Army maneuvers in 1939 (DT) (CDD) (RO) (AM).

171.4　　Lantern and color slides, some of which were created by the OCD Medical Division. The slides show types of injuries produced by various poison gases. Ca. 1942 (GI). Lantern slides illustrating methods of gas decontamination, ways to prevent contamination, and types of chemical warfare substances, ca. 1942 (GD) (GAP).

171.5　　Slides of drawings, charts, diagrams, and posters describing air raid plans, blackout regulations and equipment, and designs for bomb shelters, ca. 1942 (AR) (BD).

171.6　　A Forest Fire Fighters Service recruitment poster, 1942 (P). Color slides of posters and exhibits promoting security, recruitment for civil defense jobs, conservation, and war bonds, ca. 1942 (PDS).

171.7　　Photographs of a "service star" show sponsored by the La Junta, CO, Civilian Defense Council to honor the parents of military personnel, 1943 (L).

171.8　　Filmstrips relating to air raid precautionary measures, 1941–45 (FS).

RG 174

GENERAL RECORDS OF THE DEPARTMENT OF LABOR
1916–19 and 1948–53　　28 items

174.1　　Photographic prints of Secretaries of Labor Maurice J. Tobin and Martin P. Durkin, and showing a ceremony in celebration of the 40th anniversary of the department, 1948–53 (M). A panorama taken in 1919 showing the department's administrative personnel. (P).

174.2　　Photographic negatives documenting a miners' strike in Ludlow, CO, in 1916. The original photographic prints are filed among the textual records of the agency. (X).

RG 176

RECORDS OF THE BUREAU OF HUMAN NUTRITION AND HOME ECONOMICS
1904–39　　227 items

176.1　　Photographic negatives relating to food preparation methods and nutrition experiments and investigations, 1904–39 (HE).

RG 178

RECORDS OF THE U.S. MARITIME COMMISSION
1941–44　　150 items

178.1　　Four albums of photographic prints, graphs, charts, and plans illustrating production at the Belair Shipyard, San Francisco, CA, and the Oregon Shipbuilding Corporation, Portland, OR. The albums were presented by the shipbuilders to Adm. Howard L. Vickerey, a member of the commission. 1941–44 (PA).

RG 179

RECORDS OF THE WAR PRODUCTION BOARD
1942–45   1,602 items

179.1   Posters used in various World War II production drives instituted by the board. The majority of the posters encourage increased factory production of steel, guns, ammunition, aircraft, ships, and uniforms through teamwork, safe work habits, and efficiency. 1942–43 (WP).

179.2   Lantern slides used in training agency staff, and employees working in factories engaged in war production, 1942–45 (S) (C). Filmstrips on war production, 1942–45 (FS).

RG 181

RECORDS OF THE
NAVAL DISTRICTS AND SHORE ESTABLISHMENTS
1891–1963   ca. 3,854 items

181.1   Photographic prints of the Washington Navy Yard, the U.S. Navy's NC-4 airplane, the C-2 airship, U.S. Navy ships, and navy personnel in San Diego, CA, 1891–1919 (NC). Photographs taken at the Philadelphia Navy Yard showing the construction and repair of ships; ship identification views; shipyard buildings, shops, and offices; docks and shipways; shipyard equipment and equipment for vessels; support services; and shipyard employees. 1907–26 and 1953–63 (PS) (N). Photographic prints of buildings and employees of the New York Navy Yard and progress views of ships under construction, repair, or alteration, 1897–1955 (NA) (NYS). Photographic prints by Somach Photo Service, New York, of buildings and businesses in the Wallabout and Kent Avenue areas of New York City, 1920–41 (WM) (WA).

181.2   Photographic prints of the U.S.S. *Relief*, 1921 (PSR). Photographic prints of the U.S. Coast Guard vessel *Point Arguello*, n.d. (PSC). Photographs of Lt. Eugene Ely landing an airplane on the armored cruiser U.S.S. *Pennsylvania*. There are also a few photographs showing U.S. Navy gunnery practices. 1911–18 (PSX). Two albums of photographic prints recording the construction of the U.S.S. *North Carolina*. Completion views are also included. 1937–41 (NCB) (NCC).

RG 185

RECORDS OF THE PANAMA CANAL
1880–1979   19,200 items

185.1   Photographs relating to the construction of a canal in Panama by the French firm Compagnie Universelle du Canal Interoceanique, 1881–88 (F).

185.2   Photographs documenting the history of the construction of the Panama Canal. Photographic coverage is varied, but includes pictures of officials, workers, types of equipment, railroads, Panama Canal Company office buildings and workers' housing, and towns and cities. Also included are photographs recording visits to the canal by U.S. Presidents Theodore Roosevelt, William Howard

Taft, Warren G. Harding, and Franklin D. Roosevelt. Other celebrities visiting the canal are also pictured. In addition there are photographs showing the operation of the canal, and ships passing through the canal. 1887–1940 (G). Panoramas showing early construction of the Panama Canal, ca. 1905 (P).

185.3　Photographs collected by the Panama Railroad Company showing French canal construction and views of areas adjacent to the company's rail lines from Aspinwall to Panama City. Also included are portraits of John A. Totten and George Totten, who served respectively as a surgeon and an engineer for the company. 1880–1905 (R).

185.4　Photographs of the Panama Canal Company's ceremonial events. There are also several photographs relating to canal construction. 1937–60 (C).

185.5　Photographs (some in color) of riots and demonstrations in the Canal Zone and the Republic of Panama, 1964–79 (PR).

RG 187

RECORDS OF THE
NATIONAL RESOURCES PLANNING BOARD
ca. 1933–41　　278 items

187.1　Photographic prints collected by the board primarily from federal, state, and municipal government agencies and planning boards. The images relate to water pollution, soil erosion, irrigation, dams, floods, forestry, fishing, mining, transportation, housing, and recreation. 1933–41 (G).

RG 188

RECORDS OF THE
OFFICE OF PRICE ADMINISTRATION
1941–47　　1,896 items

188.1　Photographs from the Visual Services Branch showing exhibits, displays, posters, and other promotional activities of the agency, 1942–46 (G).

188.2　Portraits of administration officials, including Administrator Chester Bowles, 1941–47 (P).

188.3　Filmstrips, production files, scripts, cartoons, graphs, and photographic prints and negatives prepared for educational and promotional programs on rationing and conservation measures and price control, 1942–46 (FS).

188.4　Posters and original watercolors and drawings promoting price control and rationing programs, 1942–46 (PP) (PPA) (PPC).

RG 189

RECORDS OF THE
NATIONAL ACADEMY OF SCIENCES
1936–45   151 items

189.1   Photographs recording the formation, eruption, and growth of the volcano Paricutin in Michoacán, Mexico, 1936–45 (PV).

RG 196

RECORDS OF THE
PUBLIC HOUSING ADMINISTRATION
1895–1905 and 1935–67   9,605 items

196.1   Photographic prints and lantern slides showing low- and middle-income housing in the United States and slums in the United States and Great Britain, 1895–1905 (GS).

196.2   Photographic prints, including some by photographer Peter Sekaer, documenting housing projects built by the Public Works Administration and the United States Housing Authority, 1935–52 (HA).

196.3   Photographic prints of prefabricated housing constructed after World War II for housing projects in the United States and England, and pictures of low-rent housing projects in the United States, 1940–53 (M).

196.4   Photographic prints and site diagrams of housing projects completed under the 1949 Housing Act, 1949–54 (HS) (H). Binders of photographic prints representing low-rent public housing designed by architects for projects built under the 1949 Housing Act, 1951–58 (HSA).

196.5   Site diagrams and photographic prints of low-rent housing projects constructed in 30 states and Puerto Rico under the auspices of the Public Housing Administration, 1958–67 (LR) (LRH).

RG 207

GENERAL RECORDS OF THE DEPARTMENT OF
HOUSING AND URBAN DEVELOPMENT
1951–80   48,006 items

207.1   Photographs taken or collected by the Urban Renewal Administration showing areas scheduled for redevelopment, 1951–67 (UR).

207.2   Photographs relating to the construction of low-rent housing for American Indians in Arizona, Montana, New Mexico, and South Dakota, 1962–68 (I). Photographs of low-rent housing in the United States, 1963–69 (G). Photographic prints and drawings of low-income and urban housing developments in nine states; also included are photographs of the "Habitat 67" exhibit at Expo '67, Montreal, Canada. 1967–69 (LIH).

207.3   Photographs submitted by manufacturers and construction companies showing building techniques and housing production activities at prototype

196-M-2-1. *Units leaving Point Pleasant, W.Va. for Morganfield, Ky - Camp Breckenridge.* April 1944. Federal Public Housing Authority. (RG 196, Records of the Public Housing Administration)

220-TMI-41-2812-5. *Three Mile Island Alert. Anti-nuke rally - Harrisburg, PA.* April 9, 1979. EG&G. (RG 220, Records of Temporary Committees, Commissions, and Boards)

208-UNC-458. *Soviet Foreign Commissar V. M. Molotov addresses plenary session concerning Russia's views on admitting Argentina and Poland to the conference.* United Nations Conference on International Organization. San Francisco, CA. April 30, 1945. Cropped view. (RG 208, Records of the Office of War Information)

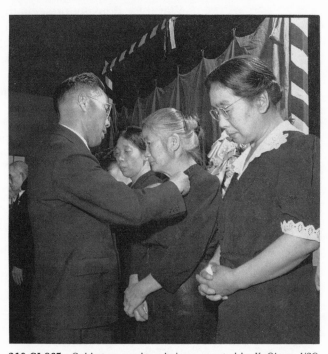

210-GI-865. *Gold stars are here being presented by K. Okura, USO representative, to mothers whose sons were killed in action.* Granada Relocation Center, CO. April 21, 1945. Hikaru Iwasaki. (RG 210, Records of the War Relocation Authority)

sites, 1969–73 (HSP). Color slides of prototype housing developments, 1970–73 (PHS).

207.4   Color slides and a few photographic prints showing plans, charts, graphs, and informational materials relating to Operation Breakthrough, a program to improve housing production processes. Included are pictures of housing designs, site plans, site models, and housing under construction. There are also photographs relating to tests conducted by the National Bureau of Standards. 1970–73 (A) (B) (D) (C).

207.5   Photographs (many in color) of projects submitted to the Department of Housing and Urban Development (HUD) for the biennial design competitions, Urban Environmental Design. Among the projects shown are housing for the elderly, inner-city redevelopment plans, commercial and retail projects, parks and recreation centers, and historic preservation plans. 1968–80 (UED). A poster announcing the HUD Urban Environmental Design competition, 1979 (P).

RG 208

RECORDS OF THE OFFICE OF WAR INFORMATION
ca. 1600–1951   ca. 206,100 items

208.1   The Office of War Information (OWI) master negative file covering all phases of U.S. wartime activity, domestic and foreign, civilian and military, and political and diplomatic, 1939–45 (N). Photographs relating to the war effort in the United States. Included are photographs of OWI staff, offices, and exhibits. 1941–46 (CO) (COKO) (DEM) (NA) (NE) (S) (SE).

208.2   Photographic prints relating to the military operations of U.S. forces during World War II and to the war effort in the United States. Among the subjects pictured are Allied and Axis political and military leaders, prisoners of war, refugees and displaced persons, U.S. military action in the European and Pacific theaters, industrial production, war bond drives, the destruction caused by the war, the liberation of areas by the Allies, concentration camps, the atomic bomb blasts over Japan, surrender ceremonies, and victory celebrations at the end of the war. Ca. 1930–45 (MO) (AA) (AAN) (MNC) (SAI) (AMC) (PA).

208.3   "Yanks in the E.T.O.": photographic prints showing U.S. Army operations in the European theater apparently assembled for an exhibit. "Lest We— Or They—Forget": photographic prints used in exhibits on Nazi concentration camps and victims. "U.S. Navy Wins Supply Battle of the Pacific": photographic prints showing the work done behind the lines to keep the forces supplied. "Rebirth of a French Town": photographic prints showing refugees returning to the town of Laval. Ca. 1941–45 (YE).

208.4   Photographic prints of U.S. and foreign wartime celebrities, including politicians, royalty, scientists, entertainers, media and sports celebrities, and military figures. Some retrospective materials are included. 1935–49 (PU) (WP) (AFP) (AP) (MCP) (PNC) (OP) (POP).

208.5   Portraits of prominent military and political figures taken by Yousuf Karsh, ca. 1943–45 (KAR).

208.6   "Life in the United States," a series of photographic prints portraying life in the United States during World War II. Shown are events, places, activities, and people considered important or newsworthy during the war. Arranged alphabetically by over 300 subjects, the pictures were accumulated by the OWI News and Features Bureau, Pictures Division. The majority of the photographs date from 1942 to 1946, but there is some retrospective coverage of colonial America and the Revolutionary War (LU) (LO). Photographs entitled "Portrait of America," 1943–45 (POA). Photographs of U.S. universities, n.d. (AU). Photographs of the funeral ceremony for President Franklin D. Roosevelt, 1945 (FDR).

208.7   Photographs used as illustrations for feature stories issued by the OWI News and Features Bureau, Pictures Division. The photographs depict American life and institutions on the homefront and show U.S. military action. 1942–46 (FS).

208.8   Photographs taken by OWI photographer Risdon Tillery, ca. 1944 (T). Photographs taken in France and Italy by OWI photographers, 1943–44 (MFI). Photographic prints of OWI outposts, 1942–45 (O). Transmitted images and photographs collected for transmission to OWI overseas outposts, 1941–45 (PCT) (WSO) (RTA).

208.9   Original watercolors, woodcuts, silk-screen graphics, and photographs made or acquired by the News and Features Bureau for use in exhibits on various aspects of U.S. life, 1942–46 (EX). Photographic prints showing U.S. architecture used in exhibits in Sweden, 1942–44 (AEX). Photographs collected for use in Stockholm, Sweden, 1941–45 (SP). Photographs used in an exhibit in Johannesburg, South Africa, n.d. (J). Photographic prints of U.S. troops assembled for an exhibit on the U.S. war effort, 1942–46 (TM).

208.10   Photographs used in OWI publications, including *USA* and *Photo Review*, 1943–46 (PP) (PR) (PRA) (PRV) (USA). Issues of *Victory* magazine and photographs used to illustrate the magazine, 1942–45 (VM).

208.11   Photographic prints from the OWI's Negro Press Section showing African Americans involved in shipbuilding and other war industries, as employees of government agencies, and as members of the Armed Forces in the United States and overseas. Also included are photographs relating to activities in connection with bond drives, and numerous images of noted African Americans. 1941–45 (NP).

208.12   Original drawings and mock-ups for cartoons promoting the war effort; and original sketches drawn by artist Charles Alston to highlight famous African Americans. Ca. 1942–45 (COM). Photographs of a variety of wartime subjects, including cartoons and scenes from Walt Disney movies, 1940–45 (D) (C) (K).

208.13   Photographs of occupational therapy programs for World War II veterans, 1943–45 (OT).

208.14   Posters, photographic prints of posters, and original art used to promote the war effort, 1941–44 (PMP) (PM) (PMO) (B).

208.15   "The Retailer Fights Inflation," a filmstrip produced by the Office of Price Administration, ca. 1942 (FSS).

208.16   Photographs and some transmitted images documenting meetings and ceremonies at the United Nations Conference on International Organization held in San Francisco, CA, 1945 (UNC) (CIO) (DIO) (DSC). Photographs taken during the Inter-American Conference on the Problems of War and Peace, Mexico City, Mexico, 1945 (MC).

208.17   Photographs documenting the visits to the United States of Presidents Romulo Gallegos of Venezuela in 1948, Vincent Auriol of France in 1951, and Miguel Aleman of Mexico in 1947, (FV). Photographs recording a visit by the royal family of Iraq to the United States, 1945 (IR).

RG 210

RECORDS OF THE WAR RELOCATION AUTHORITY
1942–46   ca. 15,200 items

210.1   Photographs taken by Dorothea Lange, Hikaru Iwasaki, Clem Albers, Tom Parker, and Charles E. Mace to document the actions of the War Relocation Authority (WRA) and the U.S. Army in the evacuation, relocation, and confinement of Japanese Americans. Included are views of Japanese Americans preparing for evacuation; the transportation of evacuees to assembly centers and relocation centers; housing at the centers; vocational, educational, and recreational facilities at relocation centers; WRA staff; and the return of evacuees to their former homes. 1942–45 (G).

210.2   Photographs showing Japanese Americans at the following relocation centers: Colorado River, AZ; Gila River, AZ; Granada, CO; Heart Mountain, WY; Tule Lake, CA; Minidoka, ID; Manzanar, CA; Topaz, UT; and Rohwer, AR. 1942–46 (CA) (CB) (CC) (CG) (CH) (CL) (CMA) (CMB) (CR) (CT).

210.3   Photographs taken by Branko Kaufmann, Gretchen Van Tassel, and Hikaru Iwasaki showing living and working conditions at the Fort Ontario Emergency Refugee Shelter for European refugees in Oswego, NY, 1944–45 (CFK) (CFZ).

210.4   "The Wrong Ancestors," a filmstrip about the World War II relocation of Japanese Americans, ca. 1943 (FS).

RG 215

RECORDS OF THE OFFICE OF COMMUNITY WAR SERVICES
1943   1 item

215.1   A filmstrip entitled "Prostitution and the War," 1943 (FS).

RG 216

RECORDS OF THE OFFICE OF CENSORSHIP
1945   4 items

216.1   Filmstrips relating to World War II telephone, postal, international telecommunication, radio, and press censorship operations, 1945 (FS).

RECORDS OF TEMPORARY COMMITTEES, COMMISSIONS, AND BOARDS

1925–26 and 1949–81   29,800 items

220.1   Photographic prints showing U.S. members of the World War Foreign Debt Commission and recording the ceremonial signings of agreements between the United States and representatives of foreign governments for the funding of debts. Most of the prints are autographed. Pictured in the photographs are Herbert C. Hoover, Andrew W. Mellon, Frank B. Kellogg, and Reed Smoot. 1925–26 (FDC).

220.2   Albums containing photographic prints showing the interior and exterior of the White House before and during renovation. The photographs were taken for the Commission on Renovation of the Executive Mansion. 1949–52 (REB) (REP).

220.3   Photographs from the President's Commission on Campus Unrest relating to its investigations of disturbances at institutions of higher learning. Shown are commission members and public hearings. Also included are photographs recording the demonstrations at Kent State University, OH, and Jackson State College, MS. 1970 (PCCU).

220.4   Photographs of the members of the National Commission on Fire Prevention and Control and commission hearings, 1971–73 (NFC).

220.5   Photographic prints of the members of the White House Conference Advisory Committee on Library and Information Services, 1979 (C). A poster announcing the conference, 1979 (CP).

220.6   Photographs (some in color) of hearings held by the President's Commission on Coal. The commission, chaired by John D. Rockefeller IV, held hearings in Denver, CO; Washington, PA; Pikesville, KY; and Washington, DC. Also included are pictures of commission members visiting mines in Wyoming and Pennsylvania. 1978–79 (CH). Photographs taken for the President's Commission on Coal to show mining communities, miners, occupational safety conditions and health facilities, and other aspects relating to life in mining communities. Many of the photographs were taken by photographers Jack Corn and Theodore Wathen. Photographer Russell Lee served as an adviser. 1979 (LC) (CS).

220.7   Color slides used in a slide presentation created by the National Commission on the Observance of International Women's Year. The slides show women's rights, roles, and opportunities for women around the world. 1975 (IWS). Posters relating to International Women's Year, 1975 (IWY). A panorama showing participants in an International Women's Year conference in Mexico City, Mexico, 1975 (IWX).

220.8   Photographic prints documenting the activities of the National Women's Conference held in Houston, TX. Pictured are delegates, conferences and meetings, and a 2,600-mile lighted torch relay. Among the women shown are such well-known individuals as Bella Abzug, Patsy Mink, Jill Ruckelshaus, Margaret Heckler, Margaret Mead, Gloria Steinem, and Coretta Scott King. 1977–78 (WC).

220.9   Photographs documenting the public meetings and hearings of the Select Committee on Immigration and Refugee Policy. Senator Edward Kennedy,

Secretary of Health and Human Services Patricia R. Harris, and other political figures are featured. 1979–81 (IMP).

220.10 Color photographic prints produced under contract for the Department of Energy and used by the President's Commission on the Accident at Three Mile Island as part of its investigation of the nuclear power plant accident. Included are aerials of the Three Mile Island plant, and pictures of the facilities and equipment inside the plant, federal agency personnel performing their duties, antinuclear rallies, the media, and press briefings. Also shown is President Jimmy Carter visiting Three Mile Island after the accident. 1979 (TMI).

220.11 Photographs of participants in the White House Conference on Small Business and Conference activities; included are pictures of Jimmy Carter, Senator Gaylord Nelson, and Small Business Administrator Vernon Weaver. Also pictured are military activities at Fort Bragg, NC, and on board two U.S. Navy vessels. 1980 (SB).

220.12 Photographs of the members of the Commission on Wartime Relocation and Internment of Civilians, as well as commission hearings in Seattle, WA, Chicago, IL, San Francisco, CA, and Washington, DC, 1981 (WR).

RG 221

RECORDS OF THE
RURAL ELECTRIFICATION ADMINISTRATION
1936–64   ca. 13,700 items

221.1 Photographs relating to rural electrification programs sponsored by the Rural Electrification Administration (REA). Pictured are REA-financed cooperatives; the construction of transmission lines; the wiring of rural homes and farm buildings; the installation of electrical appliances and equipment; installation of telephone lines in rural areas; a few pictures of REA personnel; and a few of Presidents Franklin D. Roosevelt and Harry S. Truman at REA ceremonies. 1936–64 (P) (G) (GUSF) (GA) (GS) (GIFS) (GH).

RG 226

RECORDS OF THE
OFFICE OF STRATEGIC SERVICES
ca. 1919–45   2,989 items

226.1 Photographs taken by the staff of the Field Photographic Branch of the Office of Strategic Services (OSS) Field Station in London, England, showing OSS operations, activities, and personnel. Included are photographs of the aftermath of the Allied victory in Algeria and Tunisia in 1943; photographs of preparations for the Normandy invasion; OSS facilities in England and Scotland; U.S. Navy bases in Wales and Northern Ireland; and bomb damage to London and Cherbourg, France. Ca. 1943–44 (FPL). Records of the OSS Field Station in Kunming, China, consisting of photographs of U.S. and Chinese officers and of U.S. personnel training Chinese troops, ca. 1945 (FPKU). OSS photographs from the Kandy, Ceylon (Sri Lanka), station recording training and other activities at the four OSS bases in Ceylon; military operations in Burma and the Ramree Island invasion; OSS assistance in the British push to Rangoon; and Operation Diagram—

a supply and rescue mission to east central Thailand. Also included are scenes of Rangoon after its liberation, and pictures of Bangkok, Thailand. Ca. 1945 (FPK).

226.2   Original artwork, printed materials, and photographs on display panels illustrating the activities of the Morale Operations Branch in the creation and distribution of propaganda, ca. 1943–45 (MO).

226.3   Photographs showing municipal buildings, industrial facilities, and urban centers in China, Japan, and the Philippine Islands; and topographical features of those countries, ca. 1919–43 (G).

226.4   Photographic prints of personages referred to in OSS reports, 1941–45 (P).

RG 227

RECORDS OF THE OFFICE OF SCIENTIFIC RESEARCH AND DEVELOPMENT
1942   ca. 1,000 items

227.1   Photographic negatives from Technical Division 12 of the National Defense Research Committee documenting experiments with the amphibious vehicle DUKW, 1942 (D).

RG 229

RECORDS OF THE OFFICE OF INTER-AMERICAN AFFAIRS
ca. 1800s and 1939–46   3,365 items

229.1   Color and black-and-white photographs taken or acquired by the Office of Inter-American Affairs (OIAA) and its predecessor, the Office of the Coordinator of Inter-American Affairs. Known as the Rockefeller Collection (after Coordinator Nelson A. Rockefeller), the photographs cover a wide variety of subjects relating to Latin America. Some of the subjects pictured relate to health and sanitation, the development of natural resources, industrial and commercial development, transportation and communication, tourism, and education. 1941–46 (R).

229.2   Photographs taken by OIAA photographer Alan Fisher to document Nelson Rockefeller's 1942 trip to Brazil, Secretary of the Navy Frank Knox's trip to Brazil in 1943 to inspect U.S. Navy forces, and U.S. Ambassador Adolf Berle's arrival in Brazil in 1945 (AVB). Photographic prints recording a visit to the United States by Peruvian President Manuel Prado, 1942 (PV). Photographs documenting a 1943 visit to the United States by Brazil's General Eurico Gaspar Dutra (DV). Photographs taken during a visit to the United States in 1944 by President Higinio Morinigo of Paraguay (MV).

229.3   Posters and drawings illustrating the common heritage of the countries of North, Central, and South America, the common danger each country faced from Nazi Germany, and the need for inter-American cooperation. Included are images relating to the Nazi subjugation of Poland; the Nazi obliteration of Lidice, Czechoslovakia; and 19th century Latin American leaders. Ca. 1800s and 1939–45 (PG).

233-TRP-31. *View on C Street. Round Pond.* Oklahoma. Ca. 1894.
Kennett Photo. (RG 233, Records of the U.S. House of Representatives)

221-G-5257. REA Co-op. Rush County. Indiana or Kansas. Ca. 1940.
(RG 221, Records of the Rural Electrification Administration)

RG 233

RECORDS OF THE
U.S. HOUSE OF REPRESENTATIVES
1880–96   ca. 300 items

233.1   Albumen photographic prints showing soil erosion and wharf damage to the east bank of the Mississippi River at New Orleans, LA, 1881 (NO).

233.2   Photographic prints of the wharves and harbor of Bridgeport, CT; the demolition of Flood Rock in Hell Gate channel, New York City, NY; the sinking of the vessel *Susan E. Peck* in St. Marys River, MI; and a lithograph of John E. Russell, a member of the U.S. House of Representatives from Massachusetts. 1880–1893 (M).

233.3   Card photographs taken in conjunction with the "Oklahoma Railroad Bill" (H.R. 3606, 53d Congress) showing Round Pound, Wharton, and Enid, OK; included are general views of the towns, businesses, railroad yards, and townspeople. 1893–94 (TE) (TRP) (TW).

233.4   Card photographs of the women on the Board of Lady Managers, who supervised all aspects of the 1893 World's Columbian Exposition concerning women; pictures of some of the fine arts exhibits are also included. 1896 (WE).

RG 234

RECORDS OF THE
RECONSTRUCTION FINANCE CORPORATION
1932–44   917 items

234.1   Photographs of the Board of Directors of the Reconstruction Finance Corporation, 1932 and 1938 (B).

234.2   Photographs showing the activities of the Rubber Development Corporation; rubber production in Brazil, Bolivia, Colombia, Haiti, and Peru; scenic views; corporation equipment and facilities; and agency personnel. 1943–44 (G) (M).

RG 237

RECORDS OF THE
FEDERAL AVIATION ADMINISTRATION
1860–1952   ca. 5,790 items

237.1   Photographs made or collected by the Photography Branch of the Civil Aeronautics Administration (CAA) from 1943 through 1952 to show the activities of the agency and to document a general history of aviation. Included are pictures of high-ranking CAA officials and Presidents Woodrow Wilson, Franklin D. Roosevelt, Calvin Coolidge, and Harry Truman; aviators Amelia Earhart and Charles Lindbergh; Will Rogers; historic aircraft; Washington National Airport and other airports; navigational equipment; and aerial views of U.S. cities. Among the important events pictured are the Wright brothers' flight at Kitty Hawk, NC; the flight of the *Yankee Clipper*, the crash of the *Hindenberg*, and the first airmail flight. A copy of the first aerial photograph taken in 1860 is also included. 1860–1952 (P).

NATIONAL ARCHIVES COLLECTION OF WORLD WAR II WAR CRIMES RECORDS

1940–48   5,355 items

238.1   Photographic negatives and proof sheets made from an original 8mm German motion picture film. The film seized by the U.S. Army shows Nazi mistreatment of men and women. Ca. 1940 (AF).

238.2   An album of photographic prints prepared by news photographer Otto Roesner and dedicated to Dr. Hans Frank, the German governor general of occupied Poland. The images show civil and military buildings, rallies and parades, and social and official Nazi ceremonies in Poland. 1940–41 (ORA).

238.3   Photographs relating to the International Military Tribunal for the Far East (IMTFE) trials. Shown are IMTFE staff, defendants, judges, witnesses, counsels, and general views of the courtrooms. 1946–48 (FE).

238.4   Photographs and lantern slides taken for the International Military Tribunal and the U.S. military tribunals at Nürnberg, Germany. Among the subjects shown are the courtrooms, defendants, counsels, judges, witnesses, exhibits and evidence, the press, visitors, and prisons. 1945–47 (NT) (NTA) (OMT) (LS).

RECORDS OF THE AMERICAN COMMISSION FOR THE PROTECTION AND SALVAGE OF ARTISTIC AND HISTORIC MONUMENTS IN WAR AREAS

1943–46   ca. 19,950 items

239.1   Photographs primarily documenting World War II combat damage to areas in Europe, North Africa, Palestine, the Philippine Islands, Burma, China, and the Netherlands East Indies. Included are pictures of cities and monuments showing bomb damage and the effects of vandalism, and pictures of the Allies liberating various places. Also included are pictures of looted artwork and commission employees. The photographs were collected by the commission, also known as the Roberts Commission after its chairman, Owen J. Roberts. 1943–46 (PA) (RC).

239.2   Prints used in a photographic survey of cultural institutions and monuments in Frankfurt, West Germany, damaged during World War II, 1946 (SFM).

NATIONAL ARCHIVES COLLECTION OF FOREIGN RECORDS SEIZED

ca. 1913–45   350,000 items

242.1   Photographs made by Heinrich Hoffmann, official photographer of the National Socialist Party, as documentation of Nazi activities. Included are photographs showing Adolf Hitler and associates engaged in party business and

238-OMT-II-T-13. *OMGUS Military Tribunal - Case Two. The Palace of Justice guard inspects the pass of Judge Robert M. Toms, Presiding Judge of Tribunal II, just like that of any other member of the American staff, before permitting entrance or exit to the courthouse area. Judge Toms lives in Detroit, Michigan.* Ca. 1947. (RG 238, National Archives Collection of World War II War Crimes Records)

242-JRB-3-2. *Arrival of* [Hungarian Viceroy, Admiral] *Horthy at the railroad station in Kiel.* Germany. Hitler and others. August 22, 1938. Joachim von Ribbentrop Collection. (RG 242, National Archives Collection of Foreign Records Seized)

functions; Axis leaders; Nazi officials; the construction of the Fuhrerhaus; ceremonies, rallies, and meetings; the Hitler Youth; and the cultural, social, and economic life of Germany. Also included are pictures taken in Munich during the political upheavals of 1919; at the International Water Technique Exposition in 1939; during the Spanish Civil War; and of events at the 1936 Olympic Games in Berlin and Garmisch-Partenkirchen. Ca. 1918–44 (HLB) (HLM) (HLT) (HD) (HK) (HB) (HWO) (HKL) (HMR) (HF) (HPKTC) (HPKTA) (HMC) (HFH) (HBA) (HMA).

242.2   Photographs collected by or for Foreign Minister Joachim von Ribbentrop concerning his family, social life, and career. Included are photographs of meetings, conferences, and other diplomatic functions. 1934–42 (JRA) (JRB) (JRM) (JRFA) (JRPE).

242.3   Color slides of German troops and equipment in North Africa, ca. 1941 (EAPA). Photographs of Gen. Erwin Rommel and his family; German military operations in North Africa and France; Hitler and several generals; and terrain views of North Africa. Ca. 1940–41 (EAPB) (EAPC).

242.4   Albums of photographic prints taken or collected by Eva Braun documenting her early life, her family, and her friends, as well as her life with Adolf Hitler, ca. 1913–44 (EB).

242.5   Photographs taken for propaganda purposes by photographers in the Wehrmacht and in the Waffen-SS relating to the German invasions of the Soviet Union (U.S.S.R.) and other countries. Included are pictures showing frontline action, German political leaders, military officials and troops, equipment, prisoners of war, and occupational forces. Some of the photographs relate to civilian life under German rule. 1939–45 (GAV) (GAP) (SS) (JRP).

242.6   Photographic negatives of German servicemen and other subjects, 1942 and 1944 (M).

242.7   Photographic prints taken during the trial of those accused of attempting to assassinate Adolf Hitler, 1944 (PA). Photographic prints of Luftwaffe pilots, ca. 1940–43 (GLP).

242.8   Offset reproductions of photographs used in the Spanish-language magazine *Revista Alemana* illustrating a variety of cultural, diplomatic, military, and technological subjects. Pictures of Hitler, Benito Mussolini, and Francisco Franco are included. Ca. 1938 (RA). Albums published by the Reich Ministry for Public Enlightenment and Propaganda containing photographic prints showing German life on the home and fighting fronts. The translated title of the albums is *Greater Germany in World Events—Daily Picture Reports*. 1940 and 1942 (PKA). An album of snapshots presented to Major General Erhard by Captain Rabe, 1941 (CR). Published illustrations depicting episodes in the early history of Russia (U.S.S.R.), taken by German forces from a library in the Ukraine (NP).

242.9   Sets of mounted and unmounted slides, apparently used in lectures, showing military equipment and views of German cities and rural areas, 1941–44 (LBR) (RPLA) (RPLB). Filmstrips highlighting the newsworthy events of the week, 1938–41 (BB). Filmstrips produced for the indoctrination of members of the Hitler Youth, n.d. (HJ). Filmstrips on a variety of other subjects, primarily relating to German history, n.d. (MNF).

242.10 An album prepared by the Artillery Survey Section 25 of the Bavarian Foot Artillery showing military action north of Verdun, France, ca. 1916 (KNV). Photographic prints and collotypes confiscated from the Rehse Archiv in Munich by the Allies after World War II. The majority of the images pertain to German military operations during World War I. Included are pictures of troops from Bavaria, the King and Queen of Bavaria, and Kaiser Wilhelm II. 1914–18 and 1923–36 (RH).

RG 243

RECORDS OF THE
U.S. STRATEGIC BOMBING SURVEY
1944–47   15,949 items

243.1 Photographs used in reports on the effects of Operation Strangle, a U.S. bombing operation, and on a survey of a Noball installation, a German rocket-launching site in France, 1944 (F).

243.2 Photographs taken during a survey of the effects of bombing attacks on industries, utilities, transportation, and social services in Germany, France, and Belgium, 1944–45 (E).

243.3 Photographs of United States Strategic Bombing Survey (USSBS) civilian directors, staff members, military officials in Japan and England, and USSBS installations in England, Germany, and Japan, 1945–46 (A).

243.4 Photographs used in the report, "Effects of Incendiary Bomb Attacks in Japan," 1945–47 (R).

243.5 Photographs recording atomic bomb damage to property in Hiroshima and Nagasaki, Japan. Also photographs of injured Japanese civilians. 1944–47 (H) (G) (NP) (HP).

RG 245

RECORDS OF THE
SOLID FUELS ADMINISTRATION FOR WAR
1946–47   4,100 items

245.1 Photographs taken by noted photographer Russell W. Lee and others for a Department of the Interior/United Mine Workers survey of health and housing conditions in bituminous coal-mining communities in the United States. Recorded are mine operations, mining equipment, towns, homes, medical facilities, miners, women, children, mine operators, union officials, and the medical survey members. 1946–47 (MS) (MSA).

245-MS-1463-L. *Miner. Gilliam Coal and Coke Co. Gilliam, McDowell Co., W. Va.* August 13, 1946. Russell Lee. (RG 245, Records of the Solid Fuels Administration for War)

243-NP-I-18A&B. *Before and after 7 and 12 August 1945. Nagasaki, Japan.* 1945. (RG 243, Records of the U.S. Strategic Bombing Survey)

RECORDS OF THE NATIONAL AERONAUTICS AND SPACE ADMINISTRATION

1903–69   24,692

255.1   Photographic prints, negatives, and lantern slides made or collected by the National Aeronautics and Space Administration (NASA) and its predecessor, the National Advisory Committee for Aeronautics (NACA), on the following subjects relating to aeronautics and aviation: U.S. and European aircraft; experimental craft; rockets; agency laboratories and research facilities; tests and experiments; aircraft components and construction; airports and airfields; and agency employees, aviators, and persons important in aviation history. 1903–60 (P) (RF) (PA) (RA) (LSP) (LS) (LSC) (MA) (GP).

255.2   Photographic prints relating to NACA administrative activities, including pictures of ceremonies, conferences, meetings, and Committee members and other employees, ca. 1920–58 (GF).

255.3   Photographs (some in color) of the testing, launching, and tracking of the satellites and rockets used in Project Vanguard. Also included are photographs of NASA personnel and facilities at Cape Canaveral, FL. 1956–59 (PV) (PV-CC) (PV-CCC) (PVT).

255.4   Photographic prints documenting Mercury, Gemini, and Apollo space program activities, and personnel, equipment, and facilities at the Kennedy Space Center, Cape Canaveral, FL. Included are pictures of spacecraft under construction, launch apparatus, and astronaut training programs. Several astronauts are also pictured. 1959–65 (KP).

255.5   Photographic prints of the lunar surface transmitted by television cameras on board Rangers VII, VIII, and IX, 1964–65 (RMP).

255.6   Photographs in black-and-white and color used to illustrate the final report of the Apollo 204 Review Board. The board investigated the January 27, 1967, fire that erupted inside an Apollo spacecraft during ground testing, killing astronauts Virgil Grissom, Edward H. White, and Roger B. Chaffee. Included are pictures of the accident area, a mock-up module, parts of the spacecraft, and the activities of the board. There are no photographs of the three astronauts. 1967 (AP).

255.7   Albums of photographic prints presented by the government of West Germany to commemorate visits to that country and West Berlin by astronauts Neil A. Armstrong, Michael Collins, Edwin E. Aldrin, and Frank Borman. President Richard M. Nixon and Chancellor Kurt Georg Kiesinger are also pictured. 1969 (BV) (ACAV).

RECORDS OF THE FEDERAL CROP INSURANCE CORPORATION

1936–39   648 items

258.1   Photographic negatives showing farmers working in wheat fields, harvesting, threshing, and storing wheat; and damage to wheat fields caused by

255-RA-A7-4b(3)-E2889. *Flying regularly in the transonic and supersonic speed ranges, the research airplanes are scientifically exploring new fields of flight in search for data needed to design the military and civil airplanes of the future. In the center is the Douglas X-3; at the lower left is the Bell X-1A; continuing clockwise are the Douglas D-558-I "Skystreak"; the Consolidated Vultee XF-92A; the Bell X-5 variable sweepback airplane; the Douglas D-558-II "Skyrocket"; and the Northrop X-4.* Edwards Air Force Base, CA. Ca. 1955. (RG 255, Records of the National Aeronautics and Space Administration)

270-WA-6-702. *A giant Conestoga, minus engines and instruments, became a filling station when its Fort Worth, Texas, owners couldn't find building materials.* October 1946. (RG 270, Records of the War Assets Administration)

260-CR-215-79B. *U.S. High Commissioner, Lieut. General Paul W. Caraway, received a warm welcome from Mrs. Tsuru Adaniya, 85, during a tour of Sashiki-Son. Mrs. Adaniya, who has two sons living in Hawaii, waited from early morning to meet the General. General Caraway inspected various development projects and conferred with town and village officials and the people.* Ryukyu Islands. April 3, 1961. (RG 260, Records of the United States Occupation Headquarters, World War II)

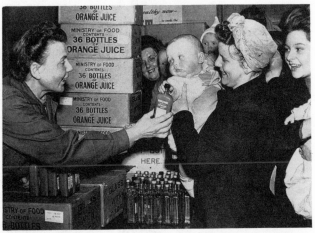

286-MP-UK-306. *An American orange concentrate distributed by the British Ministry of Food was a feature of Marshall Plan Aid to Britain. The orange juice was distributed to children as part of a child welfare scheme.* Ca. 1950. (RG 286, Records of the Agency for International Development)

drought and pests. There are a few photographs relating to cotton and other crops. Also included are pictures of farmers applying for and receiving crop insurance. 1936–39 (FCI).

RECORDS OF THE
U.S. OCCUPATION HEADQUARTERS, WORLD WAR II

Middle Ages–1972   ca. 55,000 items

260.1   Photographs taken or acquired by the Public Relations Office, Information Services Division, Office of Military Government for Germany, U.S. (OMGUS). Shown are OMGUS military and civilian personnel, U.S. government officials, military families, OMGUS headquarters, housing and recreational facilities for OMGUS personnel, and U.S. military awards ceremonies. Also included are photographs of Allied military personnel, military governors, various conferences, U.S. restitution activities, German ruins, refugees and displaced persons, CARE and other relief programs, and military operations during the Berlin airlift. 1943–49 (OMG) (MGG).

260.2   Photographs taken by the United States Civil Administration of the Ryukyu Islands showing administration officials, programs, and activities. The photographs also document the political, social, economic, commercial, and cultural life of the Japanese archipelago. Pictured also are U.S. and Japanese officials, and representatives of private organizations, businesses, and trade associations. 1949–72 (CR).

260.3   An album containing photographic prints showing Italian Benedictine abbey Monte Cassino before and after its destruction by Allied World War II bombing. Also pictured are postwar plans for the restoration of the monastery. Ca. 1939–49 (MC). Photographic prints documenting war damage to German monuments and buildings, 1946–47 (DM). Photographs of archives, libraries, and castles in 10 German cities, 1946–47 (ACL). Photographic prints used as illustrations in an OMGUS report on war damage to historical and cultural structures in Germany, 1947 (DS).

260.4   The Linz Collection—photographic negatives taken by the Dresden Art Gallery presumably as a record of art plundered by the Axis, 1940–45 (L). Photographs showing the postwar art collection, storage, and restitution activities of the Munich Central Collecting Point, 1945–47 (MP). Halftone prints of famous Germans and photographic negatives of Hermann Göring's art collection gathered by the Munich Central Collecting Point, ca. 1945 (MCCP). Photographs from the Wiesbaden Central Collecting Point showing looted art and documenting U.S. activities at Wiesbaden in the storage and restitution of art. Also shown are various exhibits of recovered art. 1945–50 (WA) (WB) (WC) (WLA) (WLB) (WLC). Halftone prints and photographic prints from the Marburg Central Collecting Point. Pictured are works of art such as paintings, sculpture, ceramics, jewelry, metal works, and religious art. Much of the art handled by the collecting points dated from the Middle Ages or earlier. 1945–47 (M).

260.5   The Einsatzstab Reichsleiter Rosenberg (ERR) Collection of photographic negatives taken by the Nazis to document art plundered from France by ERR teams from 1940 to 1943. Also included are photographic prints made from the negatives in 1945 by the United States for the Chief Counsel for Prosecution of Axis Criminality (ERR). Photographs of Polish art and Russian icons, n.d. (PC)

(RT). Photographic negatives of an exhibit held at the Jeu de Paume museum, Paris, France, in 1943 (JP). Albums containing photographic prints documenting the work of the OMGUS Offenbach Archival Depot and showing art looted from synagogues. Also an album relating to the activities of the ERR. 1946 (PHOAD).

260.6   A 1937 publication of Adolf Hitler's family lineage that includes photographs (NSD). Photographs and postcards relating to the Platterhof at Obersalzberg, ca. 1923–40 (NS) (NSA). A book relating to Ordensburg in Sonthofen, n.d. (NSC). Commemorative albums relating to the life of Ulrich Graf, ca. 1923–37 (NSE) (NSF). An album of photographic prints dedicated to Prof. Seifert, 1942 (NSB).

260.7   Halftone prints of art sent to the National Gallery of Art, Washington, DC, for safekeeping, 1945 (GU).

RG 268

RECORDS OF THE
PHILIPPINE WAR DAMAGE COMMISSION
1945–50   1,100 items

268.1   Photographic prints showing damaged buildings in the Philippine Islands and the rehabilitation of the buildings, 1945–50 (A). Photographic negatives recording the damage to and reconstruction of various Philippine government buildings and documenting rebuilding projects in 33 of the 50 wartime provinces, 1946–50 (B) (P).

268.2   Photographic prints compiled by Commissioner John A. O'Donnell to show commission office areas and housing quarters, agency personnel, and claims processing activities. Shown in a few of the photographs are commission members, Chairman Frank A. Waring, Commissioner Francisco Delgado, Philippine President Manuel Roxas and Vice President Elpidio Quirino, and U.S. Ambassador Emmet O'Neal. 1948–49 (C).

RG 270

RECORDS OF THE WAR ASSETS ADMINISTRATION
1946–49   2,800 items

270.1   Photographs of the real property or real estate assets of the administration, 1946–48 (RP).

270.2   Photographs documenting the disposal of surplus goods by the administration and the conversion of assets to peacetime use, 1946–49 (WA).

RG 277

RECORDS OF THE
NATIONAL PRODUCTION AUTHORITY
1952   1 item

277.1   A filmstrip entitled "An Introduction to the Controlled Materials Plan," which illustrates seven regulations for controlling materials necessary for defense production, 1952 (FS).

RG 280

RECORDS OF THE
FEDERAL MEDIATION AND CONCILIATION SERVICE
1959   69 items

280.1   Color slides showing the mediation work of the service, 1959 (A).

RG 286

RECORDS OF THE
AGENCY FOR INTERNATIONAL DEVELOPMENT
1948–67   ca. 31,000 items

286.1   Photographs taken by the Agency for International Development and its predecessors to document economic recovery programs in Europe under the Marshall Plan. Included are pictures of agricultural, land reclamation, educational, medical, technical, industrial, and military assistance programs. Among the countries represented are Austria, Germany, The Netherlands, Portugal, Sweden, and Turkey. 1948–67 (MP).

RG 287

RECORDS OF
PUBLICATIONS OF THE U.S. GOVERNMENT
1871–1970   ca. 9,500 items

287.1   Posters, charts, graphs, and other materials published to advertise and promote federal agency programs and policies. Some of the agencies represented are the Bureau of Biological Survey, the Bureau of Aeronautics, the National Recovery Administration, the War Manpower Commission, the Forest Service, and the Federal Home Loan Bank Board. Ca. 1900–70. Also included is an album of photographic prints taken from 1871 to 1872 by Timothy O'Sullivan and William Bell during the U.S. Geographical Surveys West of the 100th Meridian (the Wheeler Survey) conducted by Lt. George M. Wheeler (P).

RG 306

RECORDS OF THE U.S. INFORMATION AGENCY
1900–78   ca. 939,000 items

306.1   The agency's master file of photographs used in connection with the activities of the Information Service Centers in producing exhibits and illustrating press releases and publications relating to the United States. Among the subjects covered are: foreign relations and aid programs; social, economic, and cultural life; political events and Presidential activities; military activities, equipment, and weapons; visits to the United States by foreign dignitaries; and prominent U.S. and foreign personages. 1948–76 (PS) (PSA) (PSB) (PSC).

306.2   The *New York Times* Paris Bureau file of photographs covering a broad range of subjects. The focus of the file is worldwide with emphasis on Europe and the United States. Among the topics featured are: World War I; the Paris, France, riots of 1934; the Saar plebiscite, 1935; the Russo-Finnish War; the Sino-Japanese War; World War II; the post-World War II occupation of Europe and Japan; international meetings, treaties, and conferences, including the establishment of the United Nations; political, military, and social figures; actors, entertainers, and athletes; sports and the Olympic games; the Ku Klux Klan; labor strife; the 1930's Depression; industrial and technological developments; the cultures of various countries; expositions; expeditions; and scenic views of countries around the world. Ca. 1900–50 (NT). Glass negatives showing the fairgrounds and pavilions at the Paris Universal Exposition of 1900 in Paris, France (F).

306.3   Mounted photographs used in filmstrips produced or acquired by the United States Information Agency (USIA) or its predecessor, the Office of War Information, for distribution abroad by the United States Information Service (USIS). The pictures include Allied successes in World War II; political, social, cultural, and economic life in the United States, including agriculture, industry, education, and housing; and the programs of the Civilian Conservation Corps, the Rural Electrification Administration, and the Soil Conservation Service. 1942–52 (FS) (FSCE).

306.4   Photographs made or purchased by the Press and Publications Service for use by USIS or for inclusion in agency presentation albums. Subjects include visits to the United States by foreign heads of state, and other prominent persons; conferences and exhibitions; the signing of the 1963 Nuclear Test Ban Treaty; President John F. Kennedy's 1961 visit to Vienna, Austria; the 1963 civil rights March on Washington; President Lyndon Johnson's trip in 1966 to Southeast Asia Treaty Organization (SEATO) countries; Johnson's 1967 meeting with officials of South Vietnam; and the first days of Gerald R. Ford's Presidency. 1949–74 (SS) (SSM) (SSD) (DA).

306.5   Photographs of activities, programs, and exhibits at Information Service Centers in various countries, as well as pictures of center staffs, visitors, and facilities, 1948–54 (CS).

306.6   Black-and-white and color photographs relating to the industrial, scientific, cultural, political, and social life of the United States used for displays and in publications. Included are pictures of the arts, religious practices, defense, agricultural operations, various celebrations, the movie and television industry, universities and colleges, the civil rights movement, historic sites, and rural and urban life. Also in the records are photographs of Presidential nomination conventions and inaugurations, politicians, and Presidents John F. Kennedy, Dwight D. Eisenhower, Richard M. Nixon, and Lyndon B. Johnson. 1948–68 (ST) (SUB).

306.7   Mounted photographic prints and annotated issues of the publications *USIA Correspondent* and *USIA World* covering a wide variety of subjects. Some of the subjects pictured relate to the Alliance for Progress programs in Panama, civic action programs in South Vietnam, and African art. Included are pictures of various dignitaries among whom are King Faisal of Saudi Arabia, President Richard Nixon, Vice Presidents Spiro Agnew and Gerald Ford, Senator Edward Kennedy, Gov. Ronald Reagan of California, and USIA Director Carl T. Rowan. 1964–75 (USC) (USW).

306.8   Photographic prints used by USIA to publicize the social and economic programs of the Alliance for Progress, 1961–69 (AFP). Photographs taken by USIA photographers at the Organization of American States (OAS) Summit Conference held in Punta del Este, Uruguay, including pictures of attendees President Lyndon B. Johnson and Secretary of State Dean Rusk, 1967 (PDE).

306.9   Photographic prints from the USIA Press and Publication Service on U.S. involvement in Vietnam. Some of the subjects shown are military activities,

306-DR-48-25A/26. Dominican demonstrators protest U.S. intervention in their country, the Dominican Republic. 1965. (RG 306, Records of the U.S. Information Agency)

306-SSM-4B-61-32. A demonstrator at the March on Washington. August 28, 1963. (RG 306, Records of the U.S. Information Agency)

educational and agricultural programs, and refugees. 1958–74 (MVP). Photographic prints documenting U.S. military intervention in the Dominican Republic, 1967 (DR).

306.10   Black-and-white and color photographs showing life on a demonstration test farm operated as a cooperative effort of the Tennessee Valley Authority and the Soil Conservation Service, 1963 (TVA).

306.11   Photographs (some in color) of National Aeronautics and Space Administration (NASA) flights Apollo 4 through 17, Apollo-Soyuz, Gemini 9, and Skylabs 1 through 4, 1967–78. Pictured are the flight crews and their families; training programs and tests; prelaunch and launch activities; equipment; crews in orbit; moon landings; crews of the joint United States and U.S.S.R. (Apollo-Soyuz) mission; several dignitaries; several U.S. Presidents; members of Congress and governors (AP).

306.12   Negatives and proof sheets showing activities and delegates at the 1968 Democratic National Convention, Chicago, IL, and the Republican National Convention, Miami, FL. Notables pictured at the Democratic convention include Hubert Humphrey, Edmund Muskie, and Eugene McCarthy. Richard Nixon, Spiro Agnew, Nelson Rockefeller, Barry Goldwater, Edward Brooke, Gerald Ford, John Lindsay, and Ronald Reagan are among the dignitaries at the Republican Convention. There are no photographs of the Youth International Party (YIPPIES) or the riots in Chicago during the Democratic convention (DRC).

306.13   Photographs from the summer Olympic games in Mexico City, Mexico, showing the athletes, opening and closing ceremonies, several events, the Olympic village, and members of past Olympic teams, 1968 (OG).

306.14   Photographic prints of President Dwight D. Eisenhower's visits to Turkey, India, and Spain during his 11-nation goodwill tour in December 1959 showing the President, John Eisenhower, and Ellsworth Bunker; President Celal Bayar and Prime Minister Adnan Menderes of Turkey; President Rajendra Prasad, Prime Minister Jawaharlal Nehru, and Indira Gandhi of India; and Gen. Francisco Franco of Spain (EGT). Photographs of President Eisenhower and his family taken during a trip to South Korea, the Philippine Islands, Japan, and Taiwan (the Republic of China) showing parades and various ceremonies, 1960 (ET).

306.15   Photographs recording Vice President and Mrs. Richard Nixon's visit to the Union of Soviet Socialist Republics (U.S.S.R.) for the opening in July 1959 of the American National Exhibition in Moscow. Pictures relating to tours of other areas in the U.S.S.R. and a visit to Poland are also included. Shown are U.S. and Soviet dignitaries, including Premier and Mrs. Nikita Khrushchev, Frol R. Koslov, Anastas Mikoyan, Adm. Hyman Rickover, and Dr. Milton Eisenhower. In Poland the Nixons are shown with Chairman Alexander Zuwadsky. 1959 (RMN). Photographs taken of Vice President Nixon, and later as President, during several trips to Asia, Africa, the Middle East, Central America, and the Caribbean islands, 1953–74 (RNT).

306.16   Photographs taken by USIA and White House photographers showing President John F. Kennedy with ambassadors, prime ministers, astronauts, civil rights leaders, labor leaders, boy scouts, entertainers, and sports figures, 1960–64 (JFK). Photographs taken by USIS photographers and news services to document President Kennedy's trips to Central and South America, Asia, and Europe. Included are photographs of the President meeting with U.S.S.R. Premier Nikita

Khrushchev in Vienna, Austria. 1961–63 (JKT). Photographs taken by USIS in 1962 of Attorney General Robert F. Kennedy during a goodwill trip to West Germany, The Netherlands, Italy, Indonesia, Thailand, Hong Kong, South Korea, Malaysia, Taiwan (the Republic of China), South Vietnam, the Philippine Islands, and Lebanon. Ethel Kennedy and Edward M. Kennedy, who traveled with the attorney general, are also shown (RKT).

306.17 Photographs of Vice President Lyndon B. Johnson and Lady Bird Johnson touring in Southeast Asia, Europe, the Middle East, and the Mediterranean area. Shown are the heads of state of the various countries visited and other dignitaries; a meeting with Pope John XXIII; and ceremonies, military inspections, dinners, and other official functions. 1961–62 (LJT) (JGT). Photographs documenting the Vice President's 1963 trip to Denmark, Finland, Iceland, and Norway. Included are pictures of Johnson, his family, and the heads of state of the countries visited. There are also a few 1964 photographs of President Johnson's visit to Iran (JT).

306.18 Photographic negatives made from the film *Years of Lightning, Days of Drums*, 1964 (KF). Photographs documenting President John F. Kennedy's funeral, 1963 (KFU).

306.19 Photographs primarily documenting activities at the White House during Lyndon B. Johnson's Presidential administration. Some photographic coverage of Johnson while Vice President is also included. In addition, there are photographs of visiting dignitaries, Presidential trips, Johnson addressing Congress and the United Nations, and several bill-signing ceremonies. 1961–67 (JM).

306.20 Photographic prints recording Vice President Hubert H. Humphrey's trips to Europe, Africa, and Asia. Pictured are many public officials, including Nguyen Van Thieu, Ferdinand Marcos, Indira Gandhi, Willy Brandt, Queen Juliana, Charles de Gaulle, Pope Paul VI, Jomo Kenyatta, and Haile Selassie. Photographs of several U.S. officials are included. Mrs. Muriel Humphrey and Justice Thurgood Marshall, who accompanied the Vice President to Europe and Africa, are also pictured. 1966–68 (HHA) (HT).

306.21 Photographs chiefly recording the two inaugurations of President Richard M. Nixon. Also includes pictures of cabinet appointees and postelection celebrations. 1968–69 and 1973 (NIC) (RNI).

306.22 Photographic prints recording trips by Vice President Spiro Agnew to Asia, the Middle East, Africa, and Australia, 1969–73 (SAT). Color prints documenting several trips taken by Gerald R. Ford before and during his Presidential administration. There are photographs from a trip to China in 1972 and from visits to several European countries in 1975. The latter trips were taken in conjunction with Ford's attendance at the Helsinki (Finland) Conference. A few pictures of Ford at the conference are included (GRF).

RG 310

RECORDS OF THE
AGRICULTURAL RESEARCH SERVICE
1930–62   260 items

310.1   Photographs showing the effects of Dutch elm disease on trees. Shown are diseased trees, disease-resistant trees, and experiments relating to treatment of the fungus. 1930–62 (E).

RG 318

RECORDS OF THE
BUREAU OF ENGRAVING AND PRINTING
1789–1965   4,425 items

318.1   Engraved portraits of several Presidents, cabinet members, and other government officials, 1789–1965 (MP).

318.2   Photographic prints and graphics of designs and layouts for U.S. stamps and currency. There are also photographs of several U.S. Presidents, government officials, and public buildings in Washington, DC. Also included are pictures of bureau employees at work; bureau buildings, offices and shops, and equipment. Ca. 1924–42 (D).

RG 319

RECORDS OF THE ARMY STAFF
ca. 1931–66   ca. 16,780 items

319.1   Photographic prints showing U.S. military activities and operations from the World War II period through the Vietnam conflict. Pictured are a variety of subjects, including U.S. Army posts and camps, equipment and weapons; U.S. Army personnel; joint-service and North Atlantic Treaty Organization exercises and maneuvers; atomic bomb tests and Japanese atomic bomb victims; prisoners and Axis war criminals; civilian and military casualties and refugees; and postwar Japan. Also included are aerial photographs and panoramas of several foreign countries. Some of the prints are duplicates of U.S. Signal Corps photographs found in the records of the Office of the Chief Signal Officer, RG 111. Ca. 1940–66 (SF) (CE) (CF).

319.2   An album of photographic prints, probably made by Japanese officials to show favorable conditions in five World War II prisoner-of-war camps in Formosa (Taiwan). Included are pictures of prisoners engaged in animal husbandry and recreational activities, and participating in religious services. Also shown are several Allied military and civilian prisoners including Lt. Gen. Jonathan Wainwright. 1943–44 (PW).

319.3   Photographic prints taken by the Army Electronics Support Command to show communications equipment and other electronic devices, 1931–57 (AESC).

319.4   Glass negatives recording an expedition to Tibet by Dr. Ernst Schafer, a German, that were forwarded in 1950 by the U.S. Army Forces Austria for inclusion in the Army's Intelligence Document File, ca. 1940 (SCH).

RG 326

RECORDS OF THE ATOMIC ENERGY COMMISSION
1947–72   3,600 items

326.1   Photographs showing commission installations, research and experiments, notable persons, personnel, and a variety of nuclear energy-related subjects, 1947–72 (G).

RG 328

RECORDS OF THE NATIONAL CAPITAL PLANNING COMMISSION
ca. 1790–1948   588 items

328.1   Photographic prints showing flood conditions in Washington, DC, after the Potomac River overflowed in 1936 and 1942 (F).

328.2   Photographic prints, lantern slides, and drawings of Washington, DC, including views of monuments, public buildings, and parks. Also included is a ca. 1920 group portrait of the Justices of the Supreme Court. Ca. 1790–1948 (M) (S).

328.3   Photographic prints recording the construction of the Grand Coulee Dam, WA, 1934–36 (GCD).

328.4   An album of photographic prints showing waterfronts and quays in several European cities, ca. 1900 (WQ).

RG 331

RECORDS OF THE ALLIED OPERATIONAL AND OCCUPATION HEADQUARTERS, WORLD WAR II
1937–45   4,704 items

331.1   Black-and-white photographic prints taken by the U.S. Signal Corps of paintings by Japanese artists displayed in an exhibition on war art at the Ueno Museum in Tokyo, Japan. The paintings illustrate events from the Sino-Japanese conflict years to the end of World War II. 1937–45 (JWP).

331.2   Photographic prints obtained from the Civil Censorship Detachment of the Civil Intelligence Section. The photographs are of Japanese ambassadors, parliamentarians, businessmen, and other persons. Ca. 1939 (P).

331.3   Photographs taken by the Supreme Headquarters Allied Expeditionary Forces (SHAEF) during the invasion and occupation of Europe. Included are pictures of refugees and displaced persons, prison camps, military trials, war damage to cities, food rationing, SHAEF officers, and representatives of the Allied, occupied, and liberated countries. 1940–45 (CA).

331.4   Glass negatives of graphs photographed by General Headquarters, Supreme Commander for the Allied Powers (SCAP) showing prison population changes, food imports, diet levels, and other subjects relating to Japan, 1940–45 (JAP).

326-G-69-8542. *Phoebus 2A reactor being moved into test position at test cell C, Nuclear Rocket Development Station, Jackass Flats, Nevada. The reactor has been developed and tested under the joint AEC-NASA Space Nuclear Propulsion Office.* 1969. Los Alamos Scientific Laboratory. (RG 326, Records of the Atomic Energy Commission)

350-P-O-573. [Marcario] *Sakay, outlaw, and some of his companions.* Ca. 1900. (RG 350, Records of the Bureau of Insular Affairs)

332-MC-33-2. U.S. military cemetery, Saint-Laurent-sur-Mer, France. Ca. 1946. (RG 332, Records of the U.S. Theaters of War, World War II)

362-V-19A-2629-3. The office of VISTA volunteer Geoffry Steele. Location Unknown. Ca. 1970. (RG 362, Records Agencies for Voluntary Action Programs)

331.5   Printing proofs and negatives of charts, maps, graphs, posters, and photographs compiled by the staff of Gen. Douglas MacArthur for the MacArthur historical series, a planned publication. The materials relate to Japan's involvement in World War II. 1940–45 (MH).

RG 332

RECORDS OF U.S. THEATERS OF WAR, WORLD WAR II
ca. 1944–45   ca. 2,900 items

332.1   Thirty-seven albums assembled by the American Graves Registration Command to provide pictorial and historical information on temporary U.S. military cemeteries in the Azores, Belgium, England, France, Luxembourg, The Netherlands, and Northern Ireland. Each cemetery record includes a history of the area where it is located, a history of the cemetery, and a tactical history of U.S. combat operations in the area. The photographic prints relate to the histories and show military operations and units, views of the cemeteries, pictures of the communities and residents in the vicinity of cemeteries, and pictures of people paying their respects to the dead. The album relating to the cemetery at Hamm, Luxembourg, also contains photographs documenting the funeral for Gen. George S. Patton. Ca. 1944–45 (MC).

RG 336

RECORDS OF THE OFFICE OF THE CHIEF OF TRANSPORTATION
1942–45   ca. 2,000 items

336.1   Photographic prints recording the embarkation and disembarkation of military personnel and equipment from the Hampton Roads Port of Embarkation, Newport News, VA. Also included are pictures of various military support services at the port. 1942–45 (H).

RG 337

RECORDS OF HEADQUARTERS ARMY GROUND FORCES
1942–48   ca. 1,300 items

337.1   Photographs showing U.S. Army ranger training, demonstrations of amphibious combat and equipment landing techniques at Fort Edwards, MA, and the 10th Mountain Division undergoing training at Camp Hale, CO. Also lantern slides depicting various aspects of Universal Military Training, and U.S. military activity in North Africa. 1942–48 (FE) (NA) (TNG) (SL). Photographs relating to the military career of Lt. Gen. Lesley J. McNair, 1942–44 (GF).

337.2   A presentation album containing photographic prints documenting Allied air support for the D-day invasion of Europe, 1944 (AV).

RG 341

RECORDS OF
HEADQUARTERS U.S. AIR FORCE (AIR STAFF)
1954–66   ca. 8,300 items

341.1   Photographs acquired from several sources relating to alleged sightings of unidentified flying objects (UFO). The photographs were collected for Project Blue Book by the Aerial Phenomena Branch, Foreign Technology Division, U.S. Air Force. 1954–66 (PBB).

RG 342

RECORDS OF U.S. AIR FORCE COMMANDS,
ACTIVITIES, AND ORGANIZATIONS
1945–81   ca. 148,600 items

342.1   Photographs documenting U.S. Air Force activities and personnel in Germany and Japan following World War II. Included in the series on Germany are photographs showing Air Force activities during Operation Vittles, the Berlin airlift. 1945–62 (G) (J).

342.2   Photographs of European cities taken under the supervision of Col. George W. Goddard. The photographs primarily show World War II bomb destruction to cities and landmarks. 1946–48 (CGA) (CGB) (CGC) (CGD).

342.3   Color and black-and-white photographs documenting U.S. Air Force activities. Among the subjects pictured are airmen and officers; aircraft and missiles; airfields and bases in the United States and overseas; and military operations and projects including the war in Vietnam. 1955–81 (AF) (B) (C).

RG 350

RECORDS OF THE BUREAU OF INSULAR AFFAIRS
1898–1936   ca. 13,160 items

350.1   Two albums of photographic prints obtained by the bureau from the Manila Railroad Company, Philippine Islands, showing subjects such as railroad equipment, rail construction, and repair activities; and views of several provinces. Also included are photographs recording a visit to Baguio by Secretary of War William Howard Taft. 1907–16 (MR). An album of photographic prints (some hand colored) showing bridges, culverts, and artesian wells in the Philippine Islands, ca. 1909–12 (PW).

350.2   Photographic prints in albums relating to Manila and the provinces of Cebu, Mindora, Luzon, and Sulu. Included are pictures of U.S. Army camps and forts; views of villages and cities; and pictures of harbors and waterfronts, commercial enterprises, transportation facilities, and public works. Also, photographic prints showing general views of the islands and U.S. Army installations taken in 1900 by Lt. C. F. O'Keefe, 36th Infantry, U.S.V. Ca. 1899–1928 (PC). An album of photographic prints showing types of plants found in the Philippine Islands, ca. 1910 (E).

350.3   Photographic prints, negatives, and lantern slides showing Philippine agricultural methods and products; ethnic groups, customs, and crafts; industries and civil works projects; modes of transportation; educational facilities and public buildings; expositions; and views of urban and rural areas. Also included are photographs of the Philippine and U.S. military forces; Philippine and U.S. officials; and political groups and revolutionaries. 1898–1936 (P) (BS) (GS) (N).

350.4   Photographic prints of Philippine officials, 1900–1935 (O). A photographic print of members of the Philippine Commission, Washington, DC, 1904 (C).

350.5   Photographs relating to Puerto Rico showing governors, Census Bureau enumerators, police, schools, roads, and other subjects, 1901–35. Also included are photographs of Haiti, China, the Dominican Republic, Panama, Cuba, and the Virgin Islands. 1898–1935 (PR).

RECORDS OF THE
AGENCIES FOR VOLUNTARY ACTION PROGRAMS

RG 362

1964–79   ca. 44,000 items

362.1   Photographs documenting Volunteers in Service to America (VISTA) programs in the states, Puerto Rico, and Guam. The volunteers are shown visiting homes; teaching; working with migrants, American Indians, and other ethnic groups; aiding the elderly; providing legal and medical assistance; and helping the underprivileged and needy. Also included are pictures of an American Indian protest in Seattle, WA, and the aftermath of the 1967 Detroit, MI, riot. Government officials including R. Sargent Shriver and Vice President Hubert H. Humphrey are pictured. 1964–79 (V) (VS).

RECORDS OF THE OFFICE OF THE
U.S. TRADE REPRESENTATIVE

RG 364

1969 and 1978   54 items

364.1   Photographic prints (some in color) showing the 1969 signing ceremonies of the Kennedy Round Trade Agreement, and meetings of the Tokyo Round Trade Talks in 1978. Also included are informal photographs of President Jimmy Carter, Robert Strauss, W. Michael Blumenthal, ambassadors, and trade ministers (A).

RECORDS OF THE NATIONAL OCEANIC
AND ATMOSPHERIC ADMINISTRATION

RG 370

ca. 1948–70   5,019 items

370.1   Photographic prints and lantern and color slides relating to the activities of the National Operational Meteorological Satellite System, including images of meteorological instruments and equipment, early rockets, satellites, and weather conditions, 1948–70 (MSP) (MSL) (MSS).

374-OS-25. *The Fire Ball rising.* Operation Sandstone, Eniwetok Atoll.
1948. (RG 374, Records of the Defense Nuclear Agency)

RG 374

RECORDS OF THE DEFENSE NUCLEAR AGENCY
1947–48   102 items

374.1   An album of photographic prints assembled to show highlights of Task Force Seven's participation in Operation Sandstone, an atomic bomb test at Eniwetok Atoll, Marshall Islands. Shown are preparations for the detonation of the bomb, the atomic blast, and some of the effects of the explosion. 1947–48 (OS).

RG 378

RECORDS OF THE ECONOMIC DEVELOPMENT ADMINISTRATION
1963–81   ca. 28,800 items

378.1   Color and black-and-white photographs taken throughout the United States and Puerto Rico to document programs sponsored by the Economic Development Administration (EDA). The programs were designed to stimulate private sector productivity and economic growth. Among the programs pictured are municipal public works projects, historical restorations, beautification projects, agricultural and industrial programs, health and social service programs, and recreational projects; also included are photographs of housing rehabilitation plans and projects aimed at developing the economies of Indian reservations; among others, President Jimmy Carter, Vice President Walter Mondale, and several governors and mayors are pictured. 1963–81 (M) (PP) (PR) (PS).

378.2   Color and black-and-white photographs documenting the efforts of the Upper Great Lakes Regional Commission (UGLRC) to stimulate commercial and industrial growth in the area and to create jobs and protect existing employment, 1975–80 (GL).

378.3   Color slides recording EDA programs for the economic development of several Indian reservations. Shown are job training centers, planning committees, industrial parks, businesses, and recreational developments. 1974 (PI).

378.4   Portraits of EDA personnel, members of the National Public Advisory Committee on Regional and Economic Development, and Secretaries of Commerce Rogers C. B. Morton and Malcolm Baldridge. Also included are informal pictures of Secretaries of Commerce Juanita M. Kreps and Philip Klutznick, Presidents Gerald Ford and Jimmy Carter, Vice President Walter Mondale, and Chicago Mayor Richard Daley. There are a few photographs of conferences, grant signings, and other ceremonies. 1970–80 (PER).

RG 381

RECORDS OF AGENCIES FOR ECONOMIC OPPORTUNITY AND LEGAL SERVICES
1967–72   69 items

381.1   Posters advertising or recruiting for programs sponsored by the Office of Economic Opportunity (OEO) and Legal Services: the Job Corps, the Peace Corps, Foster Grandparents, Head Start, Indian Opportunities, and Volunteers in Service to America (VISTA), 1967–72 (PX).

RG 391

RECORDS OF THE
U.S. REGULAR ARMY MOBILE UNITS, 1821–1942
ca. 1776 and 1850–1950   1,605 items

391.1   Photographic prints of Fort Wingate, NM, a Zuni pueblo, and Navajo women, ca. 1866–1880 (FW). Photographic prints of the southwestern United States taken by John K. Hillers, including pictures of American Indians and pueblos, 1879 (JKH).

391.2   Photographic prints showing Emilio Aguinaldo and several insurgents, and views of the Philippine Islands, 1896–1906 (PI).

391.3   Photographic prints of officers and enlisted men of the 4th, 10th, 15th, 17th, and 19th U.S. Infantry Regiments, including the 67th New York Infantry during the Civil War and the 15th Infantry in China during World War I, 1850–1941 (IN). Photographic prints of the 1st, 2d, 4th, 5th, 6th, 9th, and 10th U.S. Cavalry Regiments, and of the 1st Cavalry and 25th Infantry engaged in amphibious training in Japan in 1950, 1850–1950 (CA).

391.4   A photographic print of Battery "C," 144th Field Artillery, California National Guard, 1939. A watercolor painted by D. W. C. Falls in 1923 of Alexander Hamilton as a Revolutionary War soldier of the Provincial Company, New York Artillery (AR).

391.5   A photographic print of the Ben Johnson League Baseball Team, Junction City, KS, 1939 (M).

RG 393

RECORDS OF
U.S. ARMY CONTINENTAL COMMANDS, 1821–1920
1917–18   145 items

393.1   Photographic prints documenting training activities and post buildings at Camp Jackson, SC, 1917–18 (CJ).

RG 394

RECORDS OF
U.S. ARMY CONTINENTAL COMMANDS, 1920–42
1925–38   775 items

394.1   Photographic prints from the Third Service Command Engineer's Office showing buildings in disrepair at several posts in the U.S. Army III Corps area, ca. 1936 (BP). Lantern slides relating to mobilization tests in the U.S. Army VI Corps area, 1933–38 (M).

394.2   Photographic prints documenting training programs at Citizens Military Training Camps at Fort George G. Meade, MD, in 1925 and Fort Monroe, VA, in 1933 (CM) (T).

394.3   An album of photographic prints of troops from Camp Stephen F. Austin during the Texas Centennial Exposition in Dallas, 1936 (SA).

RG 395

RECORDS OF U.S. ARMY
OVERSEAS OPERATIONS AND COMMANDS
ca. 1900–19   ca. 800 items

395.1   Photographic prints recording activities of the American Expeditionary Forces in Siberia, including pictures of diplomats, Bolshevik prisoners, refugees, and the military forces of other countries, 1918–19 (SE).

395.2   Photographic prints of the scenery and populace of the Philippine Islands, including pictures of Emilio Aguinaldo and other insurgents, and U.S. military activities, ca. 1900 (PI).

RG 397

RECORDS OF THE
DEFENSE CIVIL PREPAREDNESS AGENCY
ca. 1965   5 items

397.1   Filmstrips relating to the use of fallout shelters as a civil defense measure, ca. 1965 (FS).

RG 407

RECORDS OF THE
ADJUTANT GENERAL'S OFFICE, 1917–
1917–46   10,088 items

407.1   Panoramas showing troops at Camp Sheridan, AL, 1917 (CS). Glass negatives of officers, enlisted personnel, chaplains, and the secretarial staff of the Paris office of the American Expeditionary Forces, 1918–19 (EFP).

407.2   Lantern slides of military attaches in France, and the Moroccan War (the Riff War), 1925–27 (MW).

407.3   Recruitment posters used by the Citizens Military Training camps, 1924 (WP). Charts used in instructing troops in the identification of chemicals that could be used in warfare, 1942 (CW).

407.4   Original watercolors of World War II airplanes and airfields by unidentified artists, ca. 1942 (AA). Aerial reconnaissance prints of areas in the Philippine Islands, ca. 1942–45 (PI). Photographs of an LCT boat and stored supplies, ca. 1942 (LCT). Scrapbooks containing photographic prints, charts, newspaper clippings, and drawings illustrating the histories of several military units and facilities, 1940–46 (US).

RECORDS OF THE
URBAN MASS TRANSPORTATION ADMINISTRATION
1979   ca. 3,500 items

408.1   Photographs of commuter trains and light rail stations taken in 1979 for a Department of Transportation study entitled "DOT 321(b) Rail Retrofit Evaluation of Light and Commuter Rail Stations." The study was undertaken pursuant to Section 321 of the Surface Transportation Assistance Act of 1978 to determine ways to make facilities accessible and usable by the handicapped (S).

RECORDS OF THE
ENVIRONMENTAL PROTECTION AGENCY
1959–77   ca. 25,000 items

412.1   Photographic prints, negatives, and color slides taken by or acquired by the Environmental Protection Agency (EPA) and its predecessors, the National Air Pollution Control Administration and the Federal Water Pollution Control Administration, as documentation of air and water pollution in the United States and of efforts undertaken to counteract pollution. Included are pictures showing pollution caused by automobiles, industrial combustion, effluences from industrial and agricultural waste by-products, and pesticides. Also included are photographs showing the harmful effects of pollution on people, animals, fish, and the environment; pictures recording pollution control activities and quality control systems; pictures documenting agency experiments and tests; and photographs of EPA administrators Russell Train and William Ruckelshaus, other agency officials, and President Richard M. Nixon. 1959–72 (G) (GA).

412.2   Color slides taken by contract photographers for use by the EPA in its DOCUMERICA program. DOCUMERICA was a program to photographically document environmental concerns in the United States such as air and water pollution, traffic congestion, urban blight, land erosion, and the destruction of natural resources. Also included are photographs showing urban and rural areas in the United States, National Parks, the Alaska Pipeline, and people at work and relaxing. Color negatives and black-and-white photographs reproduced by EPA from the original color slides are included in the records. 1972–77 (DA) (DAS) (DAB) (DAC) (DAD) (DAF) (DAFC). Photographs taken by Ken Heyman for DOCUMERICA. Shown are people, events, and everyday activities in Mascoutah, IL. 1971 and 1973–74 (DAH). Color slides of images not included in the DOCUMERICA program, 1972–77 (DM).

RECORDS OF THE NATIONAL HIGHWAY
TRAFFIC SAFETY ADMINISTRATION
1981   214 items

416.1   Color slides from the slide program "Ease On Down The Road." The program was used to demonstrate fuel-efficient driving techniques to operators of commercial vehicles. 1981 (S).

GENERAL RECORDS OF THE DEPARTMENT OF THE NAVY, 1947–

1956–81   ca. 341,800 items

RG 428

428.1   Periscope photographs taken by the U.S.S. *Irex* off the coast of Rhode Island, 1956 (IR).

428.2   Black-and-white and color photographs showing U.S. Navy officers and enlisted men; aircraft, ships, and boats; ordnance and other equipment; training activities and facilities; bases; geographical areas; navy operations during the Vietnam war; and other subjects relating to U.S. Navy history. These photographs are a continuation of the records described in paragraph 80.3. 1958–81 (N) (K) (KN) (GX).

RECORDS OF ORGANIZATIONS IN THE EXECUTIVE OFFICE OF THE PRESIDENT

1967–79   167 items

RG 429

429.1   Photographs collected or taken for the Citizens' Advisory Committee on Environmental Quality, including pictures of committee meetings and committee chairmen Laurence S. Rockefeller and Henry L. Diamond. Some of the prominent individuals shown are Vice President Hubert Humphrey, Charles Lindbergh, Frank Borman, Lady Bird Johnson, and President and Mrs. Richard M. Nixon during a 1972 committee trip to San Francisco. 1967–76 (E).

429.2   Color and black-and-white photographic prints of Barry P. Bosworth, Alfred E. Kahn, and R. Robert Russell, officials of the Council on Wage and Price Stability, 1977–79 (W).

RG 432

RECORDS OF THE ECONOMIC STABILIZATION PROGRAM

1971–74   3,577 items

432.1   Photographs of the commissioners and other officials of the Cost of Living Council, the Price Commission, and the Pay Board. The photographs were generated by the Office of Public Affairs of the Price Commission and include pictures of George Shultz, William T. Coleman, William W. Scranton, Donald Rumsfeld, and other officials. Also shown are U.S. congressional hearings and well-known persons including Ralph Nader and Senators Jacob Javits, John Tower, Charles Percy, William Proxmire, and John Connally. Ca. 1971–74 (P) (N).

432.2   Color slides used in briefing members of the Economic Stabilization Program agencies. The slides record economic data primarily in chart and graph form. 1971–74 (ED). Black-and-white and color slides relating to the economy used in presentations to consumers, 1971–74 (PC).

391-CA-3A-44. *Colonel George S. Patton, Jr., commanded 5th Cavalry from July 24, 1938 to December 5, 1938.* Ca. 1938. Underwood and Underwood. (RG 391, Records of the U.S. Regular Army Mobile Units)

412-DAS-89. *East Boston, Massachusetts.* 1973. Michael Philip Manheim. (RG 412, Records of the Environmental Protection Agency)

452-G-1-11798-9A. Administrator John W. Warner with Ringling Brothers and Barnum and Bailey circus performers. Ca. 1976. (RG 452, Records of the American Revolution Bicentennial Administration)

RG 452

RECORDS OF THE AMERICAN REVOLUTION BICENTENNIAL ADMINISTRATION

1971–76   ca. 30,200 items

452.1   Posters designed or acquired by the American Revolution Bicentennial Administration (ARBA) and distributed as part of a campaign to encourage citizen participation in the Bicentennial, and to provide information about ARBA programs, 1974–76 (P).

452.2   Color slides used in ARBA's multimedia presentation, "Bicentennial USA." Shown are Revolutionary War reenactments, ceremonies, flags, historic landmarks, and portraits of famous Americans. 1975 (B).

452.3   Color slides taken by Frederick Figall, John Neubauer, Charles Phillips, and other ARBA staff photographers showing landscapes, historic landmarks, portraits of famous Americans, and bicentennial celebrations around the United States. The slides were taken for use in exhibits and multimedia presentations or for distribution to the media. 1971–76 (S).

452.4   Photographs taken by Frederick Figall, other staff photographers, and commercial photographers to document bicentennial events, including Operation Sail (the Tall Ships); the Smithsonian Festival of American Folklife; Expo '74, the Spokane World's Fair; the Bicentennial Wagon Train; and July 4th celebrations. Also included are pictures of ARBA officials, including John Warner and other well-known individuals: Presidents Gerald Ford and Richard Nixon, Governor Jimmy Carter, Chief Justice Warren E. Burger, Lady Bird Johnson, Queen Elizabeth, members of Congress, mayors, actors, and others. 1971–76 (G).

RG 471

RECORDS OF THE OFFICE OF SURFACE MINING RECLAMATION AND ENFORCEMENT

1957–1972   ca. 3,500 items

471.1   Color and black-and-white photographs from the Office of Surface Mining, Department of the Interior, showing mining activities, land reclamation projects, subsistence projects, and drainage and flood control efforts. The majority of the photographs were taken in Pennsylvania, but there are also pictures of localities in Alaska, Arizona, Kansas, New Jersey, Ohio, and Wyoming. 1957–72 (G).

Part II

DONATED MATERIALS

DONATED MATERIALS IN THE NATIONAL ARCHIVES

B.C.–1977   ca. 29,000 items

DM.1   **HARMON FOUNDATION COLLECTION.** Photographs primarily relating to African-American life and culture, including photographs of prominent individuals, photographs of works of art and artists, photographs relating to the work of the Visiting Nurse Association, and photographs taken by Kenneth Space of campus life at several colleges and universities. Also included are photographs of African and Asian art and images relating to Nigerian culture. B.C.–1967 (HN___) (HS) (HF-NU) (HN-AA) (HN-AC) (HN-AS) (HNE) (HNP) (HN-FAO) (HN-LS) (HN-PL) (HN-NC) (HN-SV).

DM.2   **MISCELLANEOUS COLLECTIONS.** Photographs relating to Presidents Abraham Lincoln, Theodore Roosevelt, Franklin D. Roosevelt, Woodrow Wilson, William H. Taft, Ulysses S. Grant, William McKinley, Herbert Hoover, Dwight D. Eisenhower, John F. Kennedy, and Lyndon B. Johnson; prominent civilian, political, judicial, and military personages; historic events, such as Taft signing the Arizona Statehood Proclamation in 1912; military units and events during the Civil War, the Spanish-American War, the Philippine Insurrection, World War I, and World War II; towns and buildings throughout the United States, including Washington, DC; committees and conferences; American Indians; cartes de visite of Civil War personages; and World War I posters. 1785–1967 (M).

DM.3   **ABDON DAUOD ACKAD COLLECTION.** Portraits of Justices of the U.S. Supreme Court; a group portrait of the U.S. Court for the District of Columbia and the U.S. Court of Appeals; portraits of Franklin D. Roosevelt, Eleanor Roosevelt, and Richard M. Nixon; and a group portrait of the members of the Warren Commission. Also, exterior and interior views of the Supreme Court Building and a panorama of Washington, DC, taken by William Henry Jackson. Ca. 1790–1969 (ADA).

DM.4   **MUSEUM FOR GERMAN HISTORY, BERLIN COLLECTION.** A photographic print of an 1849 drawing by Salomon Levy of Friedrich Ludwig (Louis) Biskey who fought in the United States during the Civil War (FB).

DM.5   **VICTOR GONDOS COLLECTION.** Black-and-white and color slides of several state archives buildings, 1955–67 (VGA). Photographic prints of prominent archivists, 1943–60 (VG). Photographs of foreign archives buildings, 1955–62 (VGF). Architectural drawings of archives in Georgia, Pennsylvania, and Illinois, 1955–63 (VGD). Photographic prints of American Indians, forts, the Big Horn and Yellowstone Expedition of 1876, and other subjects relating to the Indian Wars, 1851–1922 (VGG).

DM.6   **ANSCO HISTORICAL COLLECTION.** Portraits of Civil War-era personages, including Generals Ulysses S. Grant, Philip Sheridan, George Armstrong Custer, and several members of Congress, ca. 1860–69 (CA).

DM.7   **WILLIAM McILVAINE COLLECTION.** Original watercolors painted by McIlvaine showing the harbor at Veracruz, Mexico, in 1849 and Civil War subjects, ca. 1861–63 (WM).

DM.8   **LIBRARY OF CONGRESS COLLECTION.** Stereographs showing Civil War subjects, 1861–65 (CC).

DM.9   **FRANK W. LEGG COLLECTION.** Portraits of notable 19th-century men and women, including President Rutherford B. Hayes, Frederick Douglass, Henry Ward Beecher, and Nathaniel Hawthorne, 1865–84 (FL).

DM.10   **MINNESOTA HISTORICAL SOCIETY COLLECTION.** Photographs showing the construction of the Lake Bennett to Skagway Wagon Road in Alaska, 1897–99, and documenting a trip to Alaska by the U.S. Senate's Committee on Territories in 1904. Also included are photographs of exhibition halls at the Alaska-Yukon-Pacific Exposition, Seattle, WA, and the Columbia River and Puget Sound areas in Washington, ca. 1908; views of Alaska, ca. 1903; and photogravures of seals and the Pribilof Islands. n.d. (MHA). Photographic prints, lithographs, and postcards showing buildings, monuments, and statues in Washington, DC, 1866–1919 (MHW).

DM.11   **JOHN K. HILLERS COLLECTION.** Glass negatives taken by John K. Hillers showing the landscape in areas in the western United States, buildings in Washington, DC, and works of art depicting several famous battles, 1870–1900 (JH).

DM.12   **ULYSSES S. GRANT III COLLECTION.** An album of photographic prints relating to the Korean Punitive Expedition, 1871 (KWG).

DM.13   **WILLIAM PYWELL COLLECTION.** Portraits showing photographers William R. Pywell and Timothy O'Sullivan and O'Sullivan's wife, Laura Pywell O'Sullivan. Also a stereograph of Green River, WY, taken in 1872 by O'Sullivan during the King Survey, the Geological Exploration of the Fortieth Parallel (PY).

DM.14   **DAVID L. BRAINARD COLLECTION.** Photographic prints taken during the Lady Franklin Bay Expedition, 1881–84 (LFB). Photographic prints of Alaska and the Philippine Islands and snapshots and postcards from Brainard's trips to China, Korea, Russia, Finland, Panama, South America, and a Mediterranean cruise, 1884–1918 (BR). Photographic prints and memorabilia relating to the Brainard family and arctic expeditions, ca. 1884–1938 (AA).

DM.15   **WESTERN FORTS COLLECTION.** Photographs of forts and military personnel and units in the West and other areas of the United States, ca. 1887–1900 (FT).

DM.16   **UNIVERSITY OF SOUTH ALABAMA COLLECTION.** Color transparencies of works of art by African Americans, American Indians, and Mexican Americans from the University's Ethnic American Art Slide Library, 1889–1972 (SAI) (SM) (SR).

DM.17   **ORGANIZATION OF AMERICAN STATES COLLECTION.** An album of photographic prints of delegates to the First International Conference of American States, Washington, DC, 1889–90 (IAC).

DM.18   **JEFFERSON PATTERSON COLLECTION.** Photographs taken or collected by Patterson during his career as a Foreign Service officer, including pictures of his family and home, various foreign service posts, and views of Yellowstone National Park and New York. Also pictures taken during visits to Belgium, England, Egypt, France, Germany, The Netherlands, Italy, Palestine, Panama, Portugal, and Uruguay. 1896–1965 (JP) (JPA) (JPB) (JPC) (JPF) (JPM) (JPP).

DM.19   J. WILLIAM KLIE COLLECTION. Photographs of U.S. Army troops in Florida during the Spanish-American War; general views of Camp Cuba Libre, Tampa, FL; and pictures of the army transport *Red Cross*. William Jennings Bryan is also pictured. 1898 (SK).

DM.20   ALLEN N. WEBSTER COLLECTION. An album of photographic prints taken by Webster, who was with the U.S. Army Medical Corps in the Philippine Islands during the Spanish-American War. Shown primarily are views of the islands and the Filipino people. Also included are photographs of Emilio Aguinaldo with his cabinet, and his headquarters in Cavite. 1898–99 (PI).

DM.21   JOHN AND KATE EVANS COLLECTION. Six albums of photographic prints showing people and various areas in the Philippine Islands, 1900–16 (PE).

DM.22   CHARLES N. YOUNG COLLECTION. Photographs of Washington, DC, and adjacent areas in Maryland and Virginia, 1899–1943; the Philippine and Hawaiian Islands, 1900–11; Panama, 1916; France and England, 1919–27; and Pittsburgh and Gettysburg, PA, and Boston, Lexington, and Plymouth, MA, 1929–30 (MY).

DM.23   DWIGHT D. EISENHOWER COLLECTION. Microfilm of snapshots showing Eisenhower and his family, 1903–52 (DDE). Photographic prints relating to Eisenhower's funeral, 1969 (EF).

DM.24   NEIL M. JUDD COLLECTION. Photographs taken by Judd of Rainbow Bridge in Utah during the Cummings Expedition, 1909 (NJ).

DM.25   ERWIN KORNITZER COLLECTION. Photographic prints of President Theodore Roosevelt and family aboard the SS *Hamburg*, 1909 (TR).

DM.26   WOMEN'S MEDICAL COLLEGE OF PENNSYLVANIA COLLECTION. Lantern slides showing wartime activities in France during World War I, 1914–19 (WP).

DM.27   LUCIEN JONAS COLLECTION. An album of lithographs by Jonas relating to France during World War I, 1914–16 (LJ).

DM.28   HUGO H. HUNTZINGER COLLECTION. The typescript of the monograph *Forests of Porto Rico; Past, Present, and Future, and their Physical and Economic Environment* and accompanying photographic prints. The monograph by Louis S. Murphy was published as U.S. Department of Agriculture Bulletin, No. 254, October 20, 1916 (PR).

DM.29   C. S. TENLEY COLLECTION. Photographic prints recording the visit of the U.S. delegation to the First Inter-American Financial Congress, Buenos Aires, Argentina, 1916 (FFC).

DM.30   ELWYN L. WATSON COLLECTION. Photographic prints and memorabilia relating to the 419th Telegraph Battalion during World War I, 1917–19 (TB).

DM.31   GEORGE S. STEWART, JR., COLLECTION. Photographs documenting the history of the 29th Division, American Expeditionary Force, 1917–19 (GS).

DM.32 **EARNEST C. TRACY COLLECTION.** Photographic prints of military activities in northwestern France during World War I, including photographs of military and civilian notables Gen. John J. Pershing, Georges Clemenceau, and others; German prisoners of war; German artillery; and ruins. 1918 (WT).

DM.33 **DORIS McCLORY COLLECTION.** Posters used in the World War I United War Work Campaign, 1919 (UWW).

DM.34 **WILLIAM C. LANG COLLECTION.** Photographs of scenes in the U.S.S.R. taken by Lang while a member of the American Relief Administration, 1921–23 (ARA).

DM.35 **GEORGE A. CARROLL COLLECTION.** Slides documenting the history of the airship *Macon* (ZR–5), 1933–35 (AMS).

DM.36 **CHARLES RUSSELL COLLECTION.** A commemorative album consisting of photographic prints of Nazi celebrations and tributes in Nürnberg and Munich (München), Germany, 1935 (GR).

DM.37 **WILLIAM HADDON COLLECTION.** Photographic prints relating to the Federal Art Project and Federal Music Project in Massachusetts, 1936–41 (WH).

DM.38 **MAURICE CONSTANT COLLECTION.** Portraits taken by Maurice Constant of U.S. dignitaries who served during Franklin D. Roosevelt's Presidential administration, U.S. and Allied military and political leaders during World War II, and postwar U.S. politicians and diplomats, 1938–53. Duplicates of many of the images are in series 38-MCN, Records of the Chief of Naval Operations (MC).

DM.39 **ADM. EMORY S. LAND COLLECTION.** Sixteen commemorative albums containing photographic prints showing the construction and launching of merchant marine ships, 1939–48 (LA).

DM.40 **JEROME LILIENTHAL COLLECTION.** Stereographs relating to the German invasion of Poland, including pictures of German and Soviet soldiers, prisoners of war, Adolf Hitler, Polish towns, and military equipment, 1939 (SFF).

DM.41 **PARE LORENTZ COLLECTION.** Photographic negatives of midwestern industries taken by Edwin Locke, an assistant to producer Pare Lorentz, during the filming of Lorentz's *Ecce Homo*, 1939 (PL).

DM.42 **JAMES W. TALBOT COLLECTION.** Photographic prints showing the German invasion of the U.S.S.R., 1941 (GT).

DM.43 **J. ROBERT ST. CLAIR COLLECTION.** World War II posters distributed by the Office of War Information and other U.S. government agencies, (PSC).

DM.44 **SEYMOUR HOFSTETTER COLLECTION.** Color transparencies documenting the activities of the U.S.S. *Callaway* during World War II, ca. 1943 (SH).

DM.45 **WILLIAM VANDEL COLLECTION.** Photographic prints relating to the activities of the U.S. Army Counterintelligence Corps in Japan. Shown are U.S. occupation personnel, Japanese civilians and officials, and views of Japan. 1945–46 (CIC).

200-KWG-9. *Corean officer and soldiers with despatches on board the 'Colorado'.* 1871. (Donated Materials - The Ulysses S. Grant III Collection)

200-APS-64. *The last portion of pipe installation in 1976 was in the northern section of the trans Alaska pipeline in the Brooks Mountain Range, where the line was installed through Atigun Pass, elevation 4,800 feet.* 1976. (Donated Materials - The Alyeska Pipeline Service Company Collection)

DM.46   **HAROLD W. CLOVER COLLECTION.** Photographs taken by Clover during World War II including pictures of U.S. combat engineers; U.S., Russian, and German troops; casualties; U.S. and German military equipment; French and Austrian civilians; combat-damaged towns; and views of Vienna, Austria. 1945 (HC).

DM.47   **ABRAHAM ZAPRUDER COLLECTION.** Color slides made from the motion picture film taken by Zapruder of the assassination of President John F. Kennedy, 1963 (ZF).

DM.48   **ALYESKA PIPELINE SERVICE COMPANY COLLECTION.** Photographic prints showing the construction of the Alaska pipeline, 1973–77 (APS).

INDEX

Record group and donated materials collection titles appear in **bold-face** type. Numbers in parentheses refer to record groups, and other numbers refer to paragraphs.

A

Abdon Dauod Ackad Collection DM.3
Abel, Joseph, collection, 16.3
Abercrombie, Lt. William R. (photog.), 94.3
Aberdeen Proving Ground, MD, 156.12, 156.13, 171.3
Abraham Zapruder Collection DM.47
Abzug, Bella, 220.8
Acheson, Dean, 59.6
Ackad, Abdon Dauod, DM.3
Ackerman, G. W. (photog.), 33.3
Acoma Indians, 106.3
Adams, Ansel (photog.), 79.12
Adams, John, 127.2
Adenauer, Konrad, 59.6
Adjutant General's Office, 1780's–1917 (RG 94)
Adjutant General's Office, 1917– (RG 407)
Adjutant General's Office, 64.7, 77.25
Adm. Emory S. Land Collection DM.39
Advertisements, 131.1, 287.1, 381.1
Aerial bombing, 38.1, 120.4, 156.15, 165.17, 226.1, 243.1–243.5
Aerial photographs, 18.5, 18.8, 18.14, 26.2, 35.3, 38.1, 42.1, 69.6, 71.2, 77.9, 77.19, 80.5, 127.3, 165.7, 165.10, 165.14, 169.1, 171.1, 220.10, 237.1, 319.1, 407.4
Aeronautic Expedition (1917), 24.6
Aeronautics, 119.2, 255.1–255.7
Aeronautics, Bureau of (RG 72)
Aeronautics, Bureau of, 287.1
Afghanistan, 59.13
Africa, 112.2, 166.1, 239.1, 306.7, 306.15, 306.20, 306.22, DM.1
African Americans, 18.15, 35.6, 47.5, 208.11, 208.12, DM.1, DM.16
Agency for International Development (RG 286)
Agnew, Spiro, 306.7, 306.12, 306.22
Agricultural Adjustment Administration, 16.4, 145.2
Agricultural and Industrial Chemistry, Bureau of (RG 97)
Agricultural Chemistry and Engineering, Bureau of, 97.4
Agricultural Economics, Bureau of (RG 83)
Agricultural Engineering, Bureau of (RG 8)
Agricultural extension programs, 12.1
Agricultural marketing, 7.5, 16.4, 16.6, 54.1, 54.2, 54.3, 83.1, 83.2, 83.4, 83.6, 136.1, 145.1, 145.3, 145.4, 151.1
Agricultural Marketing Service (RG 136)
Agricultural production, 4.1–4.3, 7.5, 8.1, 16.4, 16.7–16.8, 48.4, 54.1, 54.3, 54.5, 54.6, 54.8, 54.9, 63.1, 83.1, 83.2, 83.6, 114.4, 119.3, 126.2, 126.5, 145.1–145.4, 151.1, 166.1, 169.1, 234.2, 258.1, 306.3, 306.6, 306.9, 350.3, 378.1
Agricultural research, 16.4, 16.7, 17.1, 54.3–54.6, 54.8, 95.1, 95.5, 97.1, 97.2, 97.3, 114.2, 306.10, 310.1
Agricultural Research Service (RG 310)

Agricultural Stabilization and Conservation Service (RG 145)
Agriculture, Department of, 7.1, 16.1–16.7, 83.6
Agriculture, Office of the Secretary of (RG 16)
Aguinaldo, Emilio, 391.2, 395.2, DM.20
AID. *See* Agency for International Development
Air Force Commands, Activities, and Organizations, U.S. (RG 342)
Air Force, Headquarters, U.S. (RG 341)
Air pollution, 97.2, 412.1, 412.2
Air raid shelters, 171.5, 171.8, 397.1
Air Service Photographic Section, 18.5
Air Transport Command Overseas Technical Unit, 18.14
Aircraft, 18.1, 18.4, 18.11, 18.12, 18.13, 24.5, 26.1, 28.2, 38.2, 72.1, 72.3, 72.4, 72.5, 72.6, 80.2, 80.3, 80.5, 80.6, 111.3, 127.1, 127.3, 156.13, 165.16, 165.17, 179.1, 181.1, 237.1, 255.1, 407.4, DM.35
Aircraft accidents, 18.10, 80.4
Airfields, 18.5, 18.8–18.10, 18.12, 71.1, 80.3, 80.6, 111.3, 127.3, 165.10, 165.16, 255.1, 407.4
Airports, 28.2, 69.3, 69.6, 162.1, 237.1, 255.1
Airship facilities, 18.3
Akron (dirigible), 72.4
Akron, OH, 72.4
Alabama, 69.1, 92.3, 142.1, 156.7, 156.10, 407.1
Alabama State Fair (1925), 92.3
Alaska, 22.2, 22.4, 22.5, 22.7, 22.9, 23.2, 26.5, 30.1, 35.8, 48.5, 48.7, 75.13, 76.2, 76.3, 92.2, 94.3, 111.3, 111.4, 111.8, 121.3, 126.1–126.3, 471.1, DM.10, DM.14
Alaska Boundary Commission, 76.2
Alaska Engineering Commission, 126.1
Alaska Game Commission, 22.9
Alaska Highway, 30.1, 79.17, 162.1
Alaska pipeline, 412.2, DM.48
Alaska Railroad, 48.7, 126.1–126.2
Alaska-Yukon-Pacific Exposition, Seattle, WA (1909), 111.4, 121.5, DM.10
Alaskan Expedition, 94.3
Alaskans, Native, 35.8, 126.1–126.2
Albatross (steamer), 22.1, 22.2, 22.5
Albers, Clem (photog.), 210.1
Albert, King of Belgium, 79.11
Albertypes, 79.6
Albright, Horace, 79.11
Albrook Field, Panama, 77.9
Albumen prints, 57.1, 57.4, 77.5, 79.4, 94.1, 94.3, 233.1
Alcohol, Tobacco, and Firearms, Bureau of, 170.1
Alcohol prohibition, 170.1
Aldredge, R.C., collection, 27.4
Aldrin, Edwin E., 255.7
Aleman, Miguel, 208.17
Alexander, Myrl, 129.1
Algeria, 169.1, 226.1
Algonquin Indians, 75.2
Alien Property, Office of (RG 131)
Allen, Lt. Henry T., 94.3
Allen N. Webster Collection DM.20
Alliance for Progress, 306.7, 306.8
Allied Expeditionary Forces, 331.3
Allied Operational and Occupation Headquarters, World War II (RG 331)

Bridges, 42.1, 59.3, 64.1, 69.3, 71.3, 77.2, 77.5, 77.19, 120.3, 165.6, 165.10, 350.1
Briggs, Lyman J., 167.1
Bristol, PA, 32.1
British Columbia, Canada, 76.2–76.3
British Royal Navy, 19.9
Broadsheets, 69.7
Broadsides, 109.1, 156.16
Brode, Wallace R., collection, 167.3
Brooke, Edward, 306.12
Browne, Charles A., 97.3
Bryan, William Jennings, DM.19
Bryce Canyon National Park, UT, 79.11
Buchanan, James, 127.2
Buchenwald concentration camp, 153.1
Budget, Bureau of the, 51.1
Buenos Aires, Argentina, DM.29
Buffalo, NY, 121.5
Buffaloes, 79.11
Bullock, D. S. (photog.), 83.5
Bunker, Ellsworth, 59.6, 306.14
Burger, Warren E., 452.4
Burke, Charles H., 75.4
Burma, 59.13, 226.1, 239.1
Butt, Capt. Archibald W., 165.7
Byrd, Adm. Richard, 26.1, 126.6

C

C.S. Tenley Collection DM.29
Cahill, Holger, 69.8
California, 16.3, 16.5, 18.4, 18.10, 18.12, 22.3, 26.6, 30.2, 30.4, 37.1, 37.2, 38.6, 48.4, 48.5, 49.2, 49.4, 54.7, 54.9, 54.11, 57.1, 57.2, 69.12, 71.2, 71.3, 75.14, 77.4, 77.7–77.9, 79.4, 79.7, 79.13, 92.6, 95.2, 111.8, 117.1, 119.4, 156.14, 165.3, 165.16, 165.17, 168.1, 171.1, 178.1, 181.1, 208.16, 210.2, 220.12, 391.4, 429.1
California National Guard, 168.1, 391.4
    144th Field Artillery, 391.4
Callaway, U.S.S., DM.44
Camouflage, 77.19, 120.3, 156.16, 171.1
Camp Cuba Libre, FL, DM.19
Camp Dennison, OH, 92.2
Camp Hale, CO, 337.1
Camp Hill, WV, 92.2
Camp Jackson, SC, 393.1
Camp Kenedy, TX, 59.10
Camp Leilehua, HI, 165.11
Camp Life (magazine), 12.5
Camp Ludington-Pere, MI, 35.3
Camp Sheridan, AL, 407.1
Camp Stephen F. Austin, TX, 394.3
Canada, 59.3, 59.10, 74.3, 76.2–76.5, 77.5, 79.7, 165.6, 207.2
Canals, 77.5, 115.1
Cape Canaveral, FL, 255.3, 255.4
Cape Eielson, Antarctica, 126.6
Capitol, U.S., DC, 48.3, 66.2
Capitol Police, U.S., 42.2
Captain Jack, 165.3

Card photographs, 49.3, 233.3, 233.4
Cardonna, Spain, 79.11
CARE, 260.1
Caribbean islands, 22.1, 127.1, 166.1, 306.15
Carlisle Indian Industrial School, PA, 75.8
Carlson, Norman, 129.1
Caroline Islands, 22.1, 38.1
Carpenters' Hall, Philadelphia, PA, 59.3
Carroll, George A., DM.35
Carter, Jimmy, 51.1, 170.1, 220,10, 220.11, 364.1, 378.1, 378.4, 452.4
Carter, William H., collection, 165.3
Cartes de visite, 92.1, 94.2, 165.1, DM.2
Cartoons, 65.1, 65.2, 188.3, 208.12
Casablanca, U.S.S., 80.4
Casiquiare River, 77.24
Castles, 260.3
Cavalry Regiments, U.S., 391.3
CCC. *See* Civilian Conservation Corps
Cebu province, Philippine Islands, 350.2
Cemeteries, 66.1, 117.1, 117.4, 120.5, 121.8, 165.15, 332.1
Censorship, Office of (RG 216)
Census, Bureau of the (RG 29)
Centennial International Exhibition (Philadelphia, 1893), 165.4
Centennial International Exposition, Melbourne, Australia (1888), 43.1
Central America, 43.2, 54.5, 127.1, 166.1, 229.1–229.3, 306.15, 306.16
Ceylon, 59.13, 226.1
Chamberlain, Clarence, 32.5
Chamberlain, F. M. (photog.), 22.1
Chambers, Lt. W. H., 19.3
Chandler, Zachariah, 48.5
Chapels, military, 24.2
Chaplains, military, 24.2, 24.6, 407.1
Charles N. Young Collection DM.22
Charles Russell Collection DM.36
Charleston, SC, 27.4, 57.2, 71.2
Charleston, WV, 156.3
Charts, 27.1, 48.5, 54.2, 72.3, 74.3, 95.3, 97.4, 171.5, 178.1, 207.4, 287.1, 331.5, 407.3, 407.4, 432.2
Chemical industry, 97.3, 142.1, 156.5, 156.7
Chemical warfare, 171.4, 407.3
Chemical Warfare Service, 70.2
Chemistry, Bureau of, 97.1, 97.3, 97.4, 136.1
Chemistry and Soils, Bureau of, 97.1–97.4
Cherbourg, France, 19.4, 226.1
Cherokee Strip, Oklahoma Territory, 49.3
Chesapeake Bay area, 22.4, 57.2
Chester, PA, 3.3, 92.2
Cheyenne Indians, 75.1, 75.2
Cheyenne River, 77.23
Chicago, IL, 26.2, 43.1, 59.3, 75.14, 77.3, 92.3, 111.3, 121.5, 165.4, 220.12, 306.12
Chicago World's Fair Centennial Celebration (1933–34), 43.1
Chichester, H. D. (photog.), 22.4
Child Collection, 19.2
Child Labor, Branch of, 155.1
Children, 47.5, 54.4, 102.1–102.2, 155.1, 245.1
Children's Bureau (RG 102)

Construction materials, 32.1, 75.8, 77.4

Consulates, U.S., 59.2, 59.4

Consumer Council of the Agricultural Adjustment Administration, 145.3

Consumer education programs, 145.3, 432.2

Consumer's Guide, 145.3

Continental Congress, 59.1

Convict labor, 30.4

Cook Islands, 22.1

Cooley, Sam A. (photog.), 165.1

Coolidge, Calvin, 16.3, 75.4, 79.2, 237.1

Coolidge Dam, AZ, 115.4

Copper River, AK, 94.3

Copper River Railroad, 126.1

Corcoran Gallery, Washington, DC, 148.2

Corn, 7.5, 54.5

Corn, Jack (photog.), 220.6

Corn Investigations, Office of, 54.5

Cost of Living Council, 432.1

Costa Rica, 76.7, 90.3

Costa Rica-Panama Boundary Arbitration, 76.7

Cotton, 5.1, 7.2, 7.5, 258.1

Cotton States and International Exposition, Atlanta, GA, 121.5

Counterintelligence Corps, U.S. Army, DM.45

Court for the District of Columbia, U.S., DM.3

Court of Appeals, U.S., DM.3

Courthouses, 121.1, 121.12

Covent Garden, London, England, 54.3

Coximer, Charles Toucey (artist), 9.1

Craig Brook National Fish Hatchery, ME, 22.6

Crayon photographic prints, 48.2

Crime prevention, 65.3

Criminals, 65.1

Crop dusting, 7.2

Crystal Cave, SD, 48.4

Cuba, 4.1, 26.1, 37.2, 92.2, 94.5, 111.3, 165.5, 165.6, 168.1, 350.5

Cummings Expedition, DM.24

Currency, 318.2

Custer, Lt. Col. George, 77.5, DM.6

Customhouses, 121.1, 121.12

Customs, Bureau of, 36.1

Customs laws enforcement, 26.1

Customs Service, U.S. (RG 36)

Customs Service, U.S., 170.1

Cyanotypes, 22.1, 22.3, 22.4, 156.13

Cyclones, 168.1

Czechoslovakia, 165.12, 229.3

D

Dagron, Rene Prudent Patrice, 64.5

Daguerreotypes, 59.2

Dairy products, 88.1

Daley, Richard, 378.4

Dallas, TX, 394.3

Dams, 114.3, 115.1, 187.1
    construction of, 69.12, 77.5, 142.3

Daniels, Josephus, 19.9, 74.3

Darling, Ding, 65.2

Data processing, 64.6

David L. Brainard Collection DM.14

Davis, CA, 54.9

Davis, Marshall (artist), 12.5

Declaration of Independence, 59.1, 148.2

Defense Civil Preparedness Agency (RG 397)

Defense Nuclear Agency (RG 374)

Defiance, OH, 74.3

de Gaulle, Charles, 306.20

Delaware River area, 32.3, 106.5

Delgado, Francisco, 268.2

Democratic National Convention (1968), 306.12

Demolition, 77.19, 233.2

Dempsey, Col. Charles A., collection, 94.5

Denmark, 54.3, 306.17

Dentistry, 112.1

Denver, CO, 75.14, 220.6

Denver, Colorado Canyon and Pacific Railroad, 57.4

Depression, 306.2

Detroit, MI, 171.3, 362.1

Dewell, Nathaniel L. (photog.), 106.5

Diagrams, 115.3, 120.1, 171.5

Diamond, Henry L., 429.1

Diederich, J. (photog.), 79.17

Dinwiddie, William (photog.), 75.2

Dioramas, 30.3

Diplomats, 59.4, 229.2, 306.16, 331.2, 364.1, 395.1, DM.38

Dirigibles, 72.1, 72.4

Disaster relief, 26.7, 92.6, 111.8, 162.1, 168.1

Diseases, 90.2, 90.4, 165.13
    children's, 102.2
    flu epidemic, 165.13
    See also Plant diseases

Disney, Walt, 208.12

Displaced persons, 208.2, 260.1, 331.3

District Courts of the United States (RG 21)

District Courts of the United States, 49.4

District of Columbia, 3.3, 16.3, 16.5, 16.6, 27.3, 33.4, 35.9, 40.2, 42.1–42.5, 48.3, 48.5, 52.1, 54.7, 59.3, 64.1, 64.2, 64.4, 66.1, 66.2, 69.4, 69.13, 70.2, 75.1, 77.4, 79.2, 79.8, 79.13, 111.10, 121.2, 121.6–121.8, 148.2, 156.1, 220.2, 220.6, 220.12, 318.2, 328.1–328.2, DM.2, DM.3, DM.10, DM.11, DM.17, DM.22

Diving bells, 19.3

DOCUMERICA program, 412.2

Dogs, 17.1

Dominican Republic, 127.3, 306.9, 350.5

Doris McClory Collection DM.33

"DOT 321 (b) Rail Retrofit Evaluation of Light and Commuter Rail Stations," 408.1

Douglass, Frederick, DM.9

Drainage, 8.1, 114.1, 471.1

Drawings, 9.1, 12.5, 15.2, 26.2, 37.2, 53.1, 57.1, 59.2, 59.4, 64.1, 77.3, 77.16, 78.1, 92.1, 120.1, 121.5, 156.4, 156.16, 168.1, 171.1, 171.5, 188.4, 207.2, 208.12, 229.3, 328.2, 407.4, DM.4
    See also Architectural drawings; Art, original

Dredging, 23.1, 77.5

Dresden Art Gallery, 260.4

Drug abuse, 170.1

Drug Enforcement Administration, 170.1
Drugs, 88.1
Drydocks, 19.1, 19.8, 71.2, 71.3, 181.1
Duane, U.S.C.G.C., 26.5
DUKW, 227.1
Dulles, John Foster, 59.6
Dunlop, Orrin E. (photog.), 76.4
Durkin, Martin P., 174.1
Dust explosions, 97.1, 97.2, 97.3
Dust storms, 114.1
Dutch elm disease, 310.1
Dutra, Gen. Eurico Gaspar, 229.2
Dwight D. Eisenhower Collection DM.23

E

Earhart, Amelia, 26.8, 32.5, 237.1
Earnest C. Tracy Collection DM.32
Earthquakes, 18.12, 30.2, 48.7, 57.2, 77.4, 92.6, 111.8, 168.1
"Ease on Down the Road," 416.1
Ecce Homo (film), (DM.41)
Economic Development Administration (RG 378)
Economic Opportunity and Legal Services, Agencies for (RG 381)
Economic Opportunity, Office of, 381.1
Economic Stabilization Programs (RG 432)
Ecuador, 59.4
Edgewood Arsenal, MD, 156.5
Education, 4.3, 12.1–12.5, 15.3, 47.2, 59.11, 69.8, 75.2–75.3, 75.7–75.9, 75.13, 119.1–119.3, 126.4–126.5, 129.2, 145.3, 165.13, 188.3, 210.1, 229.1, 286.1, 306.3, 306.9, 350.3, 350.5
Education, Bureau of, 12.1
Education, Office of (RG 12)
Education, Office of, 47.2
Educational camps, 12.5, 35.3, 119.1
"Effects of Incendiary Bomb Attacks in Japan," 243.4
Egg and poultry industry, 136.1
Egypt, DM.18
Einsatzstab Reichsleiter Rosenberg Collection, 260.5
Einstein, Albert, 16.2
Eisenhower, Dwight D., 47.4, 79.11, 79.18, 112.3, 306.6, 306.14, DM.2, DM.23
Eisenhower, John, 306.14
Eisenhower, Milton, 306.15
El Rito, NM, 8.1
Electricity, 23.3, 119.3, 221.1
Elizabeth II, Queen of England, 452.4
Ellice Islands, 22.1
Elliott, Henry Wood (artist), 22.2, 57.1, 121.3
Elwyn L. Watson Collection DM.30
Ely, Lt. Eugene, 181.2
Emden, Germany, 32.6
Emergency Fleet Corporation, 32.2
Emergency Health Services, 90.5
Emergency Management, Office of, 44.4, 121.15
Emergency vehicles, 92.2
Employment programs, 12.4
Energy, Department of, 220.10

Engineers, Office of the Chief of (RG 77)
Engineers, Office of the Chief of, 76.6, 165.5
England, 165.14, 171.1, 196.3, 226.1, 243.3, 332.1, DM.18, DM.22
    See also Great Britain
Engraved and Lithographed Portraits of Abraham Lincoln, 64.3
Engraving and Printing, Bureau of (RG 318)
Engravings, 26.2, 48.1, 59.1, 64.3, 77.3, 121.4
    See also Art, graphic
Enid, OK, 233.3
Eniwetok Atoll, Marshall Islands, 374.1
Entertainers, 208.4, 306.2, 306.16, 452.4
Entomological experiments, 7.3–7.4
Entomology, Bureau of, 16.4
Entomology and Plant Quarantine, Bureau of (RG 7)
Environmental Protection Agency (RG 412)
Erickson, H. A. (photog.), 18.4
Erosion control, 8.1, 16.4, 75.5, 114.2, 114.5
Erwin Kornitzer Collection DM.25
Ethnic American Art Slide Library, Univ. of South Alabama, DM.16
Ethnology, Bureau of, 75.2
Europe, 74.3, 78.1, 97.3, 106.5, 112.2, 114.5, 117.1, 117.4, 165.6, 210.3, 306.2, 306.16, 306.17, 306.20, 306.22, 328.4, 331.3
    architecture, 66.1
    U.S. aid to, 4.1, 286.1
    World War I, 4.1, 165.13, 165.14
    World War II, 26.1, 112.3, 208.2, 208.3, 239.1–239.2, 337.1, 342.2
Evans, John, DM.21
Evans, Kate, DM.21
Executive Office of the President (RG 429)
Executive Office of the President, 51.1
Exhibits, 4.1, 16.3, 16.5, 17.3, 19.5, 26.2, 27.1, 30.3, 40.2, 40.3, 43.1, 47.1, 48.5, 48.6, 48.8, 54.2, 54.4, 59.2, 64.4, 69.1, 69.8, 75.7, 77.3, 79.20, 80.5, 92.3, 97.1, 111.3–111.4, 115.2, 119.2, 121.5, 121.15, 127.1, 145.2, 148.1, 153.1, 162.1, 165.4, 171.6, 188.1, 207.2, 208.1, 208.3, 208.9, 233.4, 306.1, 306.4, 306.5, 412.2, DM.10
Experiment stations, 7.4, 54.5, 70.1, 70.2
Experimental farms, 16.2, 16.4, 54.4, 54.5, 306.10
Expo '67, Montreal, Canada (1967), 207.2
Expo '74, Spokane, WA (1974), 452.4
Exposition, Anniversary and Memorial Commissions (RG 148)
Expositions, 16.3, 16.5, 16.6, 19.5, 27.1, 30.4, 40.2, 43.1, 48.5, 48.6, 54.2, 54.4, 54.7, 59.2, 75.6, 77.3, 92.3, 97.3, 111.3, 111.4, 121.5, 165.4, 200.9, 207.1, 233.4, 242.1, 306.2, 350.3, 394.3, 418.2. 452.4
Extension Service (RG 33)
Extension Service, 16.4

F

Factories, 165.2
Factory cooperatives, 3.3
Factory workers, 54.1, 69.5, 74.1, 86.1

4-H clubs, 16.7, 33.2, 33.4, 75.7
Fourth International Conference of American States, 43.3
Fox, William (photog.), 94.7
France, 3.3, 4.2, 18.5, 19.4, 42.2, 43.1, 52.3, 54.2, 54.4, 63.1, 74.2, 75.8, 77.5, 80.7, 80.9, 92.5, 106.5, 111.6, 117.2, 120.1–120.5, 165.14, 165.15, 185.1, 185.3, 208.3, 208.8, 208.17, 226.1, 242.3, 242.10, 243.1, 243.2, 260.5, 306.2, 332.1, 407.1, 407.2, DM.18, DM.22, DM.26, DM.27, DM.32, DM.46
Franco, Francisco, 242.8, 306.14
Frank, Hans, 238.2
Frank Leslie's Illustrated Newspaper, 64.1, 165.5
Frank W. Legg Collection DM.9
Frankford, PA, 156.1, 156.12
Frankfurt, West Germany, 239.2
Franklin D. Roosevelt Library, 64.3
Freedmen's Hospital, DC, 48.3
French and Indian War, 111.1
Fruits, 54.1, 54.2
Fuel Administration, U.S. (RG 67)
Fuel oil installations, 32.3
Fuhrerhaus (Germany), 242.1
Fuller, Glenn L. (photog.), 114.1
Funerals, 126.3, 208.6, 306.18, DM.23

G

Galbraith, John Kenneth, 59.6
Gallaudet College, DC, 48.3
Gallegos, Romulo, 208.17
Game animals, 22.5
Gandhi, Indira, 306.14, 306.20
Gardens, 12.1, 42.1, 42.3, 54.1, 54.4
Gardner, Alexander (photog.), 75.1, 76.1, 90.1, 165.1
Garmisch-Partenkirchen, Germany, 242.1
Gas warfare, 52.2, 70.2, 171.4
Gatty, Harold, 18.13
Gemini space program, 255.4, 306.11
General Headquarters, Supreme Commander for the Allied Powers, 331.4
General Land Office, 49.1–49.2
Genoa Industrial School for Indian Youth, NE, 75.9
Geographical and Geological Survey of the Rocky Mountain Region, U.S., 57.2
Geographical Surveys West of the 100th Meridian, U.S. (Wheeler Survey), 77.8, 79.4, 106.1, 287.1
Geological and Geographical Survey of the Territories, U.S. (Hayden Survey), 57.1, 77.5, 79.6
Geological Exploration of the Fortieth Parallel (King Survey), 77.7, 79.4, DM.13
Geological formations, 49.4, 57.1, 77.8, 94.3, 106.1, 165.2
Geological Survey (RG 57), 115.2
George A. Carroll Collection DM.35
George S. Stewart, Jr., Collection DM.31
George Washington, SS, 32.5
George Washington Bicentennial Commission, 79.9, 148.1
George Washington Memorial Highway, 42.4
Georgia, 16.7, 57.2, 94.1, 112.1, 121.5, 162.1, DM.5
Gerdes, Lt. Col., 77.24

German-American Bund, 131.4
German Railroads Information Offices, 131.2, 131.3, 131.4
Germany, 5.1, 16.7, 18.5, 19.4, 32.6, 38.3, 38.6, 47.4, 59.4, 59.10, 63.1, 92.6, 111.5, 131.1–131.5, 153.1–153.2, 156.2, 156.12, 165.14, 165.15, 165.17, 229.3, 238.1–238.4, 239.2, 242.1–242.10, 243.1, 243.2, 243.3, 255.7, 260.1, 260.3, 260.4, 286.1, 306.16, 342.1, DM.18, DM.32, DM.36, DM.40, DM.42, DM.46
Geronimo, 75.1, 75.6
Gettysburg, PA, 79.3, DM.22
Gila River Relocation Center, AZ, 210.2
Gilbert Islands, 22.1
Glacier National Park, 79.11
Glaciers, 76.3, 94.3
Gleason's Pictorial Drawing Room Companion, 64.1
Glendale, AZ, 17.3
Goat Island, NY, 77.14
Goddard, Col. George W. (photog.), 342.2
Goldbeck, E. O. (photog.), 165.16
Goldberg, Rube, 65.2
Goldwater, Barry, 306.12
Gondos, Victor, DM.5
Göring, Hermann, 260.4
Government Reports, Office of (RG 44)
Graf, Ulrich, 260.6
Graf Spee (battleship), 59.4
Graf Zeppelin (airship), 18.12
Grain, 5.1, 97.1, 145.4, 258.1
Grain Corporation, U.S. (RG 5)
Granada Relocation Center, CO, 210.2
Grand Army of the Republic, 15.2
Grand Canyon National Park, 79.11
Grand Coulee Dam, WA, 328.3
Grand Teton National Park, 57.1
Grant, George Alexander (photog.), 79.11, 79.16
Grant, Ulysses S., 42.4, 127.2, DM.2, DM.6
Grant, Ulysses S., III, DM.12
Grant Memorial Commission, 42.4
Graphs, 27.1, 74.3, 97.4, 178.1, 188.3, 207.4, 287.1, 331.4, 331.5, 432.2
Grazing land, 75.5
Great Britain, 52.3, 54.3, 75.8, 76.1, 76.2, 92.5, 165.14, 171.1, 196.1, 196.3, 226.1
        See also England; Northern Ireland; Scotland; Wales
Great Depression, 306.2
Great Lakes area, 22.3, 22.4, 37.2
Great White Fleet, 80.4
Greater Germany in World Events—Daily Picture Reports, 242.8
Greeley, Maj. Gen. Adolphus W., collection, 111.8
Green Lake, ME, 22.6
Green River, WY, 57.3, DM.13
Greenland, 26.5
Griffin, Maj. T. H., 120.4
Griffiths, Maj. (photog.), 165.15
Gripsholm, SS, 59.10
Grunsonwerk Company, 156.2
Guadalcanal, Solomon Islands, 107.1
Guam, 22.1, 362.1
Guatemala, 90.3, 169.1
Guayule Emergency Rubber Plant Project, 54.11, 95.7

Hudson's Bay Company, 76.1
Hugo H. Huntzinger Collection DM.28
Hull, Cordell, 59.6
Human Nutrition and Home Economics, Bureau of
  (RG 176)
Humphrey, Hubert, 306.12, 306.20, 362.1, 429.1
Humphrey, Muriel, 306.20
Hungary, 165.14
Hunton, E. C. (photog.), 33.3
Huntzinger, Hugo H., DM.28
Hurricanes, 69.14
Hyde, F. B. (photog.), 119.2
Hydroelectric power, 115.1, 142.3
Hydrographic Office (RG 37)
Hydrographic surveys, 22.1, 23.2, 37.1
Hygiene, 90.2

I

Ice patrols, 26.1, 32.4
Icebergs, 32.4, 126.6
Iceland, 306.17
Ickes, Harold, 55.1
Idaho, 35.4, 57.1, 75.1, 76.1, 77.7, 79.6, 95.2, 210.2
Illingworth, W. H. (photog.), 77.5
Illinois, 15.5, 18.9, 26.2, 43.1, 59.3, 75.14, 77.3, 92.3, 92.5,
  111.3, 119.1, 121.5, 156.12, 156.14, 165.4, 220.12, 306.12,
  412.2, DM.5
Illinois and Mississippi Canal, 77.2
Illustrated London News, The, 64.1
Immigrants, 30.4, 90.2, 119.2, 220.9
Imperial Valley, CA, 48.4
India, 54.2, 59.13, 306.14
Indian Affairs, Bureau of (RG 75)
Indian Congress (1926), 75.6
Indian Head, MD, 38.3, 80.5
Indian Opportunities, 381.1
Indian protests, 75.13
Indian Record, 75.15
Indian Service, U.S., 75.4
Indian tribal delegations, 75.1
Indian wars, 111.1, DM.5
Indiana, 18.9
Indians. *See* American Indians
Indonesia, 59.13, 84.1, 306.16
Industrial development, 229.1, 378.1–378.3
Industrial production 4.2, 45.1, 111.1, 126.2, 126.4, 126.5,
  131.2, 151.1, 156.6, 156.11
Infantry Regiments, U.S., 391.3
Information Service Centers (USIA), 306.1, 306.5
Insects, 7.2–7.4
Insular Affairs, Bureau of (RG 350)
Inter-Allied Rhineland High Commission, 165.15
Inter-American Affairs, Office of (RG 229)
Inter-American Conference (1944–45), 208.16
Inter-American Highway, 30.1
Intercontinental Railway Commission, 43.2
Interior, Department of the, 48.2, 115.2, 115.4, 245.1, 471.1
Interior, Office of the Secretary of the (RG 48)

Interior, Office of the Secretary of the, 115.2
International Boundary Commission, 76.6
International Colonial and Overseas Exposition, Paris, France
  (1931–32), 43.1
International Conference on Safety of Life at Sea (1929), 41.1
International Conferences, Commissions, and
  Expositions (RG 43)
International Exposition, Seville, Spain (1929–30), 40.2, 48.6
International Hydrographic Conference (1919), 37.2
International Information, Office of, 59.11
International Military Tribunal for the Far East, 238.3
International Military Tribunal (Nürnberg, Germany), 238.4
International trade, 59.4, 364.1
International trade fairs, 151.1
International Water Technique Exposition (1939), 242.1
International Waterways Commission, 76.4
International Women's Year, 220.7
"Introduction to the Controlled Materials Plan," 277.1
Inventors, 64.5
Iowa, 22.4, 22.5, 69.1
Iran, 59.13, 306.17
Iraq, 208.17
Irex, U.S.S., 428.1
Irons, Col. James A., 165.12
Irrigation, 8.1, 54.3, 75.4, 75.7, 83.1, 114.1, 114.4, 115.1,
  115.3, 115.4, 187.1
Italy, 38.1, 54.2, 77.20, 165.13, 165.14, 208.8, 260.3, 306.16,
  DM.18
Iwasaki, Hikaru (photog.), 210.1, 210.3

J

J. Robert St. Clair Collection DM.43
J. William Klie Collection DM.19
Jack, John G. (photog.), 95.2
Jackson, Andrew, 59.3, 127.2
Jackson, William Henry (photog.), 57.1, 77.5, 79.4, 79.6,
  DM.3
Jackson State College, MS, 220.3
James River, VA, 71.1
James River Bridge, VA, 32.3
James W. Talbot Collection DM.42
Jamestown Tercentennial Exposition, Hampton Roads, VA
  (1907), 111.4, 121.5
Japan, 26.6, 37.2, 38.1, 59.10, 75.8, 77.25, 80.10, 84.1, 111.3,
  111.5, 165.8, 165.12, 165.17, 208.2, 226.3, 243.3–243.5,
  260.2, 306.2, 306.14, 319.1, 319.2, 331.1, 331.2, 331.4,
  331.5, 342.1, 391.3, DM.45
Japanese Americans, 210.1–210.4, 220.12
Japanese beetles, 7.4
Japanese internees, 59.10
Java, Indonesia, 84.1
Javits, Jacob, 432.1
Jefferson, Thomas, 127.2
Jefferson Patterson Collection DM.18
Jerome Lilienthal Collection DM.40
Jeu de Paume Museum, France, 260.5
Job Corps, 381.1
Job training, 35.6, 119.4, 378.1

M

Medical personnel, 112.1, 112.3–112.4, 245.1
Medical research, 52.4, 90.2, 112.2
Medical treatment, 52.2–52.4, 75.10, 90.2, 90.4, 90.5, 112.1,
  112.2, 112.3, 362.1
    See also Health
Medicine and Surgery, Bureau of (RG 52)
Mediterranean area, 306.17, DM.14
Melbourne, Australia, 43.1
Mellon, Andrew, 131.1, 220.1
Mencken, H. L., 131.1
Menderes, Adnan, 306.14
Merchant marine, 32.4, 41.3, DM.39
Merchant Marine Bulletin, 32.4
Merchant ships, 19.4, 26.3
    Japanese, 26.6
    U.S., 5.1, 32.4
Mercury space program, 255.4
Meteorology, 27.1, 27.3, 119.3, 370.1
Mexican Americans, DM.16
Mexican Pacific Railway, 165.10
Mexican Punitive Expedition, 94.7, 111.1, 165.10
Mexican War, 111.1
Mexico, 19.8, 37.1, 38.3, 54.5, 76.6, 77.12, 79.7, 94.7, 165.10,
  189.1, 208.16, 208.17, 220.7, 306.13, DM.7
Mexico City, Mexico, 220.7, 306.13
Miami, FL, 80.4, 306.12
Michigan, 18.9, 35.3, 165.2, 171.3, 233.2
Michigan Military Academy, Orchard Lake, MI, 165.2
Microfilming, 64.5
Middle East, 97.3, 106.5, 114.5, 165.6, 306.15, 306.17, 306.22
Middle River, MD, 69.12
Middlebury, VT, 17.1
Migrant workers, 145.2, 362.1
Mikoyan, Anastas, 306.15
Miles Expedition. *See* Alaskan Expedition
Military campaigns, 77.18, 111.1, 111.2
Military defenses, 38.1, 77.4, 92.2
Military insignia, 77.4, 92.2
Military installations, 77.7, 77.9, 106.1, 111.1, 165.1, 165.13,
  243.1, 243.3, 260.1
    Air Force, 77.9
    Army, 77.7, 77.9, 92.2, 92.7, 111.3, 165.11, 319.1, 350.2,
      394.1
    Navy, 80.3, 80.5, 80.6
Military medicine, 52.1–52.4, 111.1, 112.1–112.5
Military recruitment, 24.6, 24.7, 45.1, 77.21, 94.8, 109.1,
  120.6, 162.1
Military supply depots, 18.10, 38.6, 71.3, 92.2
Military training, 77.3, 77.18, 77.19, 80.3, 94.4, 111.1, 111.9,
  112.1, 120.3, 145.2, 165.13, 337.1, 393.1, 407.3
Military tribunals, 238.3, 238.4, 331.3
Military units, U.S.
    Army Counterintelligence Corps, DM. 45
    Army Forces, Austria, 319.4
    Army Ski Troops, 79.11
    Army Southern Department, 77.9
    Cavalry regiments, various, 391.3
    Corps, III and IV, 394.1; IX, 165.16
    Division, 36th, 165.15
    Engineers, 116th, 120.3
    Infantry regiments, various, 391.3

    Marine Brigade, Third, 127.3
    Mountain Division, 10th, 337.1
    New York Artillery, 391.4
    New York Infantry, 67th, 391.3
    Service Command, Third, 394.1
    Telegraph Battalion, 419th, DM.30
    U.S. Volunteers, 36th, 77.11.
        See also American Expeditionary Forces, National Guard
        units
Military vessels, 19.1–19.2, 19.4–19.9, 24.3, 24.6, 77.19, 92.4
Miller, N. B. (photog.), 22.2
Milwaukee, WI, 48.4, 156.6
Milwaukee Public Museum, WI, 48.4
Mindora province, Philippine Islands, 350.2
Mine warfare, 38.5, 74.1, 74.3, 120.3
Minerals, 70.1, 169.1
Mines, Bureau of (RG 70)
Minidoka Relocation Center, ID, 210.2
Mining industry, 57.1, 57.3, 69.5, 70.1, 77.7, 95.2, 106.1,
  126.1, 169.1, 174.2, 187.1, 220.6, 245.1, 471.1
Mink, Patsy, 220.8
Minneapolis, MN, 15.5
Minnesota, 15.5
Minnesota Historical Society Collection DM.10
Mint, Philadelphia, PA, 121.6
Mississippi, 220.3
Mississippi, U.S.S., 24.8
Mississippi River, 26.7, 77.22, 92.6, 233.1
Mississippi River Commission, 77.22
Missouri, 18.9, 43.1, 48.5, 77.23, 80.5, 92.3, 121.5
Missouri, U.S.S., 80.10
Missouri River, 77.23
Mitchell, John, 129.1
Modoc Indians, 165.3
Mondale, Walter, 378.1, 378.4
Monoplanes, 18.13
Monroe, James, 127.2
Montana, 17.1, 57.1, 79.6, 95.2, 114.4
Monte Cassino (abbey), 260.3
Monterey, CA, 79.4
Montevideo, Uruguay, 59.4
Montreal, Canada, 207.2
Monument Valley, 79.15
Monuments and memorials, 42.1, 42.2, 42.4, 64.2, 66.1, 79.1,
  79.2, 79.7, 79.8, 79.11, 79.12, 79.21, 92.5, 111.10, 117.1–
  117.4, 121.1, 121.7, 121.8, 239.1–239.2, 260.3, 328.2,
  DM.10
Moon, J. M., collection, 165.1
Moon landings, 255.5, 306.11
Moorestown, NJ, 7.4
Moqui, AZ, 106.3
Moran, John (photog.), 77.5
Morgan City, LA, 80.5
Morgan Horse Farm, U.S., VT, 17.1
Morinigo, Higinio, 229.2
Moroccan War, 407.2
Morocco, 165.12, 169.1
Morton, Rogers C. B., 378.4
Moscow, U.S.S.R., 306.15
Moseley bridges, 92.2
Mosquitoes, 112.2

Mother-of-pearl button industry, 22.14, 22.5
Motion picture stars, 53.1
Mt. Baker, 79.15
Mount Fairweather, 76.3
Mount Logan, 76.3
Mount Shasta, CA, 79.4
Mount Vernon Memorial Highway, 30.1
Moylan, Col. Stephen, 92.1
Muir, Bluford W. (photog.), 35.2
Mules, 17.1
Munich Central Collecting Point, 260.4
Munich, (München) Germany, 242.1, 242.10, DM.36
Murals, 79.12, 121.10, 121.12, 121.13
Murphy, Louis S., DM.28
Muscle Shoals, AL, 142.1, 156.7
Musée de l'Histoire de France, Paris 64.5
Museum for German History, Berlin Collection DM.4
Museums, 69.11, 79.13
Muskie, Edmund, 306.12
Mussolini, Benito, 242.8
Muybridge, Eadweard (photog.), 165.3
Mydans, Carl (photog.), 96.2

N

Nader, Ralph, 432.1
Nagasaki, Japan, 77.25, 243.5
Nanking, China, 38.1
Narcotics, 90.2
Narcotics and Dangerous Drugs, Bureau of (RG 170)
Nashville, TN, 121.5
National Academy of Sciences (RG 189), 16.2
National Advisory Committee for Aeronautics, 255.1, 255.2
National Aeronautics and Space Administration
  (RG 255)
National Aeronautics and Space Administration, 26.1, 306.11
National Air Pollution Control Administration, 412.1
National Archives Building, 64.4
National Archives and Records Administration (RG 64)
**National Archives Collection of Foreign Records
  Seized** (RG 242)
National Bureau of Standards, 167.1–167.3, 207.4
    See also **National Institute of Standards and
      Technology** (RG 167)
National Capital Parks, Office of, 79.2
National Capital Planning Commission (RG 328)
National cemeteries, 66.1, 92.5
National Child Labor Committee, 102.1
National Commission on Fire Prevention and Control, 220.4
National Commission on the Observance of International
  Women's Year, 220.7
National Defense Research Committee, 227.1
National forests, 35.8, 95.4, 95.6
National 4-H Club Camp, Washington, DC, 33.4
National Gallery of Art, Washington, DC, 260.7
National Geographic Society, 167.2
National Guard Bureau (RG 168)
National Guard units, 35.3, 145.2, 168.1, 391.4
National Heart, Lung, and Blood Institute, 90.4

National Highway Traffic Safety Administration
  (RG 416)
National Institute of Standards and Technology
  (RG 167)
National Institute of Standards and Technology, 207.4
National Institutes of Health, 90.4
National Oceanic and Atmospheric Administration
  (RG 370)
National Operational Meteorological Satellite System, 370.1
National Park Service (RG 79)
National Park Service, 35.1, 35.4
National parks, 18.8, 48.4, 79.1, 79.7, 79.8, 79.10–79.14,
  79.21, 115.2, 412.2
National Production Authority (RG 277)
National Public Advisory Committee on Regional and
  Economic Development, 378.4
National Recovery Administration (RG 9)
National Recovery Administration, 287.1
    Blue Eagle, 9.1
National Research Project, 69.5
National Resources Planning Board (RG 187)
National Socialist Party. *See* Nazis
National Women's Conference, 220.8
National Youth Administration (RG 119)
National Youth Administration, 35.7, 79.13
Native Americans. *See* Alaskans, Native and American
  Indians
Natural disasters, 18.8–9, 18.12, 23.2, 26.7, 27.1, 30.2, 48.7,
  57.2, 69.14, 77.4, 77.17, 77.22, 90.5, 92.6, 111.8, 114.1,
  114.3, 162.1, 168.1
Natural resources development, 229.1
Navajo Indians, 29.1, 75.1, 75.6, 391.1
Naval air stations, 71.1, 80.3, 80.5, 80.6
Naval Aircraft Factory, Philadelphia, PA, 72.1
Naval Districts and Shore Establishments (RG 181)
Naval Expedition and Survey of the Isthmus of Darien, U.S.
  (Panama), 77.5
Naval Flying Field, U.S., Akron, OH, 72.4
Naval Intelligence, Office of, 24.3, 26.6, 38.1
Naval Observatory, U.S. (RG 78)
Naval Operations, Office of the Chief of (RG 38)
Naval Personnel, Bureau of (RG 24)
Naval Powder Factory, Indian Head, MD, 80.5
**Naval Records Collection of the Office of Naval
  Records and Library** (RG 45)
Naval shore establishments, 71.1
Naval Supply Depot, Oakland, CA, 38.6
Naval Training Station, U.S., Newport, RI, 38.3
Naval Training Station, U.S., Sampson, NY, 71.1
Navies, foreign, 80.3
Navigation, Bureau of, 41.1
Navigational aids (aviation), 18.14, 237.1
Navigational aids (water), 23.2, 26.1–26.2
Navy, Department of the, 1798–1947 (RG 80)
Navy, Department of the, 1947–   (RG 428)
Navy, Department of the, 38.2, 38.3
Navy Hospital Corps, 52.1
Navy Hospital, U.S., Portsmouth, VA, 52.1
Navy Nurse Corps, 52.2
Navy, U.S., 19.1–19.9, 24.1–24.8, 72.1–72.6, 74.1–74.4
  facilities, 24.4, 71.1–71.3, 80.1–80.10

Navy yards, 19.3–19.5, 69.3, 71.1–71.3, 72.3, 80.3, 80.5
Nazis, 131.2, 131.4, 153.2, 208.3, 229.3, 238.1–238.4, 242.1, 260.5, DM.36
Nebraska, 27.2, 57.1, 75.9, 77.23, 119.1, 121.5
Negro River, 77.24
Negroes. *See* African Americans
Nehru, Jawaharlal, 306.14
Neil M. Judd Collection DM.24
Nelson, Gaylord, 220.11
Netherlands, 63.1, 286.1, 306.16, 332.1, DM.18
Netherlands East Indies, 239.1
Neubauer, John (photog.), 452.3
Nevada, 77.7, 77.8, 79.4
New Hampshire, 69.14
New Harmony movement, 97.3
New Jersey, 7.4, 156.12, 471.1
New London, CT, 26.1
New Mexico, 8.1, 70.3, 75.6, 77.8, 79.4, 106.3, 391.1
New Orleans, LA, 233.1
New York, 19.3, 19.5, 22.3, 23.1, 54.7, 57.2, 71.1, 71.2, 71.3, 77.4, 112.5, 117.1, 121.5, 121.6, 156.6, 181.1, 210.3, 233.2, 391.3, 391.4, DM.18
New York Air Brake Company, 156.6
New York Artillery, 391.4
New York City, NY, 69.9–69.11, 71.2, 112.5, 117.1, 121.5, 121.6, 181.1, 233.2
New York City Navy Recruiting Bureau, 24.7
New York Herald Tribune, 165.13
New York Infantry, 67th, 391.3
New York Navy Yard, NY, 19.3, 19.4, 19.5, 181.1
New York Times, 165.13
New York Times Paris Bureau, 306.2
New York World's Fair, 121.5
New Zealand, 107.1
Newport, RI, 38.3
Newport News, VA, 71.2, 336.1
"Newsmaps," 44.3
Newspaper clippings, 59.4, 111.11, 165.17, 407.4
Newsreels, 131.5
Niagara Falls, 76.4, 77.14
Niagara River, 43.2, 77.14
Nicaragua, 90.3
Nigeria, DM. 1
Nims, F. A. (photog.), 57.4
Niobrara River, 77.23
Nitro, WV, 156.3
Nixon, Richard M., 51.1, 59.13, 79.20, 255.7, 306.6, 306.7, 306.12, 306.15, 306.21. 412.1. 429.1, 452.4, DM.3
Noball installations, 243.1
Norfolk, VA, 52.1
Normandy, France, 52.3, 226.1
Norris Dam, TN, 142.3
North Africa, 239.1, 242.3, 337.1
North Atlantic Treaty Organization, 319.1
North Carolina, 57.2, 69.2, 220.11, 237.1
North Carolina, U.S.S., 181.2
North Carolina Emergency Relief Administration, 69.2
North Dakota, 114.4
North German Lloyd Steamship Lines, 131.1
Northern Ireland, 226.1, 332.1
    See also Great Britain

Northern Pacific Railroad Survey, 106.2
Norway, 306.17
Nuclear bombs, 80.3
Nuclear power, 220.10, 326.1
Nuclear submarines, 19.9
Nuclear Test Ban Treaty (1963), 306.4
Nunivak, U.S. Revenue Cutter, 26.5
Nürnberg, Germany, 238.4, DM.36
Nutrition, 90.2, 176.1, 331.4
Nuts, 54.1
NYA. *See* National Youth Administration

O

Oakland, CA, 38.6, 75.14
Observatories, 27.1, 78.1
Occupation Headquarters, World War II, U.S. (RG 260)
Occupational hazards, 28.3
Occupational safety, 70.1, 220.6
Occupational therapy, 12.3, 15.3, 208.13
O'Donnell, John A., collection, 268.2
Offenbach Archival Depot, 260.5
Office of Military Government for Germany, U.S. (OMGUS), 260.1
Ogden, H. A. (artist), 92.1, 165.4
Ohio, 18.1, 35.3, 59.3, 69.1, 72.4, 74.3, 75.14, 92.2, 156.15, 220.3, 471.1
Ohio Railroad, 59.3
Oil. *See* Petroleum industry
Oil reserves, naval, 80.8
O'Keefe, Capt. C. F. (photog.), 77.11, 350.2
Oklahoma, 48.4, 49.3, 75.2, 75.4, 75.9, 168.1, 233.3
Oklahoma National Guard, 168.1
"Oklahoma Railroad Bill," 233.3
Old Hickory, TN, 156.8
Olympic Games, 306.2
    1936, 131.2, 242.1
    1968, 306.13
    U.S. teams, 32.5, 75.8
Omaha, NE, 27.2, 77.23, 121.5
OMGUS, 260.1
O'Neal, Emmet, 268.2
Ontario, Canada, 74.3
Operation Breakthrough, 207.4
Operation Crossroads, 74.4
Operation Diagram, 226.1
Operation Sail, 452.4
Operation Sandstone, 374.1
Operation Strangle, 243.1
Operation Vittles, 342.1
Oranges, 7.5
Orchard Lake, MI, 165.2
Ordnance, 74.1–74.4, 77.3, 77.19, 80.3, 156.1–156.16, 165.13
Ordnance, Bureau of (RG 74)
Ordnance, Bureau of, 156.9
Ordnance, Office of the Chief of (RG 156)
Ordnance Corps, 77.21
Oregon, 35.4, 79.16, 92.2, 95.2, 121.5, 178.1
Oregon Coastal Areas, Committee to Investigate the, 79.16
Oregon Shipbuilding Corporation, 178.1

Reclamation, 35.6
Reclamation, Bureau of (RG 115)
Reclamation, Bureau of, 35.1
Reconnaissance maps, 77.4, 77.5
Reconstruction Finance Corporation (RG 234)
Records management, 64.7
Records storage, 32.2, 64.4
Recreational areas and activities, 12.3, 35.6, 79.1, 79.14,
    79.15, 79.21, 95.1, 111.1, 115.1, 129.2, 142.2, 162.1, 187.1,
    207.5, 210.1, 260.1, 319.2, 378.1, 378.3
Recruitment campaigns, 381.1
    Civilian Conservation Corps, 35.2
    Confederate States of America, 109.1
    military, 4.2, 15.2, 24.6, 24.7, 45.1, 77.21, 94.8, 109.1,
        120.6, 407.3
    war workers, 4.2, 47.3
Red Cross, 4.2, 45.1, 121.15
Red Cross (army transport), DM.19
Reforestation, 35.2, 35.6, 75.5, 95.6
Refugees, 4.1, 19.8, 26.1, 77.22, 208.2, 208.3, 210.3, 220.9,
    260.1, 306.9, 319.1, 331.3, 395.1
Regular Army Mobile Units, U.S. (RG 391)
Rehabilitation programs, 15.3
Rehse Archiv, Munich, Germany, 242.10
Reich Ministry for Public Enlightenment and Propaganda,
    242.8
Relief, U.S.S., 181.2
Religious services, 35.5, 306.6, 319.2
Repatriates, 59.10
"Report of the Commission of Engineers," 76.7
Report on Progress of the Works Program, 69.13
Reptiles, 22.7
Republic, SS, 32.5
Republican National Convention (1968), 306.12
Rescue operations, 26.1, 77.22, 171.2, 171.3
Reservoirs, 114.3, 114.6, 115.1, 142.2
Resettlement Administration, 96.2
"Retailer Fights Inflation, The," 208.15
Revenue Cutter Service, U.S., 26.4, 56.2
Revista Alemana (magazine), 242.8
Revolutionary War, 79.9, 92.1, 111.1, 127.1, 148.1, 148.3,
    208.6, 391.4, 452.2
Rhine River, 92.6
Rhode Island, 22.3, 35.3, 38.3, 69.14, 111.8, 428.1
Ribbentrop, Joachim von, collection, 242.2
Rice, Anthony, collection, 49.3
Richey, Frederick D., collection, 54.5
Rickover, Adm. Hyman, 306.15
Rideout, H. H. (Harry) (photog.), 79.18
Riff War, 407.2
Rio Arriba County, NM, 8.1
River, The (film), 96.2–96.3
River improvements, 77.5, 77.10, 77.14, 77.22, 77.23
Robbins, David (photog.), 69.10
Roberts, Owen J., 239.1
Roberts Commission, 239.1
Rock Island, IL, 156.12, 156.14
Rockefeller, John D., IV, 220.6
Rockefeller, Laurence S., 429.1
Rockefeller, Nelson A., 229.1–229.2, 306.12
Rockets, 255.1, 255.3, 370.1

Rockwell Field, CA, 18.4, 18.10
Rocky Mountain region, 57.2
Roesner, Otto (photog.), 238.2
Rogers, Will, 237.1
Rohwer Relocation Center, AR, 210.2
Romania, 59.4, 165.14
Rome, Italy, 38.1
Rommel, Gen. Erwin, 242.3
Ronne, Finn (photog.), 126.6
Roosevelt, Eleanor, 69.8, 75.6, 79.20, 131.1, 162.1, DM.3
Roosevelt, Franklin D., 24.6, 35.2, 47.1, 64.3, 75.6, 79.18,
    145.2, 162.1, 185.2, 208.6, 221.1, 237.1, DM.2, DM.3,
    DM.38
Roosevelt, Theodore, 127.2, 185.2, DM.2, DM.25
Rose Stereograph Company, 80.4
Rosen, Hy, 65.2
Rothstein, Arthur (photog.), 96.2
Round Pound, OK, 233.3
"Round the World Flight" (filmstrip), 18.13
Rowan, Carl T., 306.7
Rowan, Lt. A. S., 165.6
Rowe, Abbie (photog.), 79.18
Roxas, Manuel, 268.2
Royalty, 208.4, 208.17
Rubber, 54.11, 95.7, 234.2
Rubber Development Corporation, 234.2
Ruckelshaus, Jill, 220.8
Ruckelshaus, William, 412.1
Rumsfeld, Donald, 432.1
Rural dwellings, 3.3, 16.4, 33.3, 83.2
Rural Electrification Administration (RG 221)
Rural Electrification Administration, 16.4, 306.3
Rusinow, Irving (photog.), 83.4
Rusk, Dean, 59.6, 306.8
Russell, Andrew J. (photog.), 64.1, 77.3, 165.1
Russell, Charles, DM.36
Russell, John E., 233.2
Russell, R. Robert, 429.2
Russell Motor Company, Ontario, Canada, 74.3
Russia, 63.1, 77.20, 165.12, DM.14
    See also U.S.S.R.
Russo-Finnish War, 306.2
Russo-Japanese War, 165.12
*Russo-Japanese War: A Photographic and Descriptive
    Review of the Great Conflict in the Far East, The*, 165.12
Ryukyu Islands, 260.2

S

Sacaton Indian Agency, Pima, AZ, 75.2
Safety, 65.3
Safety First Exhibit, DC (1916), 40.2
St. Clair, J. Robert, DM.43
St. Elizabeths Hospital, DC, 48.3
St. George, Pribilof Islands, AK, 22.2
St. Lawrence River, 76.4
St. Louis, MO, 43.1, 48.5, 80.5, 92.3, 121.5
St. Marys River, MI, 233.2

St. Paul, Pribilof Islands, AK, 22.2
St. Thomas, Virgin Islands, 165.5
Salinas, CA, 54.11
Salt Lake City, UT, 27.3
Salt River Indian Day School, 75.8
Samoa, 19.4, 37.2
Sampson, NY, 71.1
San Diego, CA, 69.12, 165.17, 181.1
San Francisco, CA, 16.3, 16.5, 26.6, 30.2, 30.4, 54.7, 71.3,
    75.14, 77.4, 77.9, 79.4, 92.6, 111.8, 117.1, 168.1, 178.1,
    208.16, 220.12, 429.1
San Francisco Chronicle, 92.6
San Jose, CA, 75.14
San Juan, PR, 77.9
Sandbank, Harold, 59.12
Sandburg, Carl, 44.4
Sanitation, 69.1, 69.12, 90.2, 90.4, 229.1
Santa Ana, CA, 168.1
Santa Barbara, CA, 18.12
Santiago, Cuba, 165.5
Santo Domingo. *See* Dominican Republic
Saratoga, U.S.S., 24.8
Satellites, 255.3, 370.1
Saudi Arabia, 306.7
Savings Bonds, U.S., 53.2, 56.6
SCAP, 331.4
Scapa Flow, Scotland, 74.3
Schafer, Ernst, 319.4
Schneider and Company, France, 74.2
Schofield Barracks, HI, 165.11
School Garden Army, 12.1
School lunch program, 16.7
Schools, 12.1–12.3, 55.1, 69.12, 121.14, 126.4, 162.1, 162.2,
    350.5
    American Indian, 48.4, 75.2, 75.3, 75.6, 75.7
    aviation, 18.3–18.4, 18.15
    gardening projects in, 12.1, 54.4
    military, 18.3–18.4, 18.15, 19.4, 24.4
    See also Education
Schulz, Charles, 65.2
Scientific Research and Development, Office of (RG
    227)
Scientists, 7.1, 16.2, 22.7, 27.1, 90.2, 97.3, 208.4
Scotland, 47.4, 74.3, 92.5, 226.1
    See also Great Britain
Scott Field, IL, 18.9
Scott, Gen. Winfield, 15.2
Scranton, William W., 432.1
Sculpture (photos of), 16.3, 66.3, 121.10, 121.12, 121.13
Sea otters, 22.2
SEABEES, 24.7, 71.4
Seal industry, 22.1, 22.2, 22.4, 22.5, 32.4, 121.3, DM.10
Seaman, Valentine, 112.5
Searchlights, 77.16
Seattle, WA, 121.5, 220.12, 362.1, DM.10
Seger Colony, OK, 75.2
Seibert, S. R. (photog.), 165.1
Sekaer, Peter (photog.), 196.2
Selassie, Haile, 306.20
Select Committee on Immigration and Refugee Policy, 220.9
Seminole Indians, 75.2

Senate, U.S., 59.3
    Committee on Territories, DM.10
Sesquicentennial International Exposition, Philadelphia
    (1926), 19.5, 40.2, 43.1, 75.6, 97.1
Seville, Spain, 40.2, 48.6
Seymour Hofstetter Collection DM.44
SHAEF, 331.3
Shahn, Ben (photog.), 96.2
Sheep, 17.2
Shenandoah (dirigible), 72.4, 80.4
Sheridan, Philip, DM.6
Sherman, William T., 165.1
Ship models, 19.5, 19.9
Shipbuilders, 178.1, 208.1
Shipping Board, U.S. (RG 32)
Shipping Board, U.S., 41.3
Shipping industry, 151.1
Ships, 19.1–19.9, 26.1, 26.3, 32.1, 32.4, 32.5, 32.6, 41.3, 77.9,
    131.1, 165.2, 185.2, DM.39
    military, 24.3, 24.6, 26.1, 26.3, 72.3, 74.1, 74.3, 74.4,
        77.19, 80.3, 80.6, 80.9, 165.1, 165.5, 165.14, 179.1,
        181.1–181.2, 220.11
Ships, Bureau of (RG 19)
Shipyards, 19.1, 19.3–19.5, 32.1, 32.3, 71.1, 181.1–181.2
Short, C. W., 135.1
Shrimp industry, 22.4
Shriver, R. Sargent, 362.1
Shultz, George, 432.1
Siberia, U.S.S.R., 77.20, 395.1
Signal Corps, U.S., 35.2, 63.1, 77.5, 92.7, 111.1–111.11,
    319.1, 331.1
Signal Officer, Office of the Chief (RG 111)
Silk-screen graphics, 208.9
    See also Art, graphic
Sino-Japanese War, 306.2, 331.1
Sino-Japanese War (1894), 111.3
Sioux Indians, 75.2
Sitting Bull, 75.1
Sketches, 117.3, 121.1, 121.11, 121.12, 208.12
    See also Art, original
Skylab space program, 306.11
Slater, W. H. (photog.), 56.5
Slum housing, 3.3, 196.1
Smelters, 97.2
Smith, Erwin F., collection, 16.2
Smith, Hugh M., collection, 106.4
Smith, Stanton G. (photog.), 95.4
Smithsonian Festival of American Folklife, 452.4
Smithsonian Institution (RG 106)
Smokey Bear, 95.8
Smoot, Reed, 220.1
Social Security Act of 1935, 47.1
Social Security Administration (RG 47)
Social Security Board, 47.3
Society Islands, 22.1
Soil conservation, 16.4, 35.4, 114.4, 114.5, 114.6, 145.1,
    145.4
Soil Conservation Service (RG 114)
Soil Conservation Service, 35.1, 306.3, 306.10
Soil erosion, 95.2, 95.6, 114.1, 114.4, 187.1, 233.1, 412.2
Solar eclipses, 78.1

Texas Centennial Exposition, Dallas (1936), 394.3
Texas City, TX, 94.6
Thailand, 166.1, 226.1, 306.16
Theaters, 69.7
Theaters of War, World War II, U.S. (RG 332)
Thieu, Nguyen Van, 306.20
Thompson, James E., collection, 79.1
Thorpe, Jim, 75.8
Three Mile Island, PA, 220.10
Tibet, 319.4
Tillery, Risdon (photog.), 208.8
Tito, Marshal, 59.6
Tobacco, 7.5, 54.6
Tobacco and Plant Nutrition Investigations, Division of, 54.6
Tobin, Maurice J., 174.1
Tokyo, Japan, 331.1
Tokyo Round Trade Talks, 364.1
Tomb of the Unknown Soldier of the Civil War, 15.2
Tonga, 22.1
Tongass National Forest, AK, 35.8
Topaz Relocation Center, UT, 210.2
Torpedoes, 38.5, 74.1
Totem poles, 35.8
Totten, George, 185.3
Totten, John A., 185.3
Tourism, 229.1
Tower, John, 432.1
Townsend, C. H. (photog.), 22.2, 22.4
Tracy, Earnest C., DM.32
Trade Representative, Office of the U.S. (RG 364)
Trading posts, 76.1
Train, Russell, 412.1
Training programs
    census enumerators, 29.2
    Civilian Conservation Corps, 35.2, 35.6
    civilian defense, 35.2
    Coast Guard, 26.1, 26.4
    Merchant Marine, 32.4, 41.3
    military, 38.7, 77.3, 77.18, 77.19, 80.3, 127.1
Trains, 74.1
    interurban, 3.2
Trans-Mississippi Exposition, Omaha, NE, 121.5
Transportation, Department of, 408.1
Transportation, Office of the Chief of (RG 336)
Transportation Corps, U.S. Army, 77.21, 92.4
Transportation facilities, 3.3, 18.10, 30.1, 30.3–30.4, 32.1, 69.6, 75.14, 83.2, 115.1, 126.1–126.2, 127.1, 151.1, 165.10, 166.1, 229.1, 233.3, 350.2, 350.3, 408.1
Transportation industry, 69.5, 187.1
Treasury, Department of the (RG 56)
Treasury, Department of the, 121.2, 121.6
Treasury Department Building, 121.2, 121.6
Treasury Relief Art Project, 121.11
Tree diseases, 310.1
Tree varieties, 54.2, 54.4, 54.7, 95.1, 95.6
Trolley cars, 3.3
Truman, Harry S., 16.7, 47.4, 51.1, 59.6, 79.18, 111.7, 126.4, 162.1, 221.1, 237.1
Tsingtao, China, 111.5
Tulalip Agency, WA, 75.6
Tule Lake, CA, 49.4, 210.2

Tunisia, 169.1, 226.1
Tunnels, 115.1, 165.10
Turkey, 286.1, 306.14
Turpentine, 97.2
Tuskegee Army Air Field, AL, 18.15
Tuvalu Islands, 22.1
TVA. *See* Tennessee Valley Administration
Typhus, 90.4, 112.2

U

U-boats, 38.6
Ueno Museum, Tokyo, Japan, 331.1
UFOs, 341.1
Ulysses S. Grant III Collection (DM.12)
Underwood and Underwood, 94.7, 165.10
UNESCO. *See* United Nations Educational, Scientific, and Cultural Organization
Uniforms, 52.2, 77.3, 92.1, 92.2, 111.1, 127.1, 165.4, 171.2, 179.1
Unimak, U.S.C.G.C., 26.4
Union Army, 94.1, 111.2, 165.1
Union Iron Works, CA, 71.3
U.S.S.R. (Union of Soviet Socialist Republics), 38.3, 47.4, 77.20, 165.13, 165.14, 165.17, 242.5, 242.8, 260.5, 306.11, 306.15, 306.16, DM.34, DM.40, DM.42, DM.46
    See also Russia
United Fruit Company, 90.3
United Mine Workers, 245.1
United Nations, 59.9, 208.16, 306.2, 306.19
United Nations Conference on International Organization, 208.16
United Nations Educational, Scientific, and Cultural Organization, 59.9
United States-Canada boundary survey (1898), 76.3
United States Film Service, 44.4
U.S. Information Agency (RG 306)
United States Information Service, 306.3, 306.4, 306.16
United States Lines, 32.5
United States Military Railroad Photographic Album, by Andrew J. Russell, 64.1
"U.S. Navy Wins Supply Battle of the Pacific," 208.3
United States of America Typhus Commission, 112.2
United War Work Campaign (1919), DM.33
Universal Exposition, Antwerp, Belgium (1894), 43.1
Universities, 165.13, 208.6, 220.3, 306.6, DM.1
University of South Alabama Collection DM.16
University of Tennessee Experiment Station, 54.5
University of Wisconsin, 95.5
Unknown Soldiers, tombs for, 15.2, 165.15
Upper Great Lakes Regional Commission, 378.2
Urban Environmental Design competition, 207.5
Urban Mass Transportation Administration (RG 408)
Urban Renewal Administration, 207.1
Uruguay, 37.2, 59.4, 306.8, DM.18
USA (publication), 208.10
USIA. *See* U.S. Information Agency
USIA Correspondent, 306.7
USIA World, 306.7

Y

Z